A
Jewish
Book of Comfort

A
Jewish
Book of Comfort

Alan A. Kay

JASON ARONSON INC.
Northvale, New Jersey
London

This book was set in 10 pt. Galliard by Lind Graphics of Upper Saddle River, New Jersey, and printed by Haddon Craftsmen in Scranton, Pennsylvania.

Library of Congress Cataloging-in-Publication Data

Kay, Alan A.
    A Jewish book of comfort / Alan A. Kay.
        p. cm.
    Includes bibliographical references and index.
    ISBN 0-87668-589-0
    1. Mourning customs, Jewish.   2. Consolation (Judaism)—
Meditations.   3. Kay, Alan A.   4. Bereavement—Religious aspects—
Judaism.   I. Title.
    BM712.K385 1993
    296.4'45—dc20   92-43824

Manufactured in the United States of America. Jason Aronson Inc. offers books and cassettes. For information and catalog, write to Jason Aronson Inc., 230 Livingston Street, Northvale, New Jersey 07647.

In memory of and in tribute to
my beloved father, teacher, and comforter
Milton Kay, זכרונו לברכה

Contents

II. *AVELUT:* THE FIVE STAGES OF JEWISH MOURNING

III. *YIZKOR*: PRAYER IN MEMORY FOR THE DEAD

IV. PASSAGES: GOING AND COMING

Please, My Lord

Please, my lord, if the Lord is with us, why has all this befallen us?

—Judges 6:13

※

I Dare Not Go Deep in Memory

I dare not go deep in memory,
yet the pain comes.
I need to talk with you,
I see you in my mind
and know
I will never hear you again
in this world.
I dare not go deep in memory,
and yet the pain comes.

—Seymour Freedman
Mourning for My Father

※

There Is No Feeling Heart

There is no feeling heart in this world that is not broken.

—Rabbi David J. Wolpe
The Healer of Shattered Hearts

※

Introduction

A Jewish Book of Comfort is dedicated to the memory of my father and in tribute to his life as my loving father, my wise teacher, and my patient comforter. Even in his death, my father was a teacher because in his dying and death, he gently brought me to begin to walk the path of reconciliation to the truth of my own mortality.

I think my father lived as fully as he did because after his own father's sudden death, he was thrown forcefully onto that same path of reconciliation to the truth of his own mortality and stood shakingly yet defiantly to meet its challenges. My father was not led gently by the hand as I was; his father's death came without warning. I cannot say how long it took for my father to stand on his own and continue to walk the world, but he did—as we all do after the death of a loved one, however awkwardly.

My grandfather died when my father was 12. I wish I had known my father then, because he never stopped living after his father died, he just learned to live differently but with no loss of faith in either God or humankind. Not that we, as humans, are never so humble as to think we ourselves will not live forever, but such thinking is usually only youthful pride that eventually matures into acceptance of one's limited time on earth.

I am not an extraordinary mourner. To have written this book does not mean I am at home with death, nor do I expect I or anyone can ever be at home with death, but I am less afraid today of my own mortality than I was before my father's death.

I have tried to write this book with intelligence and compassion, for use as comforter in times of sorrow and in the loneliness sorrow brings. At times it will be instructive, and for some, that is a healer; but more important, it will be humane and compassionate, and for most, that is a healer.

I hope my personal narratives and the selected readings bring solace. They have been informed and enriched by Jewish custom and tradition and faith.

A Jewish Book of Comfort is not intended to be an exhausting book, and therefore it is not an exhaustive book. There will be readers who have found selections in the literature of comfort that are not found here. Those included here are personal selections that in one way or another have given me comfort and continue to do so.

A Jewish Book of Comfort is a book to be read, reread, and shared; a book to pick up for a few minutes or a few hours; a book meant to be supportive, not intrusive, and a companion, not a meddler.

❈

Readings

We Bring Our Years to an End

We bring our years to an end as a tale that is told.

—Psalm 90:9

To Everything There Is a Season

To everything there is a season,
and a time to every purpose under the heaven:
a time to be born,
and time to die.

—Ecclesiastes 3:1–2

One Generation Passeth Away

One generation passeth away, and another generation cometh, but the earth abideth forever.

—Ecclesiastes 1:4

The Chain Goes On

And so it is that as the years come upon us, we gain a greater reverence for the flow of the generations. Our seeming wisdom only adds to the mystery of those who have come before, without whom we would not be, and through whom we seem to receive little pieces of some great image of being. We are increasingly impressed with the inherited knowledge of our ancestors. More reverent toward their heirlooms. Able now to listen to the legends with greater concentration. "Inquire of generations gone by, they will tell you; ask your parents, they will inform you" (Deut. 32:7).

It is very easy. As simple as a father speaking to his son just after the boy has read from the Torah to become a Bar Mitzvah. He says, we love you and we are proud of you. You are our hope and our seed for the future. And then he says to his grown-up little boy, I remember how your grandfather, my father, was there when you were born. And how he prayed he would live to see this day when you would read from the Torah. (But the old man is absent. Died many years ago. God, how he wanted to be here.) I am sorry, my son. Now it is only you and I. The chain goes on. May I live to be present when your children read from the Torah. And if it is not meant to be for me either, then please, will you say something like this for me. Everyone cries. Drops of water, you know, are a universal symbol for resurrection of the dead.

—Rabbi Lawrence Kushner
The River of Light

❋❋

O Lord, You Have Examined Me and Know Me

O Lord, You have examined me and know me.
When I sit down or stand up You know it;
You discern my thoughts from afar.
You observe my walking and reclining,
and are familiar with all my ways.
There is not a word on my tongue
but that You, O Lord, know it well.
You hedge me before and behind;
You lay Your hand upon me.
It is beyond my knowledge;
it is a mystery; I cannot fathom it.
Where can I escape from Your spirit?

Where can I flee from Your presence?
If I ascend to heaven, You are there;
if I descend to Sheol, You are there too.
If I take wing with the dawn
to come to rest on the western horizon,
even there Your hand will be guiding me,
Your right hand will be holding me fast.
If I say, "Surely darkness will conceal me,
night will provide me with cover,"
darkness is not dark for You;
night is as light as day;
darkness and light are the same.
It was You who created my conscience;
You fashioned me in my mother's womb.
I praise You,
for I am awesomely, wondrously made;
Your work is wonderful;
I know it very well.
My frame was not concealed from You
when I was shaped in a hidden place,
knit together in the recesses of the earth.
Your eyes saw my unformed limbs;
they were all recorded in Your book;
in due time they were formed,
to the very last one of them.
How weighty Your thoughts seem to me, O God,
how great their number!
I count them—they exceed the grains of sand;
I end—but am still with You.

—Psalm 139:1–18

I

PASSAGES:
COMING AND GOING

1

✖✖✖✖✖✖✖✖✖✖✖✖✖✖✖✖✖✖✖✖✖✖✖✖✖✖✖✖✖✖

When Death Comes There Are Many Ways to Mourn

When I was 45 years old, my father, Milton, 73, died following a four-month illness with lymphoma, a malignancy but technically not cancer. Any death of a parent, or a child, or a spouse—whatever the cause and whatever the age of the one who has died or of those who survive—represents an overwhelming personal and family trauma. Although I had been a student and Jewish educator for many years, I could easily have been a lost soul after the death of my father had I not been able to call upon my own personal resources and those of my humane Jewish nuturing.

My father did not die a violent death. During the four months his body struggled to accommodate his acute condition, and his mind wrestled with itself to understand his illness, and his soul sought solace while accepting the probability of death, I believe my father's suffering was profoundly different from the suffering of patients with chronic illnesses that leave them unable to walk or speak, unable to understand the language or the behavior of those who come to share their lives with them, and unable to separate death and dying.

I have not experienced chronic, long-term illness in my family that debilitates the patient and those around the patient; I have not experienced sudden and violent death, and I cannot presume to know that trauma. But ours is an increasingly violent world and I am acquainted with others who have known such a death. Their rage will be felt eternally and they may have to find sources of comfort in addition to those I have found. They will likely evolve into noticeably different persons because they cannot have experienced such shock and not be changed.

3

For many survivors, the whole world, not just the beloved, has died. But for them, too, there can be comfort and reaffirmation in Jewish ritual and spirituality. Jewish ritual does not distinguish among deaths, nor does spirituality.

Funeral and ritual are important, because they underline the reality of death, bringing the support and warmth of fellow human beings when needed, and provide a transitional bridge to the new circumstances brought about by the death of an intimate person.

—Herman Feifel
"Grief and Bereavement"
Bereavement Care

For these survivors, faith may be not enough.

I met Julie Hilton Danan in the University of Judaism in Los Angeles, where she was a student at the Whizin Institute for Jewish Family Life, where my wife was teaching. I was doing research in the university library. At breakfast, where we met, I told her about my research. Later that morning, she found me in the library and began to talk about her grandmother's sudden and violent death two years earlier. Her paternal grandmother, 80 years old, had been assaulted and stabbed to death in her own home on the morning of the first day of Sukkot.

Julie had given a eulogy at her grandmother's funeral. She talked about her grandmother's birth in a *shtetl* in Poland, her girlhood on Manhattan's Lower East Side, and her father, Zalman's, silver *kiddish* cup, which Julie herself used at her own wedding in Jerusalem. "It was tragic that a person of such vibrancy (or anyone) should die a violent death at the hand of a psychotic killer," Julie wrote in a letter to friends after *shivah*, "but we the family have decided to focus on the eighty active years, the children and grandchildren and great-grandchildren she lived to see."

And on her flight to New Jersey from Texas for the funeral, Julie found comfort in reflecting upon selections in *Zohar, the Book of Splendor,* edited by Gershon Scholem, in particular, those of the Revelation of the *Shechinah*, or Divine Presence, experienced by those near death. There is a "beautiful, loving light experienced by those near death," Julie writes. And in those reflections Julie gained strength and insight and solace.

A king has a son whom he sends to a village to be educated until he shall have been initiated into the ways of the palace. When the king is informed that his son is now come to maturity, the king out of his love, sends the matron his mother to bring him back into the palace, and there the king rejoices with him every day. . . . Withal, the village people weep for the departure of the king's son from among them. But one wise man said to them: Why do you weep? Was this not the king's son, whose true place is in his father's palace, and not with you?

—Gershon Scholem, *Zohar*
The Book of Splendor

As I sit at my desk writing this chapter, it is midsummer, and the sound of the cicadas outside my window can be either likened to the static I hear on my radio when the station I am listening to is broadcasting too far from where I am or, conversely, likened to the rush of water in a country brook. At first, I may snarl at the static but later I will smile at the mind's picture of the peaceful run of water, and I may even be able to fill up my senses with the colors and smells and textures of the pastoral setting. As I sit here, I know my faith in Jewish ritual and God has not been tested personally by having a loved one struck by swift and awful illness and death or suffering through years of pain and debilitation, but I believe that in the face of such trauma, although my faith would be at first shaken, it would be ultimately strengthened.

I found the strength not only to survive my father's illness and death (after all, most do survive and continue to lead healthy and productive lives) but also to learn from my father's response to his own illness and to my mother's response to his illness and to his death. In retrospect, I know that my strength came from my own predisposition to the Jewish tradition, in particular to its spirituality but also to its teachings and its sensitivities and guidance as embodied in its rituals, celebrations, and folklore. Ritual, writes Rabbi David J. Wolpe in his book *The Healer of Shattered Hearts: A Jewish View of God,* "enables the believer to give specific expression to the tremendous forces swelling in his or her soul."

When my paternal great-aunt, Sally, died, my family and I went to the funeral and to the burial. At that time, my father was in Florida and unable to attend his aunt's service. I went first as my father's son and second as a grand-nephew. But I also went because I am a Jew who has always believed that visiting the sick and making *shivah* calls are among the most important *mitzvot* a Jew, or any human being, can perform. None of us are immune to illness and none of us escape death. We prepare as much for our own illnesses and deaths, for our own roles as survivors, when we offer consolation to others. And we prepare our children for their roles as comforters as well when we act as comforters in their presence. It is also within Jewish tradition to be always cognizant of one's role as a teacher. In the case of a sudden and violent death, as well as a death following a short- or a long-term illness, it is the responsibility of extended family, friends, and Jewish professionals—rabbi and cantor, in particular—to provide that nourishing, nurturing, learning environment.

As it happened, there were disappointingly few people at my great-aunt's funeral and burial, either family or friends or Jewish professionals other than a rabbi, and their absence highlighted our own presence, that of my wife, Jo, and me, and our three daughters, Corinne, Lisa, and Adina. After the burial, my family and I went back to my great-aunt's son's home. My cousin, Howard, washed his hands outside his front door, pouring water from a pitcher into a cup offered to him by his wife, Grace, who had entered the house first.

After Howard entered the house, his wife gave him a shelled, hard-boiled egg to eat. I hadn't recalled ever having seen that ritual performed. My cousin explained that it represented the cycle of life: life goes on. (I later understood that such a ritual had not been performed after the death of my Orthodox maternal grandfather, Samuel, because he had never spoken to his children about death, and so they spoke little of it to theirs, to me and my sister and our cousins. Therefore my mother did not know of that life-affirming ritual and did not perform it upon returning to our apartment after my grandfather's burial. The washing of hands was a ritual my parents knew of because in their experience it was more widely practiced, most often before leaving the cemetery and so was a ritual made available by the cemetery director and not a concern of the family.)

Washing the hands, Rabbi Maurice Lamm writes in *The Jewish Way in Death and Mourning*, "is symbolic of the ancient custom of purification performed after contact with the dead. It emphasizes the Jew's constant concern with life, its value and dignity, rather than over-zealous attention to, and worship of, the dead."

"In ancient times," Rabbi Tzvi Rabinowicz writes in *A Guide to Life: Jewish Laws and Customs of Mourning*, "the egg was regarded as a symbol of life and resurrection. Moreover, because the egg is completely sealed inside its shell, it serves as a reminder to the mourners to remain silent and refrain from casual talk. Bread is the staple food, for it 'stayeth man's heart' (Psalm 104:15)."

Later, after leaving my cousin's home, I told my wife that after 120 years, when my parents had died, I wanted a pitcher of water prepared for the washing of my hands and a shelled, hard-boiled egg for me to eat. I understood both to be life-affirming rituals about which there was no mystery. They were practical symbols that took nothing away from the departed but gave generously to the survivors. "There is strong implication that the people most successful in traversing the rapids of grief are those who possess links to a symbolic life of enduring meanings and values" (Herman Feifel, "Grief and Bereavement"). I was conscious of learning as I observed and participated in the rituals associated with dying, death, burial, and *shivah*. My cousin was being comforted by those rituals by which I myself wanted to be so comforted when the time came for me to mourn, although until the day my father became ill and the doctor told us he had three months to three years to live, I believed my parents were going to live forever.

Upon returning to my home after my father's burial, a pitcher of water and cups were on our doorstep, having been left by our neighbor Sheryl. Soon afterward, my mother, sister, aunt, and I ate our hard-boiled eggs. The rituals would not return my father to me as I had known him before his death, and neither did they diminish my pain. But I did feel I was giving something to my father by joining generations of Jews who had performed the same rituals. And I did feel I was giving something to my children because by my performing the rituals, I was connecting them to the same generations. And

I was giving something to myself because I knew that performing these rituals was part of the healing process.

In addition to the strength I derived from watching my father struggle with his disease and my mother quarrel with my father's illness, dispute its intentions, and wrestle with her own despair, a prominent source of strength during the period of my father's illness derived from my belief in God, not the anthropomorphic image of a white-bearded male comforter seated on a high throne with arms outstretched and hands open to receive me, but rather the soft caresses of my grandmother's fingers across my forehead when I was ill as a child. Herein lies the meaning of God in my life.

God exists for me not in the cosmos as a divinity that merely embodies all that lives but a real presence that is embodied in a grandmother's fingers and in all the actions of the people who conceived me, gave birth to me, raised me, and nurtured my mind and heart, my body and soul. God is not outside my human existence; God is within, because God is a part of every human existence and waits only to be discovered by each individual. "Where is God?" asks the hasidic Rabbi Menachem Medle of Kotzk: "Wherever human beings let Him in." For most people, God is discovered only when there is illness and dying and death. For me, God has always existed as a presence in my life, as an inspirer, as a comforter, as a healer.

My wife and I sat with my mother, Rose, in the hospital waiting room during my father's first operation. It is not coincidence that when the doctors came to speak with us following the surgery, they asked to do so privately, in a room down the hall from the waiting room where we had sat with little patience for three hours; it is not coincidence that the room the doctors invited us to enter was the "Meditation Room." And there, on the wall of this small, windowless room, were paintings of idyllic nature. Neither doctor nor God had planted malignant cells in my father's body, and neither God would nor doctor could perform a miracle to eliminate them. What both God and doctor now could do was comfort. And it was not insignificant that both would do this in the " Meditation Room." First, the doctors would explain and answer questions; then in the privacy of that small room, we could each call upon each other's strength to understand and accept illness and death. Later that night, I recalled some words from Rabbi Harold Kushner's book *When Bad Things Happen to Good People* that helped to make that scene in the "Meditation Room" more revealing of the life cycle drama. But it wasn't until *shivah* that I was able to read that passage again:

> How does God make a difference in our lives, if He neither kills nor cures? God inspires people to help other people who have been hurt by life, and by helping them, they protect them from the danger of feeling alone, abandoned, or judged. God makes some people want to become doctors and nurses, to spend days and nights of self-sacrificing concern with an intensity for which no money

can compensate, in the effort to sustain life and alleviate pain. God moves people to want to be medical researchers, to focus their intelligence and energy on the causes and possible cures for some of life's tragedies. When I was a boy, early summer was the most pleasant weather of the year in New York City, but it was a time of dread for young families because of the fear of a polio epidemic. But human beings used their God-given intelligence to eliminate that fear. Throughout human history, there have been plagues and epidemics that wiped out whole cities. People felt that they had to have six or eight children so that some at least would survive to adulthood. Human intelligence has come to understand more about the natural laws concerning sanitation, germs, immunization, antibiotics, and has succeeded in eliminating many of those scourges.

God, who neither causes nor prevents tragedies, helps by inspiring people to help. As a nineteenth-century *Hasidic* rabbi once put it, "human beings are God's language." God shows His opposition to cancer and birth defects, not by eliminating them or making them happen only to bad people (He can't do that), but by summoning forth friends and neighbors to ease the burden and to fill the emptiness. We were sustained in [our son] Aaron's illness by people who made a point of showing that they cared and understood: the man who made Aaron a scaled-down tennis racquet suitable to his size, and the woman who gave him a small handmade violin that was a family heirloom; the friend who got him a baseball autographed by the Red Sox, and the children who overlooked his appearance and physical limitations to play stickball with him in the backyard, and who wouldn't let him get away with anything special. People like that were "God's language," His way of telling our family that we were not alone, not cast off.

There were so many times during my father's illness that my mother thanked the doctors and nurses for their concern and efforts on behalf of my father and on her behalf as well. Speaking with us in that "Meditation Room" was the doctors' way of showing us we were not alone. Their medical skills came from training; I believe their compassion came from their humanity; I believe their humanity came from God.

Jo and I remained with my mother during the week following my father's first operation. Before his second operation, one week later, Jo returned to New York, and my sister, Barbara, arrived. We found enough strength in each other to continue to give support to our mother. After Barbara returned home, I stayed on another two weeks. I learned I needed to give my mother time and space to be alone because she had to come to know and embrace her own loneliness. And that is how I had always thought of God, as One who gave me the time and space to be alone in crisis, as One who helped me to come to know my own weaknesses, failings, loneliness, and strengths. I believe I learned my own strengths as a comforter from what I had experienced throughout my life when I witnessed others being comforted. God did not intrude, because pain must accompany loss, and that pain must be lived through. But if God did intrude, it was first as a comforter, then as a healer.

My maternal grandmother, Mary, had died in early May, one month before I became a *bar mitzvah*. I remember the night before my grandmother died, my mother received a call from the hospital informing her that my grandmother had become seriously ill. After my parents left for the hospital, I went into their bedroom, knelt at the side of their bed, and prayed. I don't recall ever having done that before, nor had I ever seen anyone in my family pray like that, but I had seen enough television shows and read enough books to have seen others pray in that manner. I didn't think of it as being a non-Jewish ritual; I just did it to get as close to God as possible. No one told me to find a *minyan*, to call our rabbi, to read a book. I took my cue from the non-Jewish rituals I had seen performed on television and in films.

My grandmother died that night. What I remember is not that God did not answer my prayer. That I had prayed to God and that my grandmother still died did not mean God had not heard me but that I had someone other than my parents (who had their own grief) with whom I could share my desire to have my grandmother live, to whom I could express myself without fear of judgment, or of being patronized, or of being dismissed. I prayed as much to have myself heard, as much to have my own soul soothed, as I did in the hope that my prayer would heal my grandmother. That she was not healed did not mean that I had not been heard.

The morning following my grandmother's death was bright and beautiful like a vivid watercolor; the world outside our apartment was awash in color. My mother stood by the living room window weeping and asking why her mother could not have lived to see a day endowed with such beauty. It is only in retrospect that I know that God both kept a distance and made a presence known at the same time that morning. On one hand, God allowed my mother to mourn, to weep and cry and sob. God, too, had lost a child, and there needed to be crying. On the other hand, God painted the day with colors "bright and beautiful" to comfort the mourner and allow her insight into God's healing powers. God does not heal the disease. God heals the spirit of both the one who is ill and the one who comforts the ill. And when death comes, God cares for the soul of the one who has died as God cares for the spirit of those who survive.

"Faith seeks to strip away the ultimacy of death," Rabbi Wolpe writes in *The Healer of Shattered Hearts*. "Given a perfect remembrance, a place where all who have lived remain unforgotten, a master memory in the universe, death is not the final editor of human aspiration. Over and against the fear of death there is the possibility of ultimate preservation and renewal. In other words, there is God."

Rabbi Wolpe writes elsewhere in his book, "Ultimately, we want to touch what God means in the most pained and private chambers of the human soul. Where anguish is greatest, the religious message is most significant. If God does not speak to suffering, to the shattered hearts of the psalmist's plea, then He must remain peripheral to our lives. That which does not touch my pain leaves me as I was. Even joy lasts and changes us only when it deepens our understanding and endurance of the pain that is part of living in an unredeemed world."

I had read no books during my father's illness. There were no books on my parents' shelves to talk to me. My sister had returned home. I kept a journal. The pen in my hand helped me to keep my balance.

"I dread the phone ringing," I wrote four days after my father's second operation. He was not conscious. "I dread the phone ringing. Not before I'm dressed and washed in the morning. What happens if the phone rings and we're told Dad's gone? How would I brush my teeth knowing Dad's gone? How would I tie my shoelaces? I mean, what do I think about when I'm tying my shoelaces and I know my Dad's gone?"

Writing in my journal steadied my hand.

I took photos of my mother and of objects and places in my parents' apartment: of my mother writing a letter to my children or to my niece and nephew, of my father's closet and his 50-year-old Royal typewriter, of my parents' books and pictures. My mother and I talked. We visited my father in the hospital three times each day. I called home every night, and my wife and I talked and I shared with her and with our children my heartache. They were in New York and I was in Florida.

And I knew when it was time for me to return home.

"I know better today than yesterday when the stirrings began or, at least, when I first recognized them, that I don't belong here any longer. I really must go home." It was two weeks after my father's second operation and he had been unconscious the entire time and I continued to write in my journal every day. "My Mom needs to be alone—with Dad and with herself. I'm not feeling well. I am full of anguish and I have not been able to get any of it out of me. You know, you're told to listen to the signals, to your body's signals. Well, my chest often feels tight, the burning in my chest and face come occasionally (especially when I stand at the foot of Dad's bed and stare into his beautiful face and stroke his feet) and I'm tired; my cheeks feel puffy and look puffy and I have a headache just about every other day. But how can I go home when I haven't spoken to Dad again?"

Writing in my journal gave me direction and perspective.

For five weeks after his second operation, my father was unconscious, and everything that could break down in his body did, except his heart and spirit. I know about his heart because the doctors, the nurses, and the heart monitors revealed how strong was his heart. "Nothing short of heroic," one doctor told us. That my father "woke up" after those five weeks and lived through Passover with us told me how strong was his spirit.

I had had no formal education in death and dying, although, as I have written, I have had much informal education; yet, when my father died, I was expected to be both a student of death education and a teacher (to myself and to my children) at the same time. I had to accept death as a natural occurrence in the life cycle at the same time that I was suffering the loss of my father, while I was expected to be helping my children do the same. Even though such education in death and dying and, later, in mourning, belongs in the home, it also belongs in the religious school and in the sanctuary and should begin before there is a house of mourning.

"The time is overdue," writes Herman Feifel in "Grief and Bereavement" "for 'death education' to assume a rightful role in our cultural upbringing as a preparation for living. It is fitting that we now recognise the psychological presence of death in ourselves from infancy on. Naturally, its qualitative form of expression will reflect such variables as individual differences, social context, and differing developmental periods. The pertinence of death education is not only for those of us in the health care professions who deal with dying, death, and bereavement but for all: in home, school, religious institution, and general culture."

A Jewish Book of Comfort is for the rabbi, the educator, and the lay leader to read and absorb in preparation for comforting others. *A Jewish Book of Comfort* is for the mourner to be comforted by and perhaps nourished by my own personal expressions of grief and comfort and those of our tradition, both ancient and modern.

A Jewish Book of Comfort is a collection of poems, short essays, short fiction, letters, sermons, insights, and readings from traditional sources such as the Bible, Talmud, and midrash *agadah* intended to serve as a devoted companion to those who have lost loved ones and to offer comfort and inspiration to the bereaving. But it is also a book for the comforters, for family and friends of the mourners, including the rabbi and cantor and lay leaders of the mourner's congregation.

Rabbi Maurice Lamm's *Jewish Way In Death and Mourning;* Rabbi Tzvi Rabinowicz's *Guide to Life: Jewish Laws and Customs of Mourning;* and Rabbi Chaim Binyamin Goldberg's *Mourning in Halachah: The Laws and Customs of the Year of Mourning* are classic modern texts on the subject of mourning; each is a gift to modern American Jewry's education in dying and death.

A Jewish Book of Comfort is meant to be a companion to these and other books explaining Jewish laws and customs of mourning, as well as a mate to books on bereavement care, such as those by Herman Feifel— *Meanings of Death* and *New Meanings of Death*. It offers literature to bring order to the chaos that sorrow gives rise to and hope to the despair that loneliness breeds.

Engagement with literature offers the bereaved the opportunity to explore his or her own personal loss through the losses of others and to share the sorrow and disorder of his or her own life with the lives of others and to find comfort and return to some order through shared experiences. Most important, reading helps the mourner to discover he or she is not alone with pain, and as the mourner explores, shares, and discovers, he or she strengthens the capacity to face the new reality created by the loss. *A Jewish Book of Comfort* is a book for reading and reflecting, in the hope that in the process, the mourner will know he or she is not alone.

In a section on "Study" in his chapter "The Manner of Mourning," Rabbi Rabinowicz writes in *A Guide to Life*, "The Psalmist says: 'The precepts of the Lord are right, rejoicing the heart' (Psalm 19:9). Our rabbis have therefore forbidden a mourner to study or even to meditate on the Pentateuch, Prophets, Hagiographa, Mishnah, Talmud, halachot (laws), or aggadot (tales). Both Ezekiel and Job throw light on this command. 'Sigh in silence' (Ezekiel 24:17) and 'None spoke a word' (Job 2:13) have been homiletically explained as 'Torah study'" Rabbi Lamm explains. "The study of Torah is not permitted during shiva, for it is considered a source of profound delight."

Rabbi Rabinowicz continues: "However, the mourner may spend his time reading the following works: the Book of Job, Lamentations, the sad parts of Jeremiah, the chapter *Eilu Megalchin* (which deals with the laws concerning mourning and excommunication), *Semachot*, and *Menorat Ha-Maor* (Candelabrum of Light) by Rabbi Isaac Aboab the Elder, a religioethical writer of the fourteenth century." Rabbi Lamm adds, in *The Jewish Way in Death and Mourning*, that the mourner may also "read the laws of mourning and study books on ethical behavior."

I have tried, in my gathering of readings, to be faithful to the tradition as shared by Rabbi Rabinowicz and by Rabbi Lamm while recognizing Rabbi Lamm's acknowledgment of an even more significant and desirable Jewish tradition because it is life-affirming. Rabbi Lamm informs us that the Jerusalem Talmud exempts from prohibitions against Torah study during mourning the scholars, students, teachers, and writers for whom the restraints would result in illness: scholars and students who would become ill if they could not study, teachers who would become ill if they could not teach, and writers who would become ill if they could not write. "The law forbids pleasure," Rabbi Lamm notes, "it does not command pain."

It is characteristic of the Jewish tradition, writes Rabbi Lamm, to study Torah in depth. For mourners to do so would mean they "may discover new understandings or glean new insights into the complex byways of talmudic logic, and this would bring [them] the sublime joy so well-known to those who have experienced the deep pleasure of scholarship."

On the other hand, Rabbi Lamm explains, the Jerusalem Talmud permits a student in mourning to write if it would cause pain because by being forbidden to write, an insight into the Torah may be forgotten. And what of the mourner who is not a "formal" student? Should he or she refrain from Torah study if in such study an insight is gained that would offer consolation? What of the mourner who is not a professional writer or even a free-lance writer? Should he or she refrain from making notes in a diary or a journal if such private writing would offer consolation?

Soon after I began writing this book, our friends Karen and Keith, having returned from a visit in Israel, presented me with a collection of poems by Seymour Freedman under the title *Mourning for My Father*. Freedman organizes his highly personal writings in the following sections: "After Shivah," "Shloshim to Yahrtzeit," and "After One Year." I suspect Freedman followed the traditions of mourning and refrained from Torah study or writing during *shivah*, but his heart must have been aching with the poems he would write later. Or, it may have been that he could not control his pen during the awful first week to have been able to write the poems he was already composing. My point is, as I amplify Rabbi Lamm's explanation of the Jerusalem Talmud's exemption, Seymour Freedman could have written his poetry during *shivah* without having violated Jewish law.

After Shivah

After the most painful grief
come the longer days
of slower sadness.

I wait alone
deep in myself
with images of you
cutting my mind
from time to time
for greater pain.

The days ahead
in which I will never be
with you again
weigh on me.
And I fear
all my life will be
one long mourning
one sadness, unending always.

—Seymour Freedman
"After the Most Painful Grief"
Mourning for My Father

During my research, I came across many personal expressions of grief—some published, others not—that highlighted the healing power of personal expression within the context of traditional mourning practices.

> I'm crying for my lost love
> And he, he cries for me,
>
> I'm crying for my love
> Through all eternity
>
> I'm crying for my lost love
> The willow weeps his tears,
> I'm crying for my lost love
> The loneliness, the fears.
>
> But the passway is locked
> And useless the key
> I'm crying for my lost love
> And he, he cries for me.
>
> —Reba Blaustein
> "Loss"
> *A Singing in My Soul*

I found this poem in a self-published booklet in the Judaica shop of the University of Judaism in Los Angeles. The poems in it are "Dedicated to all who are lonely." In an afterword, the author explains why she wrote her book:

> I wrote *A Singing in My Soul* as a catharsis for my bereavement. After 35 years of a good marriage, my husband died in one moment of a heart attack. It was the first time in my life I was really alone, and the first real disaster with which I could not cope. A friend took me to a Widowed Group, and I found my poetry helped them as it helped me. None of us wanted to concentrate on long books, but could empathize with short poems born out of sad experience and loneliness.
>
> —Reba Blaustein
> *A Singing in My Soul*

While I have tried to be faithful to the traditions and laws of mourning, I have also attempted to do so within the spirit of tradition and law as explained by Rabbi Lamm, keeping in mind that the purpose of this collection, of any collection of readings for the mourner, is to offer comfort meaningfully and with dignity. *A Jewish Book of Comfort* is for mourners like

Seymour Freedman as well as for mourners like Reba Blaustein and those who come to comfort them.

It has become customary in many American homes for visitors to the house of mourning to bring with them some food for a sharing table, and so it was in my home. But on the second night of *shivah*, our friends Arlene and Stu brought with them Rabbi Lamm's *The Jewish Way in Death and Mourning* and Rabbi Sidney Greenberg's *A Treasury of Comfort*.

Jewish expression was comforting because it offered ancient and proven wisdom. We read the laws and rituals of Jewish mourning practices and understood how we, as mourners, were following them. But during *shivah*, we were given no other direction, no other suggestions for reading—not by our rabbi, not by the congregation's lay leaders. What did our rabbi think we would do after we awoke on a *shivah* morning and throughout the day before he shared *Kaddish* with us and after he left our home to return to his?

It was not by chance that Polsky and Wozner entitled their collection of hasidic literature *Everyday Miracles*.

> Rabbi Aaron once came to the city where little Mordecai, who later became the rabbi of Lechovitz, was growing up. His father brought the boy to the visiting rabbi and complained that he did not persevere in his studies. "Leave the boy with me for a while," said Rabbi Aaron. When he was alone with little Mordecai, he lay down and took the child to his heart. Silently, he held him to his heart until his father returned. "I have given him a good talking-to," he said. "From now on, he will not be lacking in perseverance."
>
> Whenever the Rabbi of Lechovitz related this incident, he added, "That was when I learned how to convert men."
>
> —Howard W. Polsky and Yaella Wozner
> *Everyday Miracles*

Our rabbi might have found that book in the synagogue library and left it with us, suggesting we read the story that tells us that in the silence of a friend who visits us during *shivah* is a message of love and understanding, that in the rabbi's own visit, whether he speaks or not, there is understanding for what we have lost.

A rabbi who sets out for a house of mourning must be certain to bring some healing wisdom in the prayers and meditations and readings that accompany the *minyan* service for the house of mourning. A rabbi who sets forth from a house of mourning must be certain to leave behind some healing wisdom as may be found in the literature of our tradition.

Rabbi David J. Wolpe, among many writers, reminds us that the prayers and meditations and readings in the *minyan* service for the house of mourning and all the literature of our tradition are informed by a caring and healing God:

The God of the Bible speaks. But even more important, He is a God who is spoken to; who hears supplications, accusations, prayer. His action is always in question. Each prayer renews the agonizing question of Divine power unspent. But although unpredictable, He is never indifferent; although at times He seems arbitrary, he is never deaf.

—Rabbi David J. Wolpe
The Healer of Shattered Hearts

Our rabbi might have left such a book with us with words that would have helped us to understand that even in the quiet of the night when all others may be asleep, God is not asleep, and it is God who hears our breathing and listens to our prayers and feels our pain.

After *shivah,* I bought Rabbi Jack Riemer's *Jewish Reflections on Death*, a collection of eloquent expressions of grief that offered consolation because they gave rise to our own reflections on who and what we had lost. But on the shelves in my community's well-stocked bookstores, I was bewildered because I did not know what else to choose, although books by Dr. Bernie Siegel had been recommended: *Love, Medicine & Miracles* and *Peace, Love & Healing*. In his introduction to the latter, Dr. Siegel writes:

My emphasis in this new book is on self-healing, that ability given to us by our Creator and too long neglected by medicine. That does not mean that I am advocating turning one's back on the medical profession—but I also do not believe in relying on it alone. Modern medicine and self-healing need not and should not be mutually exclusive. I advise using all your options, which include your innate ability to heal, as well as what science can offer you.

—Dr. Bernie S. Siegel
Peace, Love & Healing

But my father had already died and whether my father would have been one of those "exceptional cancer patients" who could have been cured by the self-healing practices Dr. Siegel advocates, I will never know. What I do know is that my father was exceptional because his spirit never failed him, and my mother was exceptional because she never failed my father. But in the end, Dr. Siegel's books are not for mourners, nor are they for every person who suffers disease. (Rabbi Harold M. Schulweis offers considerable insight into Dr. Seigel's thesis in a moving Rosh Hashanah sermon, "Conversation with the Angel of Death," found in its entirety in the readings following this narrative.)

If we understand—as our friends did when they brought us books by Rabbis Lamm and Greenberg—that the mourner seeks refuge in the writings of our people, then the sharing table in the mourner's home—traditionally a place for food—may also be a place to set out a book for the mourner's spiritual and, yes, intellectual nourishment after the visitors have left and the food has been put away and the curtain of privacy has been drawn. It is my hope *A Jewish Book of Comfort* will be one of those set out on the sharing table.

Finally, *A Jewish Book of Comfort* seeks to include all mourners and all comforters, those who observe the traditional mourning practices and those who need to be free to read and write whatever will give them some measure of consolation.

"Just as there are manifold ways of living and dying," writes Herman Feifel, "there are many ways to mourn. . . . The route of grief appears to be one of tangled and complex pathways, with trails looping back and forth" ("Grief and Bereavement"). In the end, it is the mourner who will somehow tell the comforter how he or she wishes to grieve.

May God, the traditions of our people, your community of family and friends, and the strength of your own body and spirit guide you on your journey.

※◈※

Readings

�֍֍֍֍֍֍֍֍֍֍֍֍

My God, My God, Why Have You Abandoned Me

My God, my God,
   why have You abandoned me;
   why so far from delivering me
   and from my anguished roaring?
My God,
   I cry by day—You answer not;
   by night, and have no respite.

But You are the Holy One,
   enthroned,
   the Praise of Israel.
In You our fathers trusted;
   they trusted, and You rescued them.
To You they cried out
   and they escaped;
   in You they trusted
   and were not disappointed.

—Psalm 22:2–6

✺

I Cry Aloud to God

I cry aloud to God;
  I cry to God that He may give ear to me.
In my time of distress I turn to the Lord,
  with my hand [uplifted];
  [my eyes] flow all night without respite;
  I will not be comforted.
I call God to mind, I moan,
  I complain, my spirit fails.

You have held my eyelids open;
  I am overwrought, I cannot speak.
My thoughts turn to days of old,
  to years long past.
I recall at night their gibes at me;
  I commune with myself;
  my spirit inquires,
  "Will the Lord reject forever
  and never again show favor?
Has His faithfulness disappeared forever?
Will His promise be unfulfilled for all time?
Has God forgotten how to pity?
Has He in anger stifled His compassion?"

                                        —Psalm 77:2–10

✳✳

Give Ear, O God, to My Prayer

Give ear, O God, to my prayer;
  do not ignore my plea;
  pay heed to me and answer me.
I am tossed about, complaining and moaning
  at the clamor of the enemy,
  because of the oppression of the wicked;
  for they bring evil upon me
  and furiously harass me.
My heart is convulsed within me;
  terrors of death assail me.

Fear and trembling invade me;
 I am clothed with horror.
I said,
 "O that I had the wings of a dove!
I would fly away and find rest;
 surely, I would flee far off;
I would lodge in the wilderness;
I would soon find me a refuge
from the sweeping wind,
from the tempest."

       —Psalm 55:2–9

※※

The Lord Is My Shepherd

The Lord is my shepherd; I shall not want.
He maketh me to lie down in green pastures;
He leadeth me beside the still waters.
He restoreth my soul;
He guideth me in straight paths for His name's sake.
Yea, though I walk through the valley of the shadow of death,
I will fear no evil,
For Thou art with me;
Thy rod and Thy staff, they comfort me.
Thou preparest a table before me in the presence of mine enemies;
Thou hast anointed my head with oil; my cup runneth over.
Surely goodness and mercy shall follow me all the days of my life.
And I shall dwell in the house of the Lord forever.

       —Psalm 23

※※

The Oldest Memory

They then said that each of them should tell an old story, the story which represented the earliest thing that he could remember, from that very point where his memory began. There were both old and young people there, and they gave to the eldest among them the honor of beginning. He said: "What can I tell you? I remember when they cut the apple from the branch." No one quite understood what he meant by that, but the wise men agreed that this was indeed a very ancient memory. The second elder, who was just a bit younger than the first, was then given the honor. "Is that an old tale?" he said. "I remember that one too, but I also remember when the candle was yet burning." They agreed that this memory was older than the first, but were puzzled to find that it was the younger man who had the older memory. They then called upon the third, who was still younger. "I remember," he said, "when the fruit first began to be formed." They agreed that this was a still older memory. The fourth, who was yet younger, said, "I remember when they carried the seed to plant the fruit." The fifth claimed that he remembered the sages who contemplated the seed. The sixth remembered the taste of the fruit before it entered the fruit. The seventh remembered the aroma before it entered the fruit, and the eighth recalled its appearance in that same way. And I (said the blind beggar who was telling all this) was yet a child, but I was there too. I said to them: "I remember all these events. But I also remember nothing (*ikh gedenk gor nisht*)." And they answered: "This is indeed an older memory than all"

> —Rabbi Nahman of Bratslav in Rabbi Lawrence Kushner
> *The River of Light*

※※

The Death of Rabbi Me'ir's Sons

Rabbi Me'ir sat discoursing on a Sabbath afternoon in the House of Study. While he was there, his two sons died. What did their mother do? She laid them upon the bed, and spread a linen cloth over them. At the outgoing of the Sabbath, Rabbi Me'ir came home and asked, "Where are my sons?"

His wife replied, "They went to the House of Study."

He said, "I did not see them there."

She gave him the wine cup, and he said the blessing for the outgoing of the Sabbath. Then he said again, "Where are my sons?"

She replied, "They went to another place, and now they have returned." Then she gave him to eat, and he ate and recited the blessing. Then the woman said, "I have a question to ask you."

"Ask it."

She said, "Early today a man came here and gave me something to keep for him; now he has come back to ask for it again. Shall we return it to him or not?"

Me'ir replied, "He who has received something on deposit must surely return it to its owner."

She replied, "Without your knowledge I would not return it." Then she took him by the hand, and brought him up to the bed, and took away the cloth, and he saw his sons lying dead upon the bed. He began to weep . . . but his wife said to him, "Did you not say to me that one must return a deposit to its owner? And does it not say, 'The Lord gave, the Lord took, blessed be the name of the Lord?' "

Thus she comforted him and quieted his mind.

—*Midrash Mishle* 31:10 in Lewis Browne
The Wisdom of the Jewish People

✳❂✳

On Death and Dying

I confess that I am by no means an expert on the topic of death and dying. No one is. People have been dying ever since the beginning of time and yet we know nothing at all about it. Yet everyone of us believes, not in our heads but in our hearts, that it will happen to you and you and you—but not to me. It is a wonder that anyone recovers from a loss, that anyone can cope with the awesome, terrifying fact of mortality, and with the amputation of a loved one who has been for many years a part of oneself.

There is no simple formula, there is no religious pill that if taken often enough is guaranteed to work, and anyone who presumes to say that there is, is glib, presumptuous, and arrogant. There are some religious people who have been broken by grief, who have become bitter and angry and warped as the result of sorrow, and no one can judge them, no one can blame them, for grief can be a brutal blow. There are some nonreligious people who have been strengthened by sorrow, who have come out of the experience better and not bitter, who have been humbled, chastened, and purified by the experience, and who have emerged better able to understand and feel with and help others.

How it is that different people react to the same events in such different ways is one of the great mysteries for which we have no explanation. Yet religion, and specifically Judaism, does have some insights to offer to the mourner. It is a religion that speaks to all of life, and therefore it speaks to this experience too, for this is surely a part of every person's life. It provides a number of actions, symbols, and insights that can give comfort, consolation, courage, wisdom, and perspective to the person in grief.

The first Jewish insight is community. In your time of greatest isolation, confusion, and helplessness, the community reaches out and embraces you, and tells you that you are not alone. Ours is a group religion in time of joy and in time of sorrow. Ours is not an I-Thou relationship to God but a We-Thou relationship to God, and this is made manifest in a number of different ways during the time of grief.

What do we say when we stand at the grave? We don't know what to say. Whatever we say sounds so glib. "How old was he?"—what difference does that make? "I know how you feel"?—you don't know how I feel. "Time will heal"—it won't. Whatever we say at such a time sounds patronizing and inadequate. The tradition bids us say: "May God comfort you"—since *we* don't know how—"together with all the others who are mourning for Zion and Jerusalem!" That sounds like a strange kind of comfort. Don't I have enough with my own sorrow; must I also hear about the mourners for Zion and Jerusalem? There is a comfort in that, to know that others are also in grief, that Zion is in distress, and Jerusalem is incomplete, and that God is in exile. It sets my personal sorrow into a larger perspective and reminds me of who I am and of the community to which I belong.

You come back from the funeral and the Law states that you must eat. It is the Law because otherwise you would not, and to eat means to go on living. The Law also states that you cannot prepare the food for yourself but that others, the neighbors and the friends, must prepare it for you. This means that neighbors and friends come into the house, and you are not alone.

For seven days the minyan moves to the home, which means that at the least ten people are there twice a day. Then you go each day to the minyan and join what someone has wisely called "the fraternity of mourners." That helps to make you realize that you are not alone, that you are part of a club that everyone must join eventually, some sooner some later, and a sense of kinship and community develops among those who share this experience.

To be a Jew means to be connected horizontally and vertically—to all the Jews here and around the world, to all the Jews who ever were and to all the Jews who will yet be. It means to be Abraham's great-grandchild and the Messiah's great-grandfather and the cousin of every other Jew—be he or she in Berlin or Baghdad, Cairo or Casablanca.

The second Jewish insight to the mourner is that you are needed, that there are others worse off than you whom you can help. For one brief moment the Law gives the mourner a respite. In the hours between the death of his loved one and the burial, the Law excuses him from the yoke of the commandments, for it understands that his mind and his heart are elsewhere, that he is in no mood to pray and praise, and that anything he says at such a time could only be rote or lie. But then from the moment of burial the Law snaps him back to attention, back to duties and responsibilities, back to the world of work. It is wise in doing so for strength comes, not from resting but from helping, not from self-pity but from self-dedication, not from asking for help but from giving help. Strength comes from realizing that you are a soldier in the army of God, an army that has been diminished by the loss of your loved, and that therefore you must carry on for God's sake and for your own.

One more religious insight in the time of grief is the central religious claim that we are not simply creatures of flesh and blood, not simply a used-up machine or a collection of chemicals worth a few dollars but that we are, in some indefinable way, the children and the partners and the image of God, who come from Him and go back to Him, whose lives are a loan, a trust, a responsibility, and a gift, and whose deaths are a return, a reunion, a homecoming, and a rest.

The keys to a culture are in its words. Consider the terms for death and see what they say about the world views of the communities from which they come. The biblical term is "to be gathered to your ancestors," which means to become a part of history. It is a way of stressing the community dimension of our human existence. The classic Jewish term for death is *niftar*, which means "to be released from service." The conception is that this is the world of work, of commandments, of accomplishments, of opportunities to do things for God. That is the world of rest, of return, to which one is summoned when one has accomplished his task. The modern word is: "passed away"—a pale, vague, wishy-washy word which does not say much or mean much because we are vague and unclear ourselves in how we feel about death.

The central religious truth is that life is a loan and death a return, that after intelligence there must come trust, that after acquiring there must come surrender, and that after having there must come being.

The religious laws are meant as ways of serving God; their by-product is that they bring healing and health to the bereaved. They are immensely technical, even sometimes petty, but they prevent excess and they prevent sloughing off a loss as though nothing had happened. To say that death is not significant enough to mark in special ways is to

say that life is cheap. Many of those who do not have the time to work
out their grief in the time of loss end up spending much more time on
the psychiatrist's couch working it out later.

These three insights—that we are connected, that we are needed, and
that we are related to God—are a few of the many insights that the
tradition contains. They have been of some help to me in this, the year
of my grief and loss, and so I share them with you in the hope that they
may be of help to you. This is one area where we all stand before the
same darkness and where we all need to share whatever wisdom,
strength, and light we may have with each other.

Offered in memory of my father and teacher, Reb Eliezer ben Reb
Yosef Riemer, Louis Riemer, *niftar* on the second day of Chanukah,
5735. May his memory be a blessing

—Rabbi Jack Riemer in
Understanding Bereavement and Grief, adapted

✸✸

Conversation with the Angel of Death

The letter from Lillian came between Rosh Hashanah and Yom Kippur.

"I am writing to you as both my friend and my rabbi, driven by the
deep sadness and sense of disconnectedness that has gripped me since
this morning's Rosh Hashanah service. I am not what many would call
a religious Jew. Having come to my commitment through study as an
adult rather than through family observance as a child, my beliefs have
been shaped along lines of logic rather than those of emotion. I have
never believed in a personal God, but I take my responsibility to ethics
and ritual, to the Jewish community, very seriously. Until this morning
I have spent the High Holy Days, if not in the spirit of fear and
trembling before a God of justice, then at least in the sure knowledge
that it is appropriate to review my actions of the past year, to give real
thought to my failures, and to resolve to be a better person, a better
Jew, a better citizen.

"Until this morning. I know the central liturgy of the holiday well,
but before this year I had approached it in an abstract, intellectual
manner. This year, I could not do so. Several months ago I had surgery
for cancer, and I felt very keenly as I approached these days that in a real
sense my fate for the coming year has been written, if not in a book of
judgment, then in my own body. I look forward to health, but I may

not be granted it. As I read, the questions of the service were familiar: 'How many shall pass away and how many shall be born; who shall live and who shall die.' But the response—'repentance, prayer, and right-eousness avert the severe decree'—for the first time carried a terrifying implication. It seemed to me as I read this that my own liturgy was binding my fate to my behavior, that my illness, seen in this light, has been the result of some terrible unknown transgression, and that the ultimate punishment for failure to discover and correct it could be my death.

"I do not believe this—not with my head nor my heart. Nevertheless, as a committed Jew who takes language very seriously and believes in community prayer, I would be forced to repeat this central cornerstone over and over should I attend services for Yom Kippur. It seems today that my choice is a terrible one: to flagellate myself emotionally by joining my congregation or to spare my feelings by isolating myself from my family, my friends, my community. It is a choice I never believed I would have to make.

"I know there must be others in our congregation who sit suffering silently, as I did today, who wish to join Jews around the world at this time but find the price too high to pay. I do not write expecting an easy answer; holocaust literature has taught me there may be no answer at all. I write instead because I must, because to muffle my sadness and my anger will destroy something in the commitment I have worked so hard to build. I write from pain, hoping that from the expression of my dilemma will grow some insight, some way to cope."

There are times when religion is a matter of life and death. When it is not about getting the right seat in the sanctuary at High Holy Days, or the convenient scheduling of the Bar Mitzvah or the catered wedding.

There are times when religion, God, faith, prayer are very much taken to heart. Conversations around the hospital bed cut through the intellectual games of theology, the amenities of wishing each other "a good writing and sealing" for the New Year. Facing sickness and death, our own or our family's or our friends', the foundations of our being are shaken. You pray differently then and you think differently then. You pray and you listen hard. Lillian's letter would not let me go.

Around the same time I received the letter, I was informed that another congregant, Sandra, was seriously ill. At our first conversation, Sandra began softly, "Please, Rabbi, don't lie to me. I have a fatal form of leukemia, and I know that I am dying. The doctors have been frank with me. I have two small children who go to your school. I love them and they love me. I have wonderful parents and a marvelously supportive husband. But I cannot make sense of it all. I don't ask 'why me,' but 'what for?' Life for me has been drained of all meaning. What have I these remaining weeks or months to live for. My children have given me so much meaning. I looked forward to being their mother. But I know now that I will not be able to raise them. My future has been cut off.''

She told me that when she was in the hospital before Rosh Hashanah, a Rabbi had visited her and blown the shofar for her in the grim hospital room. She was grateful. He inquired as to the nature of her illness and then asked whether it was her practice to light Sabbath candles. She said she did and he answered, "Well then, you have nothing to worry about." He meant it as an assurance. She thought, What would he have said if she had answered no, or if he had asked her if she kept kosher. At any rate, Sandra turned away from him, buried her head in the pillow and sobbed.

I thought of Lillian's letter and Sandra's resentment. But Sandra was too agitated and too ill for theological discussion. She was inconsolable and I wanted to make her better, to cheer her spirits. A book was brought to my attention, a best-seller by Dr. Bernie Siegel, a surgeon. The book is entitled *Love, Medicine & Miracles*, and its subtitle read "Lessons learned about self-healing from a surgeon's experience with exceptional patients."

In my eyes Sandra was an exceptional patient. I read the book quickly. It was filled with statistics, evidence, anecdotal accounts of patients successfully coping with death-threatening cancers, and cases of multiple sclerosis, arthritis, diabetes, heart disease, AIDS. It offered eyewitness and hearsay accounts of terminally ill patients who beat the odds. Resilient, adaptable, confident, with an unquenchable will to live, they defied the gloomy prognostications of their doctors, stuck their tongues out at their lugubrious predictions and refused to curl up and die.

The book is full of illustrations and quotes, stories of the triumph of hope and love and will. These were the exceptional patients who refused to go gentle onto the operating table, whom—according to Siegel—doctors don't like because they are inquisitive, demanding, aggressive, bad patients who refuse to surrender. These are the patients who don't look at the physicians or surgeons as M.D.s—an acronym for Medical Deities—and who if they are not satisfied, change doctors.

Before reading the book, Sandra told me of the doctors' terrible prognosis. I told her that doctors are not prophets and that according to the Sages, "prophesy in our times has fallen into the hands of children and fools." "Sandra," I said, "remember doctors are not gods." Sandra liked that, told it to her doctor, who responded, "Well, neither are rabbis." I had my come-uppance.

Now I had a book written by a surgeon of oncology to shore up her spirits. The book I gave Sandra started out with a bold statement from Norman Cousins' *Anatomy of an Illness*, "Patients divided themselves into two groups. Those who were confident they would beat back the disease and be able to resume normal lives and those who resigned themselves to a prolonged and even fatal illness."

Those who had an optimistic view had a higher percentage "discharged as cured" than the others in the tuberculosis sanitorium where Cousins was sent. There appears to be a "physiology of optimism." There are peptide molecules in the body releasing "wonder drugs within": endorphins, interleukins, interferons.

I like Norman Cousins ever since I heard about his advocacy and practice of watching Marx Brothers films as a form of therapy. My own cardiologist I decided has no sense of humor.

Siegel throughout maintains that " instead of turning fighters into victims, we should be turning victims into fighters." The book is sprinkled with success stories of exceptional patients whose *attitude* and will gave them hope and extended their lives. I meant the Siegel book to help her. But it boomeranged on her. The book angered, then saddened her. I re-read the book this time through Sandra's eyes.

For Sandra, and for others I have talked to since, the success of the exceptional patients was her failure, their victories her defeats, their cures her misery. "What's wrong with me. I have tried, God knows I have tried. I have gritted my teeth. Taken the chemotherapy, the medicines. I have given love and been loved in turn. Why can't I will myself into wellness like those others."

Psychological literature speaks of "survivors' guilt," those tortured by their good fortune to survive while others fall. Soldiers who have seen their buddies wounded and killed while they leave the battlefield unscathed; survivors of concentration camps who witnessed the suffering and murder of their fellow inmates while they are spared. Sandra was suffering from "victim's guilt," the guilt of the ordinary, the unlucky, the condemned. She couldn't forgive herself for her unexceptionality.

I read it again and then read Siegel's new book, *Peace, Love & Healing*, a clone of the first book, to understand Sandra's reaction. There Siegel quotes with favor a novelist who writes that "illness doesn't strike randomly like a thief in the night. Certain kinds of people at certain points in their lives will come down with certain ailments. You can almost predict it.''

Ray Berti, a college professor in Massachusetts battling throat, bone marrow and other types of cancer for fourteen years, finally sees the light. ''The critical thing for me was when I said to myself, 'Ray, somehow or other you're causing it. I am the cause.' '' Paradoxically, the book which intended to offer her morale, to rid the patient of passive dependency, delivered a double whammy. First, she felt responsible for her lack of attitude that made her susceptible to the disease, and now she felt responsible for not snapping out of it.

I understand Siegel's argument that patients become too acquiescent, too passive, too dependent; that patients frequently abandon their responsibility. The reversal of that dependence was popularized two decades ago among psychological cults. As one of the celebrated psychologists put it, ''I am me. Therefore everything that comes out of me is authentically mine because I alone chose it. I own everything about me. My body, my mind, my eyes. I own my fantasies, my dreams, my fears, my triumphs, my failures, my mistakes. I own me and therefore I can engineer me. I am me and I am okay.''

If you are indeed all that, you have no one to blame but yourself, you are the cause. I have a rabbinic friend who a few years ago found himself immobilized, his bodily movements painfully restricted. The paralysis was shown not to be organic. He consulted all kinds of doctors and psychologists and was recommended to a psychologist whose specialty is hypnosis. After going there, he told the doctor, ''I'm not being helped.'' ''You will be helped,'' said the psychologist, ''when you're ready.'' So the failure to recover was a failure of will. Not can't but won't blocks your cure.

Paul Cowan, the author, in his last article for The Village Voice (May 17, 1988) before his death from leukemia, comments on the need to confront the awesome, mysterious power of his disease. ''Otherwise, if the leukemia cells re-enter my bone marrow, I run the risk myself for relapsing and if I continue to weaken, of raging at my psyche instead of fighting back.'' The dark side of faith in will is self blame.

This is part of the new tyranny of the will. We live in a climate of desperate voluntarism. We are raised to believe in the omnipotence of the will. We have been read to in our childhood and pass its theology on to our children [about] the little engine chugging its way up the mountain with the endless refrain: ''I think I can, I think I can, I think I can, I think I can . . . '' until triumph flashes, ''I knew I could.''

We live in a culture of will and wish. Peter Pan reaches out to the audience to have it pray with the hands to revive Tinker Bell. And we do it. Faith will revive. Faith will resurrect. Faith will redeem. Faith will cure . . . if you only believe yourself into recovery. Will is the secular form of faith. Will can move mountains and remove illness. Things just don't happen. We choose them. We make ourselves sick and well.

So Siegel declares, "Psychologists long ago discovered that emotions can be modified merely by adopting the facial expression of contrary emotions." Indeed Dr. Paul Ekman of U.C. at San Francisco distinguishes 18 anatomically different types of smiles. It calls to mind Dr. Smiley Blanton, a popular psychologist, who would convince his audiences that with their cooperation, he could convert their sadness to happiness. He would instruct his audience to smile and when they parted their lips and showed their teeth, challenged them to be simultaneously sad. "When you smile," he concluded, "you control your emotions." Smiling has made you happy. Photographers have developed this philosophy into a photogenic technique. "Look happy, Rabbi," they instruct me, asking me to stop eating and stand behind the other seated guests. I don't look happy because at the moment I'm not happy, and smiling is not the appropriate expression now. "Say *cheese*," the photographer advises. I obey and later, after the film has been developed he boasts that he had captured my happiness. Others, seeing the picture, comment on my joy. In truth, however, the photographer had not immortalized happiness, he had only captured "cheese."

The triumphalism of the will ignores what wisdom understood: the limitations of will. I can will my smile—I cannot will my happiness. I can will my eating, I cannot will my hunger. I can will going to sleep, I cannot will my dreams. I can will knowledge, I cannot will wisdom. I can will my self-assertion, I cannot will my courage. I can will shaving, combing, dressing up—I cannot will my joy. I can will purchasing flowers, perfume, candies—I cannot will love. I can will fasting, the recitation of the litany of transgression—I cannot will remorse. I can will opening the prayer book and Bible—I cannot will belief. "A wink is not a blink." One I will, one I do not. I can will many things, but I cannot will my will.

During my own illness I recall feeling frightened and sad and later at night turning to a channel which fortuitously, was showing "A Night at the Opera," a Marx Brothers classic. Norman Cousins' counsel did not work with me. I did not laugh. The Marx Brothers were not funny, nothing was funny. I could not will feeling funny. Should I have felt failure because of my inability to laugh? How have I no sense of humor now that I need it?

Judaism celebrates freedom of will. It has from the time of the Bible on struggled against pre-destination theologies, against fate. But there is a deeper wisdom in Judaism—a Reality Principle—that knows the limitations of will. Judaism presents a more balanced portrayal of the human condition.

"By dint of force are you born. By dint of force you die." And that helps me interpret differently the "who shall live, who shall die" prayer that troubles Lillian.

"How many shall pass away and how many shall be born; who shall perish by fire and who by water, who by earthquake and who by plague." I do not know. For these matters are not matters of will—neither my will, your will, or God's will. For me the litany refers to natural events, births, deaths, accidents, sicknesses over which I have no control. They are not God's punishments or rewards. What then are they? If they are not the "acts of God" are they the acts of the Devil?

The Talmud (Avodah Zarah 54b) is helpful here. It refers to "the ways in which Nature pursues its course." The Talmud uses this expression in arguing against a simplistic explanation of patently immoral events. The sages ask, "Suppose a man stole a measure of wheat and then sowed it in the ground." Clearly it would be right for that wheat not to grow. That would be the "din," the judgment were this a case brought to the rabbinic courts. But "*the world pursues its own natural course*" and as for the fools who act wrongly (i.e., for those who stole the wheat) "they will have to render an account." They offer another illustration: Suppose a man has intercourse with his neighbor's wife. It would be morally right that she should not conceive but we must acknowledge that "the world pursues its natural course," and as far as the transgressors who act wrongly are concerned, they will have to render an account.

I understand the sages to be cautioning not to confuse biology with morality; not to confuse the procreative process with the process of the law; not to confuse physical laws of nature with moral laws. *Every event has a cause but not every cause is morally determined*. Every event has a reason for occurring, but not every event has a purpose in occurring. The cancer I have is not God's curse for my sin. The heart attack is not God's punishing rod to whip me into repentance. *Not all events are judgments*.

There are consequences to my taking a contaminated needle for the sake of transfusion. My contraction of AIDS is a consequence but a consequence is not a punishment, and a reason explaining why a sickness occurs is not a moral judgment. The infant born addicted may be a consequence of the substance abuse of its parent, but consequence is not purpose or judgment or justification for the addiction. Such distinctions must be drawn if we are not to condemn ourselves to lives of masochistic dread and guilt or to turn God into an indiscriminate punisher.

Nature is not God. And to treat nature as if it were God would convert every fact into a moral judgment. An earthquake into God's smoldering anger against sinners, rainfall into a reward. That outlook breathes a spirit animism that sees ghosts in rocks and waters, in lesions in the skin and leprous rashes. That theology turns sadomasochistic. Unintentionally, it turns God into a mysterious sadistic God and man into a masochist with a taste for suffering.

Those who seek desperately for justification of evil and suffering frequently turn to the "Helen Keller defense" popularized in a poem. "At birth deny a child vision, hearing and the ability to speak and you have a Helen Keller. Raise him in abject poverty and you have an Abraham Lincoln. Stab him with rheumatic pain until opiates are needed and you have a Steinmetz."

The truth in the argument is that there are people who can make virtue out of necessity, who can transcend suffering and use it to spur them on to greatness. The falsehood in the argument is in pointing to heroism and courage as justification for human suffering, agony and death. That mentality would argue that poverty is good because it gives people an opportunity to be charitable; that sickness is good because it offers medical science challenge, that suffering is good for it tests character. With some theologies, the facts of sickness, suffering and death are converted into divine intention. Purpose is read into calamity by interpreting it as either God's punishment or God's reward. What "is" is turned into what "ought to be."

Dr. Siegel writes, "I suggest that patients think of illness not as God's will but as our deviation from God's will." He thinks patients must acknowledge "the absence of spirituality" in their lives. To avoid blaming God and therein the assumption of the patient's responsibility, Siegel inadvertently turns the patient into a scapegoat.

To see in illness a deviation from God's will is a retrograde piety. Who shall end up in hospital or hospice and who shall remain healthy is not a matter of will, divine or human. If it were, life would be filled with false guilt, blame and accusation. Sickness would justify the infantile unending taunt: "It serves you right. You get what you deserve." Susan Sontag (*AIDS and Its Metaphors*) recalls painfully the fictions of responsibility

that attended her becoming a cancer patient. Cancer was regarded as a
disease to which "the psychically defeated, the inexpressive, the re-
pressed" are particularly prone.

As I reflect on the book, I find it fascinating to see how saturated this
society is with the need to blame, to find fault. It is as if there cannot
be any explanation of events without someone to fault. How remarkable the Talmudic insight "nature pursues its own course."

Elsewhere Dr. Siegel contends, "I feel that all disease is ultimately
related to a lack of love . . . that all disease is ultimately related to the
inability to give and accept unconditional love."

That bit of generalizing philosophy unintentionally adds insult to
injury. Sandra loved deeply, loved her family, her friends; she was
involved in the synagogue, with the developmentally disabled. She was
gifted with social conscience. Inadvertently, Siegel ends with blame of
the failed patient for not having the right kind of self-love or altruism.
He is caught up in a secular guilt trip.

I return to Lillian's letter and to the conversation I had with her. For
her the "who shall live and who shall die" prayer sent a shiver in her,
a threat of future punishments for past transgressions. And the more
hopeful conclusion that Repentance, Prayer, and Charity would avert
the evil decree rubbed salts in her wounds. Had she not lived, repented,
prayed, and been charitable before she contracted her illness? And is that
illness a "decree," a verdict, a judgment upon her from up high? How
should she understand the prayer? How do I pray the "netaneh tokef?"

For me, the Netaneh Tokef questions, with which the prayer opens,
mean that there are areas in life over which I have no control. It confesses
my creatureliness, my dependence on nature. There are amoral features
in nature which should not be explained as if nature were a rabbinic
tribunal. Part of the prayer expresses the Jewish reality principle. I accept
the law of nature, the withering of the leaves, the breaking of the boughs,
the miscarriages in birth, the congenital and non-congenital disease. I
accept the limitations that nature places on me. Moreover, Judaism does
not encourage me to pray for a suspension or modification of the laws
of nature. Judaism's reality principle calls prayers that seek to reverse the
laws of nature, that pray that what events take place did not *"tefillat
shov,"* vain, empty prayers. Jewish faith is not magic.

Much as I would desire it I cannot pray away the damage done to my
heart nor pray away the tumor from my colon nor will the growth of
arms and legs onto my paraplegia.

But that wisdom of acceptance is not the acceptance of impotence,
that reality principle does not paralyze the proper areas and functions of

my mind, heart and will. That is the meaning of "turning, prayer, and charity." Those are the areas over which I do have control. I cannot alter the world of nature outside, but I can effect the world within. As Albo in the *Ikarim* asserts, my prayer actions do not change God; they change me (IV Chapter 18).

Maimonides (Hilchoth Avodah Zarah 11–12) offers a crucial distinction between the healing of the body and the healing of the spirit (refuath ha-guf; refuath ha-nefesh). "To read a scriptural verse or place a Torah or a pair of tefilin on a child so that he may sleep is not only the way of diviners and fortune tellers, but it uproots the Torah—for they who practice in this manner make the Torah a healer of the body whereas the Torah is a healer of the spirit."

Jewish faith-healing does not pretend to cure the cancer with the willful laying on of the hands. God is not found in the leukemia. God is found in the character and meaning latent in the patient. Meaning is not in the deafness or blindness or muteness or lameness—that is nature's course, not God's will. But how we respond to nature calls upon our intelligence, our hope, our faith.

When Sandra asked what meaning in life remained to her which was tied up to her raising her children, we explored the possibilities of meaning. Sandra agreed that she wanted to raise them to be strong, to help them learn how to cope with the abrasiveness of life, how to face the challenge of adversity. Are these not the wishes of a mother?

"Your children, Sandra, know how sick you are. And you are teaching them lessons they will cherish the rest of their lives. Sick and suffering, you teach them how to love, how to cling to faith. Living, you teach. Dying, you teach dignity, courage and meaning. And so it is with your husband and your family and your friends. Sandra, you are meaning. There is a midrash that informs that 'the righteous are informed of the day of their death so that they may hand the crown to their children.' "

I would not lie to her or Lillian or to myself. Who shall live or die, how long I shall live is not in our control. And God whom I worship is no enemy of mine, no implacable, inaccessible Judge. God is my ally, my strength and my friend. And as I tap into the curative forces within the soul into which God breathed life I may make my life a blessing. Tshuvah, Tefillah, and Tzedakah cannot save me from death, but they can give me more life.

—Rabbi Harold M. Schulweis

II

✕✕✕✕✕✕✕✕✕✕✕✕✕✕✕✕✕✕✕✕✕✕✕✕

AVELUT: *THE FIVE STAGES OF JEWISH MOURNING*

2

✕✕✕✕✕✕✕✕✕✕✕✕✕✕✕✕✕✕✕✕✕✕✕✕✕✕

Aninut: *From Death to Burial*

Aninut is the first stage of the Jewish mourning period and includes death (*mavet*) and burial (*kavorah*). At the moment following death, each of the immediate survivors becomes an *onen*, "a person in deep distress, a person yanked out of normal life and abruptly catapulted into the midst of inexpressible grief" (Rabbi Maurice Lamm, "A Parable," *Understanding Bereavement and Grief*). Funeral arrangements are made. With some exceptions, burial occurs within 24 hours after death.

The *Chevra Kadisha*, the Holy Society, or the staff of the funeral home prepares the body for burial, called *taharah*. The preparation includes washing and dressing the body in *tachrichim*, burial garments, usually shrouds of white linen. From the moment of death until the burial, a *shomer*, or watcher, keeps guard over the body.

A eulogy for the funeral service is prepared and includes *hesped*, praising of the deceased for his or her worthy qualities, and *bechi*, expression of the grief and the sense of loss experienced by the mourners and the entire Jewish community.

Before the funeral service, *keriah* is performed, the rending of the garment, a sign of grief. The funeral service itself includes scriptural readings, concluding with *El Malay Rachamin*, "O God, full of compassion."

Pallbearers escort the coffin from the funeral parlor to the hearse and at the cemetery, from the hearse to the grave, stopping seven times as the rabbi leads the mourners in prayer. The grave is filled, and the burial *kaddish* and the memorial prayer, *El Malay Rachamin*, are recited.

DEATH (*MAVET*)

"Alan, I think he's gone." My mother's voice was calm. Her thoughts collected. Her pain was so deep it would not break the surface until the sanctuary service; but then, with all her hope for my father's recovery, not a miraculous one but one resulting from response to medical treatment, my mother had feared my father's death for four months, and her outrage had already and so often been expressed. Now that he had died, there was a certain assurance that in death his body was at peace and his soul was being gently cared for; but there was no less anguish.

My mother told me she was standing at my father's bedside in the Ft. Lauderdale, Florida, hospital, holding my father's hand in one of hers while her other hand held the telephone receiver. I was at the other end in New York. We were linked. But my heart ached not to have been physically with them. My father's hospital room was clean and well lighted. His bed had just been freshened and he wore a clean white sheet over his body.

My mother told me she had kissed my father's forehead and had watched his eyes stare into a world she could not see, then close and remain closed. "When death is finally established," writes Rabbi Rabinowicz, "the eyes and mouth are gently closed by the son or the nearest relative. Jacob was assured that Joseph would render this final filial service (Genesis 46:4)" (Rabbi Tzvi Rabinowicz, *A Guide to Life*).

"God called to Israel in a vision by night: 'Jacob! Jacob!' He answered, 'Here.' And He said, 'I am God, the God of your father. Fear not to go down to Egypt, for I will make you there into a great nation. I Myself will go down with you to Egypt, and I Myself will also bring you back; and Joseph's hand shall close your eyes'" (Genesis 46:2–4).

What is this world I believe my father looked into before he died? Perhaps it is a "glimpse of the divine"; perhaps it is the world of his mother and father and of theirs. "Legend has it," Rabbi Rabinowicz writes, "that the dying are granted a glimpse of the Divine. 'Thou canst not see My face, for men shall not see Me and live' (Exodus 33:20); in other words, a man cannot see God in life but only in death." In a note to this reference, Rabbi Rabinowicz adds: "Zohar, Vayyechi 281b: 'At a time of a man's death he is vouchsafed to see his dead relatives and companions from the other world.' Also p. 226: '. . .the eyes which have just beheld a holy vision should now dwell on a sight of different character.' "

I remember the words of my wise friend Lou Rivers, who shared with me this same legend before one of my visits with my father during his illness. I had remarked to my friend how distant my father had seemed to both me and my mother during an earlier visit.

"Remember," my friend said, "your father had a father and he had a father who had a father and so on. And when a child is in crisis, he will seek the comfort of his parents. When your father withdraws, he withdraws not from your love or from your mother's love, but from his own fear. Only a parent can accept a child's fear unconditionally. Your father, as any child, knows this to be true." I had only to look to the genealogies in the Torah to know death is only a link in the chain of life and that there is comfort in knowing one's own generation is warmly embraced by past generations. "And, be ever mindful," my friend added, "no one has lived forever." In Ecclesiastes it is written: One generation passeth away, and another generation cometh, but the earth abideth forever.

This is the record of Adam's line.—When God created man, He made him in the likeness of God; male and female He created them. And when they were created, He blessed them and called them Man.—When Adam had lived 130 years, he begot a son in his likeness after his image, and he named him Seth. After the birth of Seth, Adam lived 800 years and he begot sons and daughters. All the days that Adam lived came to 930 years; then he died.

When Seth had lived 105 years, he begot Enosh. After the birth of Enosh, Seth lived 807 years and begot sons and daughters. All the days of Seth came to 912 years; then he died.

When Enosh had lived 90 years, he begot Kenan. After the birth of Kenan, Enosh lived 815 years and begot sons and daughters. All the days of Enosh came to 905 years; then he died.

When Kenan had lived 70 years, he begot Mahalalel. After the birth of Mahalalel, Kenan lived 840 years and begot sons and daughters. All the days of Kenan came to 910 years; then he died.

When Mahalalel had lived 65 years, he begot Jared. After the birth of Jared, Mahalalel lived 830 years and begot sons and daughters. All the days of Mahalalel came to 895 years; then he died.

When Jared had lived 162 years, he begot Enoch. After the birth of Enoch, Jared lived 800 years and begot sons and daughters. All the days of Jared came to 962 years; then he died.

When Enoch had lived 65 years, he begot Methuselah. After the birth of Methuselah, Enoch walked with God 300 years; and he begot sons and daughters. All the days of Enoch came to 365 years. Enoch walked with God; then he was no more, for God took him.

When Methuselah had lived 187 years, he begot Lamech. After the birth of Lamech, Methuselah lived 782 years and begot sons and daughters. All the days of Methuselah came to 969 years; then he died.

When Lamech had lived 182 years, he begot a son. And he named him Noah, saying, "This one will provide us relief from our work and from the toil of our hands, out of the very soil which the Lord placed under a curse." After the birth of Noah, Lamech lived 595 years and begot sons and daughters. All the days of Lamech came to 777 years; then he died.

When Noah had lived 500 years, Noah begot Shem, Ham, and Japheth.

—Genesis 5

"There are no new kinds of tears: we cry the same tears as did David for his child" (Rabbi David J. Wolpe, *The Healer of Shattered Hearts*):

"The king was shaken. He went up to the upper chamber of the gateway and wept, moaning these words as he went, 'My son Absalom! O my son, my son Absalom! If only I had died instead of you! O Absalom, my son, my son!'" (2 Samuel 19:1).

I visited my father again soon after talking with my friend. This visit was also a journey because I had a mission. In my innocence, I thought I could look into my father's eyes to have confirmed what my friend had told me.

My father and I sat alone at the dining room table. He sat at the head of the table, as he always did, leaning forward as he was accustomed to doing when eating, sipping from a spoon plain chicken soup my mother had prepared. His lips were pursed as if he were going to kiss the soup before it entered his mouth. I sat to his left, listening to the whisper of liquid passing his lips.

I could not ask my father to look at me. I was also frightened that he would. What would I see? I wanted to see beyond death to the promise of eternal life.

I was frightened because once before when we had sat as we were then sitting, my father looked at me and talked about death. It was one month earlier. We were having breakfast at the end of a five-day visit. My mother had told him the chemotherapy would begin that week. He was looking directly into my eyes; his eyes were wide and clear but they seemed to be emitting a bright light. Later, I read in Proverbs: "The spirit of man is the lamp of the Lord, searching all the inward parts." Was God already revealing himself to my father? I sensed a familiarity I had never before experienced with my father, as if I had been invited to share in his inner being, closer than any touch, or any word, as if my father were inviting me to "look in, look in, see what's happening to me and see what I can see." But then all he did say was about the chemotherapy: "It's the only chance I've got. If it doesn't work, I'm a dead duck." What a strange metaphor for my father to use. What a cliche, as if that was all he had left, the tried-and-true, like chicken soup. Was it only fear I saw in his eyes then? Later, when I recalled that moment, I sank into despair that I didn't hold him in my arms at that time and squeeze the fear out of him.

But this visit was different. This time something strange and wonderful happened. As my father and I stared into each other's eyes—and all this occurred between blinks—he suddenly wasn't looking at me but through me, beyond me, and for the first time since my father's illness, he gave *me* comfort.

After my mother told me my father had died, I told her I loved her and that I would come down to Florida to accompany her and my father to New York for the funeral. No. She wanted my sister and me to make the arrangements for my father's funeral in New York and she would prepare to leave her apartment and fly up to New York with her sister and her husband (my Aunt Dubby and Uncle Irving), who lived nearby.

"I'm fine," she assured me. "I really am."

Later that evening, after friends had left our home, I sat alone with the journal I had kept since my father first became ill.

"I am comforted by the fullness with which Dad and I had a relationship," I wrote. "I am full with my father and that blesses me. I took full advantage of every opportunity to be with him these four months. I grabbed at him. I have left nothing undone. I am comforted by my mother's strength. She fought for his life and for their life together. I am comforted by my belief that Dad had come to an acceptance of his death before he died, so when he did die, he wasn't afraid. He saw into a world we could not see. He saw the world of his mother and father. I am comforted by my belief in God. Would I want another minute with my dad? Of course! But I am not angry or resentful of God because one day I will be with Dad again and I want him to know his life remains alive in mine." In the Talmud it is written: "The righteous need no memorials, their words and deeds are their remembrances. The righteous even after their death are called alive." And Proverbs emphasizes this eternal life: "A good man leaveth an inheritance to his children's children."

Aninut is the first stage of the Jewish mourning period. As soon as my mother told me that my father had died, "Alan, I think he's gone," I became an *onen*, as my mother and my sister, Barbara, had become, as my father's sister, Lettie, had become. I had suddenly become a part of my father's death and apart from the rest of the world.

An *onen* is "one who is troubled" or "sorrowful" (Genesis 35:18): "But as she [Rachel] breathed her last—for she was dying—she named him [her newborn] Ben-oni; but his father called him Benjamin." And *Ben-oni* may be translated as "son of my suffering."

Rabbi Lamm writes: "The *onen* is a person in deep distress, a person yanked out of normal life and abruptly catapulted into the midst of inexpressible grief. He is disoriented, his attitudes are disarranged, his emotions out of gear. The shock of death paralyzes his consciousness and blocks out all regular patterns of orderly thinking. 'The deceased lies before him,' as the sages said, and, psychologically, he is reliving the moment of death every instant during the period" (Rabbi Maurice Lamm, *The Jewish Way in Death and Mourning*).

Seymour Freedman expresses similar "deep distress" in one of his poems.

Why does the human being,
why did my father,
have to end his days
in suffering and pain?

Could not G-d who loves us
find a more dignified and joyful way,
to deliver us?

Why didn't my father die peacefully
quietly
in his sleep,
without the restless struggling
and the agony of the end?

Why did my father's last moments
have to be among
and like,
the most terrible
he had known
in his life?

—Seymour Freedman
"Why Does the Human Being"
Mourning for My Father

Whether death comes after a long, painful illness or suddenly, the survivor "is a person in deep distress, a person yanked out of normal life and abruptly catapulted into the midst of inexpressible grief." Rabbi Lamm did not write his book nor Rabbi Tzvi Rabinowicz his during the "shock of death." Neither did Seymour Freedman write his poetry during the shock of his father's death. As a matter of fact, Freedman's poem is found in the first section of his collection under the general title "After Shivah" to suggest he could not, would not write during the first seven days after burial. It seems reasonable to assume that during *aninut* and during *shivah* itself, Freedman was in the "midst of inexpressible grief" and could not write and did not think he would ever again. Also, as I have written earlier, the traditional prohibition against any such writing, at least until the end of *shivah*, would have kept Freedman from putting pen to paper.

That I was not "shocked" by my father's death did not lessen my pain; that I was not "disoriented" did not lessen my distraction; that my consciousness was not "paralyzed" did not lessen my despair; that I was able to read and write even after being told my father had died did not make me any less devoted to Jewish tradition or to my father. Feifel reminds us, "The route of grief appears to be one of tangled and complex pathways, with trails looping back and forth" (Herman Feifel, "Grief and Bereavement").

"In order to survive the emotional crisis [of a loved one's death] you must mobilize all the elements in your personality that make for stability—your values, your outlook on life, and your faith. You have to face your grief honestly. You must not be afraid of a confrontation with reality" (Rabbi William B. Silverman and Dr. Kenneth M. Cinnamon, *When Mourning Comes*).

I did mobilize all the elements in my personality that make for stability in my life: my value in caring for others here, my mother, and my father's body; my outlook on life, which included caring for my children and my wife; and my faith in *olam haba*, the world to come.

After speaking with my sister, I made arrangements both with the funeral director to have my father's body flown to New York and with the rabbi to have him meet with me and my mother the day after her arrival in New York. I called my daughter who was away at school and, at home, I sat with my other two daughters and my wife, and we consoled each other. My mother, too, gathered her strength. She made her own airline reservation and took care of obtaining copies of my father's death certificate and whatever other business she needed to attend to before leaving for New York.

How profound was that great gap suddenly created in my personal life and in the life of my family? I could feel and hear my heart beat and almost nothing else. My mother had lost her only husband; I had lost my only father; my children had lost their only grandfather, my wife's father having died before we were married; my wife had lost her only father-in-law. And what of my sister and her family and my father's sister and hers? Each of us had lost a "one of a kind."

"For many survivors, the whole world, not just the beloved has died" (Herman Feifel, "Grief and Bereavement"). At the moment I replaced the receiver on the cradle of the telephone after hearing my mother tell me, "I'm fine. I really am," and for that one moment when recovery seemed impossible, my whole world had died along with my father. But as my wife reached out to me and I to our children and then they to me, my world was reborn and gave me footing again, although without my father, I will always walk with a limp.

"Life is never the same after you've lost a loved one," my friend Karen's father Bernard Shawn had written in his journal. "Everyday demands are met; needs are taken care of; life goes on in its usual uneventful pattern. But there is a difference—the wholeness of your life has been damaged. It is as though some part of you lies buried with the beloved whom you have lost.

"Life between those who love is a matter of sharing, and it is this sharing which is no more. All the little things, the seemingly unimportant things you've shared become important. . . . There is an immense emptiness which can never be filled. There may be others to whom you can turn for love—a wife, perhaps, a husband, brothers and sisters, friends, and they give back love and consolation, and you are solaced and your grief assuaged. But still a part of you is gone—the loss of anyone beloved is, in fact, inconsolable. Life has changed—a corner deep within you remains forever empty."

But what of the *onen*, the mourner about whom Rabbi Lamm writes, the one for whom the "shock of death" paralyzes and blocks out all regular patterns of orderly thinking? Then it must be the community of family and friends and synagogue that mobilizes, and, more than anyone, it is the rabbi who must provide guidance, even direction. That rabbis find it increasingly difficult to do so, not only because time does not permit but also because they are not well trained for bereavement care, may best be illustrated by the following news article:

> In New York, the Riverside Memorial Chapel is underwriting a program to train members of the clergy to provide free counseling. It is run by Jacob Goldberg, a retired rabbi with a degree in counseling who has developed an eight-session program for mourners.
>
> They need someone who will "help them go through their legitimate and deep turbulent emotions," he said. "Clergy don't learn this."
>
> In remote towns and big cities, such services are proliferating. Funeral homes and hospitals are redefining their purpose, and clinics and private practitioners are springing up to provide help to the living after the funeral.
>
> Books on bereavement seem to come out daily. Self-help groups are organizing to meet the needs of a wide variety of people, including those coping with suicide, murder and death from AIDS.
>
> Death is as old as life, but people have lost some of the supports that used to help them cope. These days, Americans have greater geographic mobility, smaller, fragmented families and looser ties to community and religious organizations. More than ever, they are turning to strangers for solace.
>
> —Trish Hall
> "Solace after Bereavement"
> *New York Times*

Bereavement care is rooted in Jewish tradition, noted in the Torah, and debated in the Talmud. Jews need not go outside their tradition for ritual nor outside their community for consolation. In more religious communities, these roots are feeding family trees whose leaves have been falling, whose branches have been cut off. But in less religious Jewish communities, even among their rabbis, the roots themselves have not been nurtured.

My father died on a Monday afternoon. Although his body would be flown to New York the following Tuesday morning and my mother would arrive that Tuesday evening, at my mother's request the burial would take place on Thursday rather than on Wednesday. My rabbi asked me to convey to my mother his concern that in delaying the burial, even by one day, she was perhaps denying my father's death.

"Assure the rabbi I'm okay," my mother told me Tuesday morning from

Florida. "I know my husband has died but I need today to make some arrangements for the care of the apartment and to pack my clothing. I don't know how long I'll be in New York. And I'll need tomorrow to rest after my flight and to speak with the rabbi. And I don't want to rush these last few hours." My mother knew exactly what she needed for herself and what she was doing for herself.

"It is obligatory upon Jews to bury the dead as soon as possible. Early burial was not due entirely to the exigencies of the hot climate of the Holy Land, as it is sometimes said. Rather, it was considered humiliation of the dead to leave them unburied" (Rabbi Tzvi Rabinowicz, *A Guide to Life*). We shall not allow a corpse to remain overnight but it must be buried the same day (Deuteronomy 21:23). And so, Jewish law has come to recognize burying the dead within 24 hours following death.

"However," Rabbi Rabinowicz continues, "a delay in burial is permitted if it is 'for the sake of honor,' e.g., for the purpose of making a coffin or providing shrouds, or to enable relatives and friends to pay their last respects [*Sanhedrin* 47a; *Yoreh Deah* 357:1]. Rabbi Lamm explains that the rabbis allowed a delayed burial for the "completion of forms and papers" as my mother had need to do; in addition, she was coming from a great distance and she appropriately asked for and was given the time she needed.

When I spoke with the funeral director Monday after my mother's phone call, he asked me if I wanted my father buried in the traditional shroud or in his own clothing. Again, I was unprepared for the question. I had "heard" about the shroud, but at that point I had not read a book on Jewish laws and customs associated with death and burial; I did not have the books of Rabbis Lamm and Rabinowicz on my shelf. And I did not recall the preparations for my grandparents' burials to have the information I needed.

"The garments in which the dead are clothed are known as *tachrichim,* from the Hebrew root meaning 'to wrap up,' " Rabbi Rabinowicz writes. "The shrouds should be made from fine white linen. Neither a hem nor a knot of any sort should be made in the shrouds. No corpse must be shrouded in less than three garments. Some pious people even prepare their shrouds during their lifetime, basing the practice on the verse from Amos: 'Prepare to meet thy God, O Israel' (Amos 4:12). It is also a custom dating from talmudic times to bury a dead man in the woollen *tallit* (prayer shawl that he used during his lifetime, with the fringes deliberately rendered ritually unfit)."

I told the funeral director I needed to speak with my mother, that it was her decision what clothes my father's body would wear in death. The funeral director thanked me and assured me that he and his staff would act as the *Chevra Kadisha,* the Holy Society, to prepare my father's body for burial, the preparations being called *taharah*. My father's body would not be left alone, according to Jewish tradition. One of the funeral directors would serve as a watcher, or *shomer*. Rabbi Lamm details the preparations of the body for burial in a chapter in *The Jewish Way in Death and Mourning* titled "A Guide to the Chevra Kadisha."

I called my mother and repeated the question the funeral director had asked me. She said she didn't know how my father's body should be dressed but she would bring my father's clothing with her and would decide once we were together.

My mother arrived at John F. Kennedy International Airport in New York on Tuesday evening. During the drive to our home, she retold the events of the entire weekend and those leading up to and following my father's death. Her words were spoken in great sadness, and the strain of the previous 24 hours, of the previous 48 hours, and of the previous 4 months were evident in the deliberateness with which she chose her words and in the mist in her eyes. Her storytelling was part of her grief process, and my listening was part of mine.

My house was quiet when we arrived. Jo was waiting for us. The lights in the house were dimmed to complement the great sadness we all felt. It seemed appropriate to have the lights low, as if to say the light of life has been extinguished. But tradition would have it the other way. "The soul of man is the lamp of the Lord" (Proverbs 20:27). Also, "The mystics have pointed out that the numerical value of the letters of the Hebrew phrase ner daluk (a kindled light) and the Hebrew word Ha-Shechinah (the Divine Presence) add up to 390" [1 Samuel 31:13; 2 Samuel 1:22; Joel 1:17; Zechariah 7:4–7, 9] (Rabbi Tzvi Rabinowicz, *A Guide to Life*).

There are, as well, other reasons for not dimming lights at death. Rabbi Rabinowicz writes, "In the Torah portion Tetzaveh (Exodus 27:20- 30:10), which is read during the week of the seventh of Adar (the traditional date for commemorating Moses' death), the opening verse states that the children of Israel were commanded 'to bring pure olive oil beaten for the light to cause a lamp to burn continually' (Exodus 27:20)."

Before my mother went to bed that Tuesday night, she took from a suitcase my father's clothing, including some socks and shoes he had bought before he died but had never worn.

"I guess if he's going to see his parents, he should look his best," my mother said.

We said nothing more that night. There was nothing more to say. We left each other to "sigh in silence" (Ezekiel 24:17).

※※

Readings

Oh, My suffering

Oh, my suffering, my suffering!
How I writhe!
Oh, the walls of my heart!
My heart moans within me.

—Jeremiah 4:19

I Am Racked with Grief

I am racked with grief;
sustain me in accordance with Your word.

—Psalm 119:28

Deliver Me, O God

Deliver me, O God,
for the waters have reached my neck;
I am sinking into the slimy deep
and find no foothold;

I have come into the watery depths;
the flood sweeps one away.
I am weary with calling.

                              —Psalm 69:2–4

❋

I Am Weary

I am weary in my sighing, and I find no rest.

                              —Jeremiah 45:3

❋

There Is but One Step

There is but one step between me and death.

                              —1 Samuel 20:3

❋

On My Part, I Will Not Speak with Restraint

On my part, I will not speak with restraint;
I will give voice to the anguish of my spirit;
I will complain in the bitterness of my soul.

                              —Job 7:11

❋

Refuge

Early morning, I sit on my
    terrace upon the canal.
The sun is rising from the
    east, spreading its
irridescent rays upon the
    calm water.
A boat with its churning
    motor passes slowly by,

> making the water swirl
>   around. It kicks up the
> frightened, fleeing fish.
> They find a place of
>   refuge, far from harm.
> Why, then, can't I?

—Beatrice Lipsett in *The Journal Project*

✳✳

The Spirit of Man Is the Lamp of the Lord

The spirit of man is the lamp of the Lord
Searching all the inward parts.

—Proverbs 20:27

✳✳

Maariv

He faced the darkening window as he stood
to say the evening prayer.
And those who moved about him there,
the strangers, who were all his own,
giving him neither scorn nor care,
left him the more alone.
His old eyes
echoed the dimming skies. His fingers
fluttered, as tho' he sought
to catch the faded fringes of his thought,
the while he warmed his aching bones
with words of praise
that lit like sunset the cold end of days.
And as he prayed,
a feeble patriarch in a thin old coat,
drawing about him like a sacred shawl
the comfort of his ancient ritual,
the room grew wide, and wavered . . .
Thru the dusk,—
on velvet paws, inscrutable-eyed, remote,
the desert rose.

Out of the east, licking the dunes like flame,
tawny and purple, came the climbing caravans,
whose colors died among the hilly sands,
and flared again
against the sands.
And still flowed forward, travelling to find
some gold oasis bright with sudden fruit,
but might not ever leave
the oblivious sands behind.
And at the desert's edge,
creeping between the heavens and the sand,
carrying households on their restless road,
driving their flocks, themselves beneath the goad,
striking their tents at dawn and wandering on:
the chosen seed,
the eternal aliens pass.
They know the feebleness of desert streams,
the indurate darkness of the grave they know,
the thoroughfares of war,
the burning feet that can go forth no longer, and must go,
the burning eyes that look to withered grass
and green, untrampled dreams.
Have they not made their covenant with One
stronger than desert sun?
One who surrounds them like encompassing wind,
who is above them like the night, and under
their feet like patient earth, and in their ears
a low terrible thunder.
How might they else
bear the long burden of this dusty heat,
the long strange way
among strange people always,
the long day of labor that is seasoned with slow tears
and by the rapid thieving years is snatched
too soon away.
How might they bear
to see their children eat the broken bread
of homely custom, staled,
now they are fed not by their own.
How might they bear
to hear their fathers in defeat

muttering the evening prayer,
when every dusk comes down on a new loss,
and seems familiar since it, too, will pass.
They keep an ancient covenant; they have heard
the desert's heart beat with a sacred Word
credited and unknown.
They do not fear
stars in their cruel courses, which are shewn to be
His handiwork; they do not dread
men, strangely made
in His unthinkable image.
Their tented bed
is safe beneath His hand,
who are His pride. . . .
The sand
vanished. The darkness changed,
as the old man, from the security of his solitude,
turned to the world, and sighed.

—Babette Deutsch in
The Menorah Journal

BURIAL (*KAVORAH*)

The day after my mother's arrival in New York saw a visit with our rabbi, Jay Rosenbaum, in his office in Temple Emanu-el of East Meadow. My wife, Jo; my mother, and I attended. "The rabbi's role is one of giving spiritual support and guidance. At this time of emotional vulnerability, when family feelings run high and when there are no easy answers to mitigate irreparable loss, great strength and comfort can be found in religious observance" (Rabbi Tzvi Rabinowicz, *A Guide to Life*). For us, that sacred observance, which began the moment of my father's death with preparations for a Jewish funeral, would continue in the form of our meeting with our rabbi. The rabbi should make a prefuneral call on the bereaved family to take time to get to know the family should they not be members of the congregation, Rabbi Rabinowicz informs us. Our rabbi was new to our congregation and knew little of my family. My mother and father had lived out of state. We preferred to meet the rabbi in the synagogue, not in our home, because the synagogue was another home to us and where we wanted to be that morning.

The three of us walked arm in arm along the synagogue building's main corridor to the rabbi's study, with my mother between Jo and me. It wasn't that my mother was too weak to walk unaided, but Jo and I needed both to show our support for her and to have her need ours. And I needed my mother's.

A congregant was walking toward us, approaching as if out of nowhere, as though she had, in fact, been waiting for us to arrive. Jo and I knew her; my mother did not. She embraced my mother and said tearfully, "I'm sorry." Then she hugged Jo and me. "My father died this time three years ago," she told us. What more graphic illustration of the link between mourner and community than one of empathy. What more telling moment in Jewish communal life than recognition of the oneness of our people in time of crisis. What more spiritual embrace than the arms of a kindred soul. "Religion is community. It is the way people learn to relate to each other and to belong to each other in truly human ways" (Rabbi Harold Kushner, *Who Needs God*). As we continued walking, we passed the memorial plaques—some lighted— on both walls of the corridor. This will become a new place in the synagogue for me to visit, I thought. I am now among the mourners. My body quivered and I was glad my arm was linked with my mother's.

My mother and the rabbi spoke for more than one hour in the library next to the rabbi's study. Occasionally Jo and I would share a thought or clarify a point, but we were as much interested in what my other had to share as was the rabbi.

My mother knew what she wanted the rabbi to say and what she did not want him to say. Praise my husband for being a decent human being and a kind and wonderful husband and father and grandfather and brother. Do not make him into a god. Praise him for his accomplishments. Do not forget his struggles. Remember his many friends and those who came to him for professional and personal advice. Remember that they will be lost without him. Remember him for having lived a full and meaningful life. Do not forget he could have lived more.

> Following the lesson of Abraham, the first patriarch of the Jewish people, who eulogized his wife, Sarah, the purpose of the eulogy is twofold. First is hesped— the praising of the deceased for his worthy qualities. Second is bechi—expressing the grief and the sense of loss experienced by the mourners and the entire Jewish community. Very wisely, the Jewish tradition requires the eulogizing of the deceased to be kara'vi, balanced and appropriate. It may not grossly exaggerate, or invent, qualities that the deceased did not in fact possess . . . In addition, the mourners should remember that although the deceased may have been undistinguished in many ways, and lacking certain moral qualities, there is also a substratum of goodness and decency in all men which can be detected if properly sought.
>
> — Rabbi Maurice Lamm
> *The Jewish Way in Death and Mourning*

David's eulogy for Saul and his son Jonathan is among the Bible's most poignant:

> Your glory, O Israel,
> Lies slain on your heights;
> How have the mighty fallen!
> Tell it not in Gath,
> Do not proclaim it in the streets of Ashkelon,
> Lest the daughters of the Philistine rejoice,
> Lest the daughters of the uncircumcised exult.
>
> O hills of Gilboa—
> Let there be no dew or rain on you,
> Or bountiful fields,
> For there the shield of warriors lay rejected,
> The shield of Saul,
> Polished with oil no more.
>
> From the blood of slain
> From the fat of warriors—
> The bow of Jonathan
> Never turned back;
> The sword of Saul
> Never withdrew empty.
>
> Saul and Jonathan,
> beloved and cherished,

Never parted
In life or in death!
They were swifter than eagles,
They were stronger than lions!

Daughters of Israel,
Weep over Saul,
Who clothed you in crimson and finery,
Who decked your robes with jewels of gold.
How have the mighty fallen
In the thick of battle—
Jonathan, slain on your heights!
I grieve for you,
My brother Jonathan,
You were most dear to me.
Your love was wonderful to me
More than the love of women.

How have the mighty fallen,
The weapons of war perished!

—2 Samuel 1:19–27

My mother's elbows leaned on the long conference table as she spoke to the rabbi, her hands often clasped. Her composure was remarkable and she seemed to gain strength as she spoke about my father. The rabbi wrote as she spoke and asked few questions. One might have thought my mother had prepared in advance all she wanted to say. Perhaps she had. She must have relived her life with my father every day of the 4 months he was ill. And she must have loved my father very much every day of those 4 months to have so cherished their 48 years together that she could speak so lovingly of them.

Later, my mother asked me if I wanted to speak at the funeral. No, I did not. I had not thought about doing so although I had listened to other mourners at other funerals talk about their fathers. I had not thought about doing so because I did not think I would have the composure to stand at my father's coffin, face my family and friends, and speak of my love for my father. "Every man has a unique image," writes Rabbi Lamm. I trusted my family and friends to know my loss; they knew my father. I trusted my mother to share my father's life clearly enough so the rabbi would find the words to draw the images that would help the congregation of mourners remember my father as they knew him, as we knew him. Also, I did not want to speak because I did not want to leave my mother's side during the funeral service.

In addition, I believed that even if no one spoke, the chapel would still resound with words, so spiritual is death, so sanctified, so full of God. "God is full of compassion for the distress of the soul" (Rabbi Abraham Joshua

Heschel, *God in Search of Man*). I believed that even if no one spoke, in the silence would I have heard God's compassionate words: "Something sacred is at stake in every event" (Heschel).

Because we have to call upon our greatest resources to bear the burden of the death of a loved one, we must find in ourselves—I found in myself—during that awful first week "a center of faith"; for me, that center of faith was knowing that even without a word being spoken, my father would exist in memory as he had in time (Rabbi David J. Wolpe, *The Healer of Shattered Hearts*).

> . . . there is a blessed immortality in the echoing renown of one's life on earth. "A good life hath put few days; but a good name endures forever" [Hasdai Crescas, OR ADONAI, III, Kelal 2 and 4]. The life of an individual ends in extinction, but not the life of his people, nor the good things which a man has built, nor the noble causes which he has served, nor his memory or influence.
> —Rabbi Abba Hillel Silver
> *Where Judaism Differed*

"God is the beginning of a partial answer that human beings have to death. Zochair Kol Hanishkachot. God remembers all the forgotten. There is no forgetting before God. Every person, achievement, deed, is touched by eternity. There is no lost or wasted word in the unredeemed epic of human history" (Wolpe). "God is also in the great gift of remembrance," writes Rabbi Sydney Greenberg in *Words to Live By*.

But the son's remembrance—or the promise of God's—"cannot wipe out the infamous sting. Agonies of oblivion remain for all, the great as well as the 'common man'" (Wolpe).

"It eases, this Divine kiss, the unyielding edges of death."

> One of the most beautiful passages in Jewish literature is the Midrashist's description of the death of the greatest prophet of the Jewish tradition, Moses. Not only on account of the fear of being forgotten did Moses struggle, but because life was filled with promise he had not yet realized—to walk in the land to which he had brought the people. The logical, seemingly inevitable culmination of Moses' life was stolen away. In the dark pathos and bittersweet resolution of Moses' death scene as told by the Rabbis, all the themes of death, memory, and God are interwoven in a remarkable way.
>
> When Moses realized that his death had been decreed, he fasted, put on sackcloth, and drew a small circle on the ground. Then he stood inside of the circle and proclaimed before God: "I will not stir from this spot until You reverse Your decree." Moses continued to lament and pray before God, until the heavens and earth—the entire order of nature—trembled.
>
> God decreed that Moses' prayer go unanswered; his fate had been decided. But so powerful did Moses' prayers become, like a sword which rends everything it touches, that all the gates of heaven had to be sealed to prevent the supplication from penetrating to the throne of the Almighty.

Still, Moses prayed, pleading with God: "Master of the universe, You know how hard I strived to teach the people of Your words and will. I journeyed with them, contended with them, and now that they are to enter the land will You exclude me from their joy? Is this the recompense for all my struggle?" God answered only, "The time of your death has come."

Moses would not cease praying, reminding God of their time together: "Master of the universe, remember that day when You revealed Yourself to me, speaking to me from the burning bush. Recall the forty days and nights we were together on Mount Sinai, where I learned Your law to teach to the people. I beg of You—do not now hand me over to the angel of death." God calmed Moses' fears with a heavenly voice that said, "Do not be afraid. The time comes to all mortals to die. I Myself will attend to your burial."

Upon hearing those words, Moses stood up and sanctified himself like the angels. God Himself came down from the very heights of heaven to take away the soul of Moses. And God took away the soul of His servant Moses with a kiss. And God wept (combined from Deut. R. 11, Midrash Petirat Moshe, and parallels).

In various versions of the Midrash this scene is much expanded. The components remain essentially the same. Moses cannot be fully reconciled to death. He mourns and pleads. In one version of the story, Moses physically fights off an angel sent by God to reclaim his soul! God finally bolts the heavens because Moses summons all his power to struggle against the inevitable lot of being human. For Moses, as the Rabbis knew, death was no sweeter or easier than it is for the more pedestrian run of humanity. The greatest prophet, like the humblest pauper, is not exempt from fear. The man of God too trembles at the prospect of being no more.

Moses is given the comfort of being taken by God. His death is not so much a finality as a separation. Still, it is painful enough. Even after such a life, the prospect of death is sufficiently agonizing to cause this servant of the Lord, whom the Bible depicts as a tower of faith and strength, to offer anguished cries of injustice, to plead, to cry. But the strange softness at the end of the Midrash is suggestive of something deeper. It eases, this Divine kiss, the unyielding edges of death. Moses dies too soon. That is his tragedy and it cannot be changed. He dies in the arms of eternity, and that is his comfort and his hope.

To die too soon is a tragedy known to more than patriarchs and prophets. As the Midrash teaches, "No one leaves this world with even half of his desires fulfilled" (Eccl. R. 1:13). The proper biblical span, based upon the life of Moses, was set at 120 years. This symbolic number says, with the fullness of realism, that we all die too soon. Even when the end is accepted with apparent equanimity, it is, after all, the equanimity of inevitability. There is no choice. Death has prepared the path for acceptance by taking others whom one loves. It gradually strips capacity and appetite, smoothing the way with the persistence of pain and physical decline.

—Rabbi David J. Wolpe
The Healer of Shattered Hearts

On the day following our visit with the rabbi and after the funeral service, the drive from the funeral home to the suburban cemetery was quiet. There was probably some talk, although I remember none of it; there were surely whispers when we spoke only to ourselves; there was weeping. My father would be buried on May 4, 4 months to the day of his first operation and of his seventy-third birthday. And it was in the middle of spring and such a glorious middle of spring.

I recall now staring out of the limousine window at the country trees, at the brown and green grass along the parkway curb, at the rush of the colors of cars. And as I sit here and write, I recall another spring day in May, 33 years before, watching my mother stare out of another window—our living room window—the morning after her mother's death.

I have written earlier that that morning following my grandmother's death was bright and beautiful like a vivid watercolor whose paint had not yet dried and that my mother stood by the living room window whispering and weeping and asking aloud why her mother could not have lived to see a day endowed with such beauty. The day of my father's death was such a day; the day of my father's funeral was such a day.

Perhaps God kissed the earth where my mother looked that day 33 years ago; perhaps God did so again when my father died. Sometimes, "He is all over one like a comforter made of sunlight" (Roger Rosenblatt, "The Face of God," *Life*).

"It eases, this Divine kiss, the unyielding edges of death."

Roger Rosenblatt, editor at large and columnist at *Life* magazine, was one of many who responded to the question "Who is God?" in the December 1990 issue of *Life*.

Rosenblatt wrote that upon his arrival in Israel for his first visit in 1975, he was notified that his father had suffered a heart attack. There were no return flights until morning, so he drove to Jerusalem to visit the Western Wall and prayed that God would spare his father's life.

On the flight back to the States after that night in Jerusalem, I was one of but four or five passengers scattered about the jetliner. I sat by the blue window in the near empty plane, and I realized that I was about to lose both my father and my bearings. I was certain, without being told, that he had died while I was in flight. Many new responsibilities would befall me, my mother's care primarily, and I had no doubt that I was not equal to any of them.

I wanted it all not to be happening. I knew that death was a part of living, but I did not want to be touched by death. "You are casting me into a terrible darkness," I told my God. He told me: "No. These things just happen. You will do the best you can. And I will be nearby, when it occurs to Me to be nearby."

As if to demonstrate His seeming casual approach to my fear and grief, New York was socked in with the deepest fog in its history when my plane attempted to land. I could not get down to my father. We were diverted to Dulles airport in Washington, D.C., where I phoned to learn that, yes, my father was dead. Soon the fog dissipated, and I was on my way home to a life changed forever.

The stars shone cold and with a fierce unblinking brightness. The earth below sparkled like an endless gaudy bracelet up America's east coast. I tried to cry, but that would come later—years later, actually, when I would fully realize how permanent an absence death creates, that what one misses after an hour, one misses that much more after years. And the years go on. Instead of crying, I prayed. At least, I sort of prayed.

I'm not sure if my God was with me then or not. But I observed His planet and His stars, and felt that whatever stretched out before me was as full of kindness as of threat, as sensible as it was mystifying, as good as it was bad. I was comforted in spite of myself. And I thanked Him without knowing it.

—Roger Rosenblatt
"The Face of God"
Life

Roger Rosenblatt observed God's planet and God's stars, places where God had kissed the universe, and he thanked God because he was comforted. "It eases, this Divine kiss, the unyielding edges of death."

But what of death in winter? in darkness? ". . . to God even darkness is light" (Freema Gottlieb *The Lamp of God*).

"Those who have witnessed a western sunset," writes Rabbi Sydney Greenberg in *Words to Live By*, "know that the most enchanting time of day is often around evening. After the hot summer sun sets, while nature breathlessly waits for the light to be rolled away before the darkness, the sky is suddenly clad in the spectacular brilliance of multicolored light. These indescribable gorgeous colors are the day's afterglow.

And when the day is done, what of these "indescribable gorgeous colors"?

Because the farther the light travels from its source the dimmer it becomes, darkness, paradoxically, is often an indication of a light so powerful that it is invisible to the eyes. This kind of darkness, far from being a negation of light is that Hidden Treasure that God concealed when He created the world—the darkness that contains all color. Even the effect of darkness is to reveal what otherwise would be invisible.

—Freema Gottlieb
The Lamp of God

If there is God's Divine kiss on earth and on the stars, how could we not believe it is on man's soul as well. "God," writes Rabbi Wolpe, "is intimately tied to the night . . . when the spirit, unable to forget itself by being lost in the day or distracted, must sleep or seek. It is the time to look for the God who waits within." And what will we find within? In Proverbs, we read: "The spirit of man is the lamp of the Lord . . ." (Proverbs 20:27).

Light is what we will find within.

" 'The word of God in itself is like a burning flame," Rabbi Heschel quotes Rabbi Yaakov Yosef of Ostrog, "and the Torah that we received is merely a part of the coal to which the flame is attached. And yet, even in this form it would have remained beyond our comprehension as long as we are mortals. The word had to descend further and to assume the form of darkness ('arafel) in order to become perceptible to man.' "

Light of understanding and comfort we will find within.

It was late morning when we left the synagogue building after our meeting with the rabbi. The rest of the day was lost in memory and reverie and, as the day before, in several phone conversations with my sister. When my mother and I talked, we talked only about my father and the preparations for the funeral the next day. We spoke late into the evening all the words we would have shared with the congregation of mourners had we decided to deliver the eulogy ourselves. The day was a gift to our sorrow.

We awoke early the next morning and waited patiently, yet tearfully, for the limousine to take us to the funeral parlor. The long, sleek black limousine was a stark intrusion into our personal grief. It was a car no one knew, and the ride was both too short and far too long. Our eldest daughter, Corinne, drove the family car with her two sisters, Lisa and Adina, as passengers. My sister and her family would meet us at the funeral parlor. Her children, David and Samantha, would join our daughters for the drive to the cemetery after the service.

The funeral parlor was just another building when we arrived, but as soon as the first cousin stepped forward as we emerged from the limousine, the building became, like the hospital where my father had spent most of the 4 months during his illness, a weight upon my chest unlike anything I had ever before felt.

Family and friends continued to arrive and we continued to tell my father's story, crying as we did so. Each face was another moment in my father's history; each offer of condolence was another break in our hearts. When my mother went into the sanctuary to stand alone at my father's coffin before anyone else entered, she uttered a cry that pierced the hearts of all who heard. Soon, the rabbi called us into the family room adjacent to the sanctuary. It was time for *keriah,* rending of the garment. Another moment in my father's history; another break in our hearts.

"The origin of this practice of keriah (rending) is found in the Divine Command, given expressly to the priests Aaron, Eleazar, and Ithamar after the death of Nadab and Abihu: 'Let not the hair of your heads go loose, neither rend your clothes' (Leviticus 10:6). From this explicit prohibition, it is inferred that everyone else must perform keriah, those who have lost a father, mother, wife, husband, brother, sister, son or daughter, or half-brother or half-sister" (Rabinowicz).

From earliest times, the rending of garments has been regarded as a sign of grief. When his sons brought him Joseph's bloodstained coat, "Jacob rent his garments" (Genesis 37:34). When the goblet was found in Benjamin's sack, his brothers "rent their clothes" (Genesis 44:13). When David heard of the death of Saul, "he took hold of his clothes, and rent them; and likewise all the men that were with him" (2 Samuel 1:11).

> My father died suddenly when I was forty-three; I was in a daze. Right before the funeral service, the rabbi cut the lapel of my jacket to symbolize the cutting of the fabric of one's life. I was jolted into the realization that my life had been rent apart by the death of my father.
>
> As the garment was being cut, I said a prayer acknowledging that God is the true judge. It was incredibly painful to say that God had judged correctly in my father's death, but it was absolutely essential to the process of grieving. The prayer cut through my denial. Regardless of whether I thought his death was wrong, I had to accept that there is a truth in the divine order of things, and that my father's death was a part of that order.
>
> —Phyllis Toback
> "Kaddish"
> *Invisible Thread*

"Then Job stood up and rent his mantle" (Job 1:20). I stood in front of the rabbi on his right; my mother was next to me; my sister, Barbara, next to her, and my Aunt Lettie, my father's sister, next to Barbara. Behind the rabbi at a short distance stood my wife and our three daughters and my sister's husband and their son and daughter.

> Meet all sorrow standing upright. The future may be dark, veiled from the eye of mortals—but not the manner in which we are to meet the future. To rail at life, to rebel against a destiny that has cast our lines in unpleasant places, is of little avail. We cannot lay down terms to life. Life must be accepted on its own terms. But hard as life's terms may be, life (it has been finely said) never dictates unrighteousness, unholiness, dishonor.
>
> —Rabbi J. H. Hertz in Rabbi Tzvi Rabinowicz
> *A Guide to Life*

But to meet the need to be angry, writes Rabbi Lamm,

> Keriah may serve also as a substitute for the ancient pagan custom of tearing the flesh and the hair which symbolizes the loss of one's own flesh and blood in sympathy for the deceased and which is not permitted in Jewish law: "You are children of the Lord your God. You shall not gash yourselves or shave the front of your heads because of the dead. For you are a people consecrated to the Lord your God: the Lord your God chose you from among all other peoples on earth to be His treasured people" (Deuteronomy 14:1–2).
>
> —Rabbi Maurice Lamm
> *The Jewish Way in Death and Mourning*

Rabbi Rabinowicz points out that although "the prohibition against cutting the flesh was addressed only to the priest, the law was extended to all Israel as God's children. 'If a man made any cuttings for the dead,' says the Mishnah [Mishnah Makkot 3:5], 'he is liable to forty stripes.' "

Rabbi Lamm continues, explaining that the "halachic requirement to 'expose the heart' (that is, that the tear for deceased parents must be over the heart), indicates that the tear in the apparel represents a torn heart. The prophet Joel chastises the Jew to rend the heart itself, not only the garment over the heart, indicating that the external tear is a symbol of the broken heart within": "Rend your hearts/Rather than your garments,/And turn back to the Lord your God" (Joel 2:13).

Rabbi Lamm offers insight into this custom from the Jerusalem Talmud as well (*Moed Katan* 3:5):

> The "exposing of the heart" is performed because the mourner has lost the ability to fulfill the biblical command to honor father and mother. We suffer deeply when we can no longer give love to our beloved. Of course, respect for parents can, and should, be expressed after their deaths, but, according to many authorities, it is rabbinic, rather than a biblical enactment. Keriah, thus, also symbolizes the rending of the parent–child relationship, and confronts the mourner with the stabbing finality of this separation, expressed on his own clothes and on his own person for all to see.
>
> —Rabbi Maurice Lamm
> *The Jewish Way in Death and Mourning*

Rabbi Rabinowicz notes that for men, "the jacket, sweater, or vest is used, and for women, either the dress, blouse, or sweater. The use of a black ribbon for keriah is not permitted." Rabbi Lamm offers a passionate and powerful admonition against the use of a black ribbon pinned to the garment the mourner is wearing as a substitute for tearing the garment itself.

> The rending of the clothes expresses the deepest feelings of sorrow and anguish. It is the symbol of a broken heart and a genuine mark of separation from one who was dearly beloved, with whom one had a blood relationship, or ties of matrimony.
>
> The grief we express at such moments taps the deepest wells of humanity, and the manner in which we manifest it should be equally authentic. The anguish is exquisite and, one might even say, sacred, and the way in which we express it should be no less sacred. It is appropriate that this form of release of sorrow be sanctioned by faith and by centuries of ancient custom, going back often to biblical times.
>
> How shallow, how disappointing, how pitiably trivial therefore, to symbolize these authentic sentiments not by an act of historic and religious significance, but by the little black ribbon or button—invented by enterprising

American undertakers! Tradition calls upon us to tear our garments, to put the mark of the broken heart on our own clothing—and not to vent our feelings on a meaningless and impersonal strip of cloth pinned on us by a stranger.

Keriah is too personally meaningful to substitute for it a petty gimmick, the expression of penury, rather than grief, thereby desecrating our own most genuine human experiences.

Nevertheless, if for some reason the ribbon has been used at the funeral service, the mourner should make a tear in the proper clothing upon his return home.

—Rabbi Maurice Lamm
The Jewish Way in Death and Mourning

Although there are those who find funeral directors intrusive, I did not. The funeral director who acted on behalf of my family was patient and caring, from my first phone call to him to the day I selected the coffin with my brother-in-law, Jerry, who was performing the *mitzvah* of helping the bereaved; (having lost a father-in-law to whom he was very close, Jerry was among the bereaved as well). Our rabbi did not give us the option of having our garments torn. As we stood next to each other facing the rabbi, the funeral director pinned black ribbons on our clothing.

A Jewish Book of Comfort is not intended to replace consultation with a rabbi on matters of *halachah* and tradition or with family members on matters of custom. As members of a Reform congregation, my family might have sought the advice offered in *Gates of Mitzvah: A Guide to the Jewish Life Cycle* (edited by Simeon J. Maslin and produced by the Committee on Reform Jewish Practice of the Central Conference of American Rabbis. If we had, we would have read: "Keriah, the rending of one's garment or the symbolic cutting of a black ribbon, is left to the discretion of the rabbi and family" (Maslin). Not having read the book, not having been directed to it, we relied upon our rabbi. In retrospect, however, I would have wanted—and perhaps my mother would have wanted, as well, to have discussed the options before the funeral service. After all, we did have the time. Families must, to the extent possible, be given ample opportunity to participate in decisions regarding mourning practices. But there was so much to do that we could not have thought of everything ourselves.

Like so many rituals in the mourning process, the rending of one's clothing is custom and not law, referred to in the Talmud (*Moed Katan* 24a) and the *Shulchan Aruch* (*Yoreh Deah* 340:1). We are reminded that the practice arose out of Reuben's and Jacob's actions when both brother, first, and father, later, heard of the alleged death of Joseph:

When Reuben returned to the pit and saw that Joseph was not in the pit, he rent his clothes. Returning to his brothers, he said, "The boy is gone! Now, what am I to do?'' Then they took Joseph's tunic, slaughtered a kid, and dipped the tunic in the blood. They had the ornamented tunic taken to their father, and they said, "We found this. Please examine it; is it your son's tunic or not?" He recognized it, and said, "My son's tunic! A savage beast devoured him! Joseph was torn by a beast!" Jacob rent his clothes, put sackcloth on his loins, and observed mourning for his son many days.

—Genesis 37:29–34

There we stood in the family room in more pain than we could ever have imagined, facing our rabbi and behind him my father's other "children"—his daughter-in-law and son-in-law and grandchildren. Together with them, we formed a tableau of anguish. What would it have mattered then whether I ripped my jacket lapel or my mother the neck of her dress? How often had I seen her tear the air with desperate fingers during the months my father lay ill? How recklessly had I clawed the back of my father's oldest friend, Hymie, when I sobbed in his embrace moments before our rabbi called us into the family room for *keriah?* There are many ways to perform *keriah*.

Devorah, Asher Lev's tormented wife in Chaim Potok's *The Gift of Asher Lev,* had survived concealed for two years in an apartment in a Paris neighborhood before the city was liberated near the end of World War II. Her father had perished in Auschwitz, her mother in Budy, a small camp for women near Auschwitz. The news about the horrible way in which her mother died "came in bits and pieces" to Devorah. And she performed *keriah* in her own way out of her own despair.

Each piece of information had somehow to be conveyed to Devorah and each was greeted by her with increasing disbelief and horror, and each was a separate blow. The sadness grew within her until she seemed to exist only as a dark nimbus of melancholy, and even Max could no longer cheer her with his talk and his drawings. Once he showed her a drawing and she looked at it and he left it with her, and when he came back for it he found it torn to shreds. It was a very long time before he left her alone again with one of his drawings.

—Chaim Potok
The Gift of Asher Lev

And so the funeral director pinned the black ribbon on my left side, on the lapel of my black suit jacket, close to my heart. And he did the same for my sister. For my mother and my aunt, as customary for spouses and siblings, the ribbon was pinned to the right side of their dress but still no further from their heart. We recited the blessing as one: "Blessed art Thou, O Lord our God, King of the Universe, the true Judge."

Keriah performed, the funeral director quietly escorted the grandchildren to the chapel and to their second-row seats where my sister and I had sat, in another chapel, a generation before, when our grandparents, at different times, were eulogized. Then sitting in the first row were our parents and aunts and uncles and their spouses. On this day, because it was our father's funeral, my sister and I sat in the first row facing our father's coffin. For every season . . . .

I sat between my wife and my mother; my sister, Barbara, sat between her husband, Jerry, and our mother with our Aunt Lettie sitting next to Jerry. We were linked by our sorrow as we were during *keriah*, as we would for the rest of our lives in a way none of us had ever been before.

The rabbi's voice alternately rose and fell according to my own attention to what he was saying. If the moment was a realization of the truth of my father's body lying in that coffin, tears blinded me and the sounds of my internal agony deafened me; if the moment was no more than a scene in daydream, I heard the rabbi's words loud and clear but knew there was no truth to the claim that my father had died. That our tradition calls upon us to sit together facing the coffin in which the body of our loved one lies, accepting the order and decorum of the service, is at once remarkable arrogance and welcome benevolence: tradition comforts in time of crisis, and benevolence assures us we are not alone. It was no dream.

Our rabbi guided us through the service, beginning with a recitation of Psalm 23. The psalm was followed by other scriptural readings and the finely sculptured eulogy embracing my father's life—his past and his present, his accomplishments and his goals—and I felt great pride and sorrow. "Jewish law," Rabbi Adin Steinsaltz writes in *The Strife of the Spirit*, "prescribes that all eulogies made at funerals are to life and to the surviving members of the family."

I met Dr. Bert Levin in Jerusalem several years ago and we have corresponded since. I sent him an essay I had written about my apprenticeship as a writer and as a son, originally as an introduction to a collection of my father's own short stories, which I had printed for his seventy-second birthday gift and revised after his death.

In Dr. Levin's letter to me after having read my essay, he included a remembrance of his own father and mother:

> My Dad, a tailor, died at age 89, my mother at 92. I have often thought of the positive influence my father had on me, especially in my first 13 years when we (including my two older brothers) lived in the back of the shop, my exposure to Dad thus being all day daily. His hard work, his skill, his pride in his noncompromising skill, his make-do with little, his love of America (he had fled the Czar's army), his contributions to the needy (from a near-empty purse), his Socialist bent (Abe Kahan was his idol) but his recognition that Jews needed to support the synagogue no matter that he had little time to use it (he worked 6½–7 days per week for many years), and his love of people (oh how he loved!) each certainly influenced my behavior as a child and the mold of my personality

as an adult. What a compliment when people would say, "You look more like Rose but you act like Max." Mom certainly influenced my behavior pattern in other ways, but less so than Dad. He's gone now for 20 years but I think of him often and sometimes tearfully.

We are always eulogizing our loved ones who have died and, often, at times when we least expect we will. We never know what another might say or write or do that will remind us. Sometimes, the eulogies that most make our hearts ache are not the ones heard in a sanctuary but the ones we speak to ourselves and to others who will listen many years later.

My father's funeral service concluded with the recitation of *El Malay Rachamin*:

> O God, full of compassion, Thou who dwellest on high! Grant perfect rest beneath the sheltering wings of Thy presence, among the holy and pure who shine as the brightness on the heavens, unto the soul of _____ who has gone unto eternity, and in whose memory charity is offered. May his repose be in paradise. May the Lord of Mercy bring him under the cover of His wings forever, and may his soul be bound up in the bond of eternal life. May the Lord be his possession, and may he rest in peace. Amen.

> —Rabbi Maurice Lamm
> *The Jewish Way in Death and Mourning*

We left the chapel and returned to the limousine for the drive to the cemetery, my Aunt Lettie now joining us for the ride. In the first car behind us were the grandchildren; in the car in front of us, my father.

The decision had been made by my mother to have my father buried in his own clothes, those she had brought with her to New York from their home in Florida. His *tallis* was draped around his shoulders. Rabbi Lamm writes about the "democracy of death" in his discussion of the *tachrichim*—shrouds—the garments in which the dead are traditionally clothed.

> Jewish tradition recognizes the democracy of death. It therefore demands that all Jews be buried in the same type of garment. Wealthy or poor, all are equal before God, and that which determines their reward is not what they wear, but what they are. Nineteen hundred years ago, Rabbi Gamaliel instituted this practice so that the poor would not be shamed and the wealthy would not vie with each other in displaying the costliness of the burial clothes.
>
> The clothes to be worn should be appropriate for one who is shortly to stand in judgment before God Almighty, Master of the universe and Creator of man. Therefore, they should be simple, hand-made, perfectly clean, and white. These shrouds symbolize symbolic purity, simplicity, and dignity. Shrouds have no pockets. They, therefore, can carry no material wealth. Not a man's possession

but his soul is of importance. The burial society or funeral director has a ready supply of such shrouds available.

—Rabbi Maurice Lamm
The Jewish Way in Death and Mourning

Rabbi Rabinowicz adds, "No firm rule concerning shrouds was laid down in early times, but from the sixteenth century C.E. it became the general practice to use white shrouds."

Clothing the body of the deceased in a shroud, like the performance of *keriah*, may provoke dissension among family members, even within oneself. Novelist Philip Roth writes about preparing his father's body for burial:

Later in the day, at the bottom of a bureau drawer in my father's bedroom, my brother came upon a shallow box containing two neatly folded prayer shawls. The older tallis I took home with me and we buried him in the other. When the mortician, at the house, asked us to pick out a suit for him, I said to my brother: "A suit? He's not going to the office. No, no suit—it's senseless." He should be buried in a shroud, I said, thinking that was how Jews were buried traditionally. But as I said it I wondered if a shroud was any less senseless—he wasn't Orthodox and his sons weren't religious at all—and if it wasn't pretentiously literary and a little hysterically sanctimonious as well. I thought how bizarrely out of character an urban earthling like my insurance-man father, a sturdy man rooted all his life in everydayness, would look in a shroud even while I understood that that was the idea. But as nobody opposed me and as I hadn't the audacity to say, "Bury him naked," we used the shroud of our ancestors to clothe his corpse.

—Philip Roth
Patrimony

My mother wanted my father to be dressed as she knew him all his life, no, not as the "accountant-man father" but as the careful but not overly deliberate dresser, neatly attired even when casual, always pleasing to look at, and ever respectful of propriety.

Our rabbi did not ask about the clothes my father's body would wear. "The dead may be buried in ordinary clothing or in shrouds," it is written in *Gates of Mitzvah*. As I have written, the funeral director informed me during my call to him after learning of my father's death that he had a ready supply of shrouds available. But he, too, left the decision to my mother.

Should my father have been buried in what was familiar or in a cold foreign garment taken from a shelf in a storeroom in the funeral parlor? He would, after all, be wearing his own *tallis*, whatever its individual style and material value, not one provided by the funeral director.

My father was not among those pious people, to whom Rabbi Rabinowicz refers, who "prepare their shrouds during their lifetime, basing the practice on the verse from Amos: 'Prepare to meet thy God, O Israel' " (Amos 4:12). No, my father's body would be clothed in the warmth and history of the familiar, and draped around his shoulders would be the *tallis* with whose fringes I played when I was a boy at his side in the small synagogue on Legion Street in Brownsville, Brooklyn.

My mother (and I) made the decision about my father's dress with intention and after careful consideration. My mother had more than 24 hours after my father's death, including the flight to New York carrying a suitcase full with his clothing, to think about how my father would be dressed in death. I, too, had that time to think. My mother was being quite serious when, before she went to bed the night she arrived from Florida with that suitcase, she said to me, "I guess if he's going to see his parents, he should look his best." And if he is going to "stand in judgment before God Almighty, Master of the universe and Creator of man," he should be dressed in death as the man he was in life and be judged by the way he lived in the clothing he wore.

Rabbi Herman E. Schaalman helps me express my thinking on the choice my mother and I made:

> Finally it all depends on whether I am ready to live my life in relationship to God, in response to Him, in my acceptance of His being Commander of me as His covenant partner, giving life to the berit—the covenant—by my mitzvah response. And while I have and retain the freedom of choosing my specific means of response at a given moment, the essential fact of my life will be my intention to respond. And once my feet are set on this road, then even what at one time appears opaque and incapable of eliciting my response may do so at another time. The number of mitzvot I thus choose to perform is not nearly as important as is the fullness of my awareness and intention, for it is likely that in time I may hear the authentic "voice of God" in many mitzvot than at first I could have imagined.
>
> —Rabbi Herman E. Schaalman
> "The Divine Authority of the Mitzvah"
> *Gates of Mitzvah*

The essential fact of my life as a Jew has been the "fullness of my awareness and intention" to live my life as a Jew. When my father died in the hospital near his home, he was bathed in the white linen of his sheet, his gown, and his blanket: "No corpse must be shrouded in less than three garments," Rabbi Rabinowicz reminds us. At the time of his death, my father wore the clothing of his tradition. At the time of his burial, he wore the clothing of his history. I have always tried to live my life in relationship to God and to others I love, so my choices have been informed by my love for both.

When the hearse entered the gates of the cemetery, my body shivered. I wanted to go back and start the day all over again. The day was moving too quickly, although I also thought it was moving too slowly. Maybe it was moving at just the right pace.

I had spoken with my mother on the Wednesday before the funeral about who would be pallbearers. I had suggested my father's son-in-law, Jerry, and his son, my father's grandson, David; my father's brother-in-law, my uncle Irving, and his son, my father's nephew, Stewart; my father's cousin, Howard; and my father's oldest friend, Hymie. My mother agreed. Although I could have joined them as a pallbearer, I chose to remain with my mother. The pallbearers had accompanied the coffin from the funeral parlor to the hearse, and now they would escort the coffin to the grave. "Thou shalt surely bury him" (Deuteronomy 21:23).

Our limousine parked a short distance from the grave and, as planned, the cars of the pallbearers passed us. As we walked to the grave, my father's family and friends were already carrying his coffin, preceded by the rabbi who was reciting Psalm 91.

This Psalm has been ascribed by Bible commentators to Moses, or a poet under his influence. It is said to have been recited at the building of the Tabernacle in the desert. Others ascribe it to a dialogue held between David and Solomon, or recited by them, at the dedication of Jerusalem and the Temple. It is referred to as the "Song of the Spirit," guarding man against the evil that surrounds him. It is an expression of confidence that God will watch over His people, and that nothing will again befall them because they trust in the Lord.

—Rabbi Maurice Lamm
The Jewish Way in Death and Mourning

O you who dwell in the shelter of the Most High
   and abide in the protection of Shaddai—
 I say of the Lord, my refuge and stronghold,
   my God in whom I trust,
   that He will save you from the fowler's trap,
   from the destructive plague.
He will cover you with His pinions;
   you will find refuge under His wings;
   His fidelity is an encircling shield.
You need not fear the terror by night,
   or the arrow that flies by day,
   the plague that stalks in the darkness,
   or the scourge that ravages at noon.
A thousand may fall at your left side,
   ten thousand at your right,
   but it shall not reach you.

You will see it with your eyes,
   you will witness the punishment of the wicked.
Because you took the Lord—my refuge,
   the Most High—as your haven,
   no harm will befall you,
   no disease touch your tent.
For He will order His angels
   to guard you wherever you go.
They will carry you in their hands
   lest you hurt your foot on a stone.
You will tread on cubs and vipers;
   you will trample lions and asps.

"Because he is devoted to Me I will deliver him;
   I will keep him safe, for he knows My name.
When he calls on Me, I will answer him;
   I will be with him in distress;
   I will rescue him and make him honored;
   I will let him live to a ripe old age,
   and show him My salvation."

—Psalm 91

"It is a great mitzvah to escort the dead to their last resting place," writes Rabbi Rabinowicz. "The Mishnah lists 'escorting the dead' among the deeds 'the fruit of which a man enjoys in this world while the stock remains for him in the world to come.' " Rabbi Rabinowicz goes on to explain that in talmudic times during the funeral procession, it was the custom to stop seven times and make lamentations over the dead (Ketubbot 2:10; *Bava Batra* 6:7; *Oholot* 18:4; *Bava Batra* 100b). It is still customary to halt several times (at least three times) on the way to the grave when Psalm 91 is recited. "The seven halts," Rabbi Rabinowicz tells us, "are symbolic of the seven times the word hevel (vanity) occurs in the Book of Ecclesiastes [Ecclesiastes 1:2; *Bava Batra* 100b]. The number seven, too, corresponds to the days of the world's creation and also to the seven stages that man experiences in his lifetime [Ecclesiastes 1:2; *Bava Batra* 100b]. With each stop, the fact of ultimate death teaches us to avoid the life of vanity, to be creative and kind, to repent of evil, to walk in the path of goodness."

My father's coffin was lowered into the grave "with [his] head facing toward the west and [his] feet toward the east, and all those who [were] present [said]: 'May he come to his place in peace' " [Exodus 18:23] (Rabinowicz).

I knew I had wanted to participate in the filling of my father's grave. But I also knew that although Jewish tradition prescribed that the family of the deceased remain at the graveside for the lowering of the coffin and the refilling of the grave, there are families who choose not to do either or at least not to refill the grave. And, as much as I, too, was afraid to hear the thunder of mortality as the earth fell from the shovels of the mourners onto the wood coffin, I knew I had to hear the closing sounds of my father's burial to allow me to begin the next part of the mourning process having left nothing undone. And in so doing, I would have paid the fullest respects to my father's body. "It is a signal honor and duty to help in shoveling the earth to cover the casket," informs Rabbi Lamm.

> Psychologically, the heart-rending thud of earth on the casket is enormously beneficial. In proclaiming finality, it helps the mourner overcome the illusion that his relative still lives; it answers his disbelief that death has indeed claimed its victim; it quiets his lingering doubts that this may be only a bad dream. The earth-filling process dispels such illusions and starts the mourner on the way to recovery and reconciliation.
>
> —Rabbi Maurice Lamm
> *The Jewish Way in Death and Mourning*

When it was time to refill the grave, I turned to my mother. "Mom." She knew what to do. After she replaced the shovel in the mound of earth at the foot of the grave, I took my turn. Then my sister. Soon there was a waiting line. And soon the grave had been refilled and the earth was still.

Although according to Rabbi Rabinowicz the prayer *Tzidduk Ha-Din* is recited when the grave is completely filled, Rabbi Lamm advises that this prayer, justification of the divine decree, may be recited "immediately before, or immediately after, the body is interred (depending on local Jewish usage) when the reality of the grave confronts the mourners."

The *Tzidduk Ha-Din* prayer, Rabbi Rabinowicz writes, begins with the affirmation, "The Rock, His work is perfect for all His ways are judgment." The prayer's "themes are resignation and submission to the inscrutable will of God, belief in the immortality of the soul, and the affirmation of the principle that there is a Heavenly Judge who will recompense everyone 'according to his ways and according to the fruit of his doings.'"

TZIDDUK HA'DIN
צדוק הדין

The Rock, his work is perfect, for all His ways are judgment: A God of faithfulness and without iniquity, just and right is He.

The Rock, perfect in every work, who can say unto Him, "What workest thou?" He ruleth below and above; He ordereth death and restoreth to life: He bringeth down to the grave, and bringeth up again.

The Rock, perfect in every deed, who can say unto Him. "What doest thou?" O Thou who speakest and doest, of Thy grace deal kindly with us, and for the sake of him who was bound like a lamb, O hearken and do.

Just in all Thy ways art thou, O perfect Rock, slow to anger and full of compassion. Spare and have pity upon parents and children, for Thine, Lord, is forgiveness and compassion.

Just art Thou, O Lord, in ordering death and restoring to life, in whose hand is the charge of all spirits; far be it from Thee to blot out our remembrance. O let Thine eyes mercifully regard us; for Thine, Lord, is compassion and forgiveness.

If a man live a year or a thousand years, what profiteth it him? He shall be as though he had not been. Blessed be the true Judge, who ordereth death and restoreth to life.

Blessed be He, for His judgment is true, and His eye discerneth all things, and He awardeth unto man his reckoning and his sentence, and all must render acknowledgment unto him.

We know, O Lord, that Thy judgment is righteous: Thou art justified when Thou speakest, and pure when Thou judgest, and it is not for us to murmur at Thy method of judging. Just are Thou, O Lord, and righteous are Thy judgments.

O true and righteous Judge! Blessed be the true Judge, all whose judgments are righteous and true.

The soul of every living thing is in Thy hand; Thy might is full of righteousness. Have mercy upon the remnant of the flock of Thy hand, and say unto the destroying angel, "Stay thy hand!"

Thou art great in counsel and mighty in deed; Thine eyes are open upon all the ways of the children of men, to give unto every one according to his ways, and according to the fruit of his doings. To declare that the Lord is upright; He is my Rock, and there is no unrighteousness in Him.

The Lord gave, and the Lord hath taken away; blessed be the name of the Lord. And He, being merciful, forgiveth iniquity and destroyeth not. Yea, many a time He turneth His anger away, and doth not stir up all His wrath.

The prayer has three major themes:

1. God ordained this dreadful end, and His decree is justified. God gives to each his due, in accordance with reasons He alone knows. Although we may not understand His ways, we know that there can be no imperfection in Almighty God.

2. We pray that God be merciful to the survivors. Although He has taken the life of this dear one, may He, in His great mercy, spare the lives of the remainder of His flock and stay the hand of death. Even at this most personal moment of grief, the Jew must concern himself with unselfish thoughts and pray for all of humanity.

3. God's decree must be accepted. To the very end we must remember that as God in His kindness was beneficent to give us this dear one and bring him into life, He is the same just God when He beckons that soul to return to Him. "The Lord has given and the Lord has taken." We thank the Lord for the years that were given to us. "Blessed be the name of the Lord."

—Rabbi Maurice Lamm
The Jewish Way in Death and Mourning

Following *Tzidduk Ha-Din* Psalm 23 was recited, then the Burial *Kaddish* and, finally, the Memorial Prayer *El Malay Rachamin,* "O God full of compassion." We would whisper no more words that day at the grave. We looked again at the mound of earth that completely covered the grave, turned, and, passing between two rows of other mourners, returned to our limousine.

"May the Almighty comfort you among the other mourners of Zion and Jerusalem."

✳

Readings

✖✖✖✖✖✖✖✖✖✖✖✖✖✖✖✖

My Heart

I feel my heart turn over.

—Chaim Potok
The Gift of Asher Lev

✖✖

Do Not Comfort Thy Fellow

Do not comfort thy fellow in the hour that his dead lies before him.

—Talmud

✖✖

Death as Estrangement

I do not exist;
I am not I;
I am an alien in the land of the living.

—Emanuel Feldman in
Jewish Reflections on Death

✖✖

But Who Is Now My Comforter?

But who is now my comforter?
To whom shall I pour out my soul?
Whither shall I turn?
All my life my beloved companion hearkened
to my troubles, and they were many, and
comforted me so that somehow they would
quickly vanish. But now, alas, I am left
to flounder in my woe.

> —Marvin Lowenthal, trans.
> *The Memoirs of Gluckel of Hameln*

❋

Hear My Cry, O God

Hear my cry, O God,
heed my prayer.
From the end of the earth I call to You;
when my heart is faint,
You lead me to a rock that is high above me.
For You have been my refuge,
a tower of strength against the enemy.
O that I might dwell in Your tent forever,
take refuge under Your protecting wings.

> Selah.

O God, You have heard my vows;
grant the request of those who fear Your name.
Add days to the days of the king;
may his years extend through generations;
may he dwell in God's presence forever;
appoint steadfast love to guard him.
So I will sing hymns to Your name forever,
as I fulfill my vows day after day.

> —Psalm 61

❋

A Palace in Flames

There are those who sense the ultimate question in moments of wonder, in moments of joy; there are those who sense the ultimate question in moments of horror, in moments of despair. It is both the grandeur and the misery of living that makes man sensitive to the ultimate question. Indeed, his misery is as great as his grandeur.

How did Abraham arrive at his certainty that there is a God who is concerned with the world? Said Rabbi Isaac: Abraham may be compared to a man who was traveling from place to place when he saw a palace in flames. Is it possible that there is no one who cares for this palace? he wondered. Until the owner of the palace looked at him and said, "I am the owner of the palace." Similarly, Abraham our father wondered, "Is it conceivable that the world is without a guide?" The Holy One, blessed be He, looked out and said, "I am the Guide, the Sovereign of the world" [*Genesis Rabbah* chap. 39].

—Rabbi Abraham Joshua Heschel
God in Search of Man

On Weeping for the Dead

It is regarded as unnatural not to weep for the dead.

—Rabbi Tzvi Rabinowicz
A Guide to Life

Mourning

"My son," says Ben Sira, "let thy tears fall over the dead, and as one that suffereth grievously begin lamentation. . . . Make bitter weeping and make passionate wailing, and let thy mourning be according to his desert, for one day or two, let thou be evil spoken of; and so be comforted for thy sorrow."

—Rabbi Tzvi Rabinowicz
A Guide to Life

Kaddish

In modern America, you're not supposed to cry, you have to be strong.
But in traditional Jewish culture, crying is accepted and valued. It isn't
seen as a sign of pain—it's a sign of healing and recovery.

—Phyllis Toback in
Invisible Thread

❋

My Grandmother

When my grandmother died
The birds sang.
The whole world with her kind deeds
And her good heart rang.

When they lifted my grandmother from the bed,
And laid her on the floor,
Everybody wept, because
The kind old lady was no more.

My grandfather walked up and down the room,
With anger in his eye,
Because he had promised grandmother,
He would be first to die.

When they bore her into the town,
All the Christian folk cried,
And the Greek Catholic Priest lamented,
That such a good woman had died.

Only when the Shamash took his knife,
To cut in their clothes the mourning slash,
My uncles and my father cried aloud,
Like prisoners under the lash.

—Moshe Kulback in
The Golden Peacock

❋

Grandfather Dies

My grandfather came home at night from the field,
Made his bed, and said the Prayer of those about to die.
He stared hard at the world around him,
Saying to all his last goodbye.

My uncles and my father, his sons, stood silent,
Their hearts were heavy: they couldn't speak.
Grandfather sat up in his bed, slowly,
And addressed them in a voice trembling and weak.

And this is what grandfather said to his sons,
The big, burly fellows, the sturdy ones:
You, Ortche, my eldest, you are the prop of the family,
The first in the field, and the last to come home.
The earth knows the feel of your plough.
Like in rich soil may your seed grow.

Rachmiel, who can compare with you in the meadow?
Your scythe works like fire in the corn.
The snakes know you in the swamps, and the birds in
    their nests.
May you be blessed in stable and barn.

You, Samuel, man of the river,
Always with a net and fish in your hand,
You have the smell of the fisherman about you.
Be blessed on the water, and on the land.

Night was falling, the sunset glow
Came through the window. No one stirred.
My uncles and my father stood dumbly,
Listening to my grandfather's last word.

Then my grandfather drew his knees together,
And lay down in the bed.

And closed his eyes for ever.
Not one tear my father and my uncles shed.
A bird sang in the forest.
The sunset glow went out.
And my father and my uncles stood there,
With their heavy heads bowed.

—Moshe Kulback in
The Golden Peacock

❋

Explaining Death to Children

For children as well as adults, the ceremony surrounding death is of enormous significance. The Jewish faith suggests rites that play a vital role in the healing work of grief. The bereaved must realize that a loved one is gone and that the void must be filled gradually in a constructive way. He should not suppress memories or the disturbing, even guilt-producing recollections which are an inevitable part of all human relationships. Rather, shock and grief are structured by definite and solemn procedures. Joshua Liebman in *Peace of Mind* points to the wisdom of the Hebrew sages in assigning a definite period of mourning participated in by the entire family.

The wise parent should discuss the Jewish customs relating to death in a gentle and nonthreatening manner. The child should not have to wait until the death of a loved one to be hurriedly and frantically informed by a weeping mother that people are buried in special gardens or that stones or plaques are placed on each grave to indicate who is resting there. It is suggested that one explain the realities of death under more ideal circumstances, rather than with retroactive interpretation in the face of grief.

When death does occur, a child from approximately the age of seven on should be encouraged to attend the funeral. To shut a youngster out of this experience might be quite costly and damaging to his future development. He is an integral part of the family unit and should participate with them on this sad but momentous occasion. However, if the child is unwilling, he should not be forced to go or made to feel guilty because "he let the family down." If he does not attend the funeral, it may be wise to provide an opportunity at some later time to visit the cemetery and see the grave.

In Judaism, from the moment that one learns of the passing of a dear one, there are specific religious rituals to be followed which help to order one's life. The Jewish funeral is a rite of separation. The bad dream is real. The presence of the casket actualizes the experience. It transforms the process of denial to the acceptance of reality. The service itself is relatively brief and is devoted to prayers and to a description of the loved one's life and qualities that might be perpetuated by the living. By the child's attendance he, too, offers his last respects, feels enriched by being part of this person's existence, and through his presence is able to express publicly his own love and devotion. All the emotional reactions a child is likely to have to death in the family—sorrow and loneliness, anger and rejection, guilt, anxiety about the future, and the conviction that nothing is certain or stable anymore—can be considerably lessened if the child feels that he knows what is occurring and that adults are not trying to hide things from him.

Rabbi Earl A. Grollman
Explaining Death to Children

※※

A Funeral

Together with my two cousins and three others, I stepped over to the coffin. We lifted it off the trestles and slowly carried it—how astonishingly light it was!—up the center aisle of the synagogue as another elder, who walked before us, recited a Psalm. The air seemed suddenly stifling; I could not breathe. I worried about Rocheleh. We were outside. I inhaled deeply the cool air. The crowd silently parted as we came through, and there was the hearse, black and gleaming in the sunlight, and then the coffin was inside behind the curtained windows and someone was guiding me toward a glistening black limousine.

I sat next to my father in the back seat. There were two other men in the car, colleagues of my father whom I had known since childhood. We rode in silence. The cortege of funeral cars was two blocks long. My father sat gazing out the window. We drove through ruined streets and graveyard neighborhoods. A moment after we swung onto the Interboro Parkway, my father sat back and put his hand over his eyes. He remained in that position until we reached the cemetery.

The cars came to a halt in the section of the cemetery that contained the graves of Ladover Hasidim. I walked on the gravel road to the hearse and helped remove the casket. The crowd stood in silence. An elderly man, reciting from the Book of Psalms, led the procession to the edge of the open grave. I looked into the earth, saw the deep wounds made by the wielded shovels of the gravediggers, who stood idly by, watching. Abruptly, I felt my legs go weak and a sudden careening of the world. All around me were the muted sounds of weeping. My uncle's white-pine casket was lowered into the earth, the gravediggers swiftly and adroitly maneuvering the straps and then standing aside. My aunt sobbed and sagged into the arms of one of her daughters. My father stood beside me, biting his lips, all of him rigid. The starched white collar of his shirt, visible above his dark coat, glinted in the sunlight. I saw my mother in the crowd, her face ashen. Devorah, I knew, was not there: she had taken the children back to my parents' home.

My uncle's two sons began to fill in the grave. I took a shovel from one of the gravediggers, dug with it into the reddish-brown earth heaped along the rim of the grave, and lifted and let earth and pebbles and stones fall into the grave; heard the hollow sounds of the stones and earth striking the wood. My father took the shovel from me, and a moment later someone took it from him. My aunt stood nearby, loudly sobbing. The open grave filled rapidly. My uncle's two sons stood before the mound of raw turned earth and recited through tears the special Kaddish that is said at the grave of one newly buried. The crowd stirred, moved, divided itself into two lines between which the members of the immediate family moved through murmured words of consolation: "May God comfort you together with all the mourners of Zion and Jerusalem." My aunt walked supported by her two daughters. The cars began to fill up for the return journey.

—Chaim Potok
The Gift of Asher Lev

✳❈✳

Strange Envy

Envy
Those who stand bent before the casket
    wiping away their tears.
Envy memories of
    Warm embraces, gentle humour,
    birthdays, anniversaries,
joyous meals around the Sabbath
    table.

Pity those who cannot cry
tears long
dried into resignation,
surrendering the promise.

Pity the dried-eyed sadness
of those who can only dream of that
which could have been, or should have been.

Pity those who regret what should have been said
   or left unspoken—
loves lost, joys missed,
hopes abandoned.

Pity memories in subjunctive moods—
"if only he had, if only she had, if only I had."

Envy the mourners
who with sweet-bitter nostalgia
slowly recite the Kaddish.

—Rabbi Harold M. Schulweis

✺

The Passing of Tzirel Dvorah Siegel

To me, he was always Grandpa Bill. But Grandma called him Velvel—the same name she used since the day her aunt made the match some time in the last century in Poland. Velvel, a Little Wolf. When her Velvel died, we knew Grandma Tzirel would go on for six or eight or ten months, but no more. Not that life was not worth living any more—her Holy Books told her that Life was Good as long as it was given to you to live. Still, she thought, it would be proper after fifty-five years of marriage, to set her final house in order, instruct her children, then join her husband in the Other World of her immense, unbending faith.

We never joked with Grandma Tzirel. I know now that she was the stern mover of all the family affairs, though I had always seen her merely as a scarecrow-thin woman with a bent back and a cane. She sat in front of their small store day after day, emaciated, but strong as the Cossacks who tried to slaughter her and her Velvel, before I would be born. Long before. Next to my stocky Zeyde, she was a stick, and had they not been my grandparents, I might have thought of them as Laurel and Hardy: comic, out of place in a small New Jersey town populated by Irishmen and Italian clammers, and highschool hoods roaming the amusement park on the boardwalk down the street, out for a night of hellraising fun.

She was shrivelled before I got to know her, and even from pictures from her youth I cannot tell if she was ever pretty. That she was wise, no one disputes. Hers was a harsh wisdom befitting an age of unquestionable parents and unrebellious children. Everyone knew my father would never *not* become a doctor.

I don't believe she cried that Sabbath night and day while Velvel's body lay stretched on the bed. She sat there reading her pageworn books, without cursing or damning or demanding an answer from her God, who understood Yiddish better than Hebrew. She was then, as she was to be the following Fall—even as they placed her in the ground—a presence and focus of all who carried her blood.

When I was three or four, she made me put on a midget Tallis and forced me to recite the Shema before I could have my orange juice. It was her household, and she would not have her grandchildren grow up like *goyyim*. I recited according to her wish, repeating word-for-word after her, enchanted by the Hebrew word "Bom," which sounded so much like "bomb" to me. I smiled, imagining myself watching rockets' red glare and explosions everywhere. She felt immense satisfaction from watching the expression on my face, and I thought I had fooled her. I thought she was thinking I loved my Judaism and would be her Rabbi someday, leading the family in Kaddish for her, year after year at a reverent service that would call to mind her commands and statutes. But I was only laughing at a funny-sounding Hebrew word.

As always, though, she foresaw what I would never see: that for all her Old Country smells and intonations, I would come back to her, and love her, even when I fought her and weakly threw off this Law and that Custom. . . . as if I were getting even with a woman already fifteen years decomposed in the dirt of a cemetery so far away from her native Poland she would never have dreamed of such a graveside setting in her wildest fantasies. She was left there on an expectedly rainy day, as if her wrath and domination were straining Nature's storehouses to soak us to the skin. As if she were saying, even in death, "Stop kvetching! You'll be through with me soon enough. Are you so delicate you can't stand a little rain while you're putting away your grandmother?"

Counting the wood, the coffin we carried couldn't have weighed more than a hundred pounds.

We never get sentimental about her. Grandma Tzirel. She would have laughed at any of us who would speak about her with affection. None of us hated her, not really. But it wasn't love. There was too much fear.

Grandma Tzirel was born a hundred years ago in a now-vanished village—to haunt us, I think. She knew her purpose and meaning, and we pass it on to our ignorant children, this indelible omnipresence, feeling the chill of her extraordinary light.

Danny Siegel
Between Dust and Dance

✵✵

God Works Miracles

I can believe in the reality of God, despite the things that have happened in my family and in the families of people I care about, because I have seen Him work miracles. Not like the miracles of the Bible, suspension of natural law, splitting the sea, bringing the dead back to life—God works miracles today by enabling ordinary people to do extraordinary things.

—Rabbi Harold Kushner
Who Needs God

✵✵

Death

With the death of a husband you lose your present; With the death of a parent you lose your past, and with the death of a child you lose your future.

—Norman Linzer
Understanding Bereavement and Grief

✵✵

Protect Me, O God, for I Seek Refuge in You

Protect me, O God, for I seek refuge in You.
I say to the Lord,
    "You are my Lord, my benefactor;
    there is none above You."
"You are my Lord, my benefactor;

As to the holy and mighty ones that are in the land,
   my whole desire concerning them is that
   those who espouse another [god]
   may have many sorrows!
I will have no part of their bloody libations;
   their names will not pass my lips.
The Lord is my allotted share and portion;
   You control my fate.
Delightful country has fallen to my lot;
   lovely indeed is my estate.
I bless the Lord who has guided me;
   my conscience admonishes me at night.
I am ever mindful of the Lord's presence;
   He is at my right hand; I shall never be shaken.
So my heart rejoices,
   my whole being exults,
   and my body rests secure.
For You will not abandon me to Sheol,
   or let Your faithful one see the Pit.
You will teach me the path of life.
In Your presence is perfect joy;
   delights are ever in Your right hand.

                    —Psalm 16

❈❈

Out of the Depths I Call You, O Lord

Out of the depths I call You, O Lord.
O Lord, listen to my cry;
   let Your ears be attentive
   to my plea for mercy.
If You keep account of sins, O Lord,
   Lord, who will survive?
Yours is the power to forgive
   so that You may be held in awe.

I look to the Lord;
   I look to Him;
   I await His word.

I am more eager for the Lord
  than watchmen for the morning,
  watchmen for the morning.

—Psalm 130

❈

The Face of God

"You are casting me into a terrible darkness," I told my God. He told
me: "No. These things just happen. You will do the best you can. And
I will be nearby, when it occurs to Me to be nearby."

—Roger Rosenblatt in *Life*

❈

God, You Are My God

God, You are my God;
  I search for You,
  my soul thirsts for You,
  my body yearns for You,
  as a parched and thirsty land that has no water.
I shall behold You in the sanctuary,
  and see Your might and glory,
Truly Your faithfulness is better than life;
  my lips declare Your praise.
I bless You all my life;
  I lift up my hands, invoking Your name.
I am sated as with a rich feast,
  I sing praises with joyful lips
  when I call You to mind upon my bed,
  when I think of You in the watches of the night;
  for You are my help,
  and in the shadow of Your wings
I shout for joy.
My soul is attached to You;
Your right hand supports me.

—Psalm 63:2–9

❈

After My Death

After I am dead
Say this at my funeral:

There was a man who exists no more.

That man died before his time
And his life's song was broken off halfway.
O, he had one more poem
And that poem has been lost
For ever.

He had a lyre,
And a vital, quivering soul.
The poet in him spoke,
Gave it all his heart's secrets,
His hand struck all its chords.
But there was one secret he kept hidden
Though his fingers danced everywhere.
One string stayed mute
And is still soundless.

But alas! all its days
That string trembled,
Trembled softly, softly quivered
For the poem that would free her,

Yearned and thirsted, grieved and wept,
As though pining for someone expected
Who does not come,
And the more he delays, she whimpers
With a soft, fine sound,
But he does not come,

And the agony is very great,
There was a man and he exists no more.
His life's song was broken off halfway.

His life's song was broken off halfway.
He had one more poem
And that poem is lost,
For ever.

—Hayyim Nahman Bialik, trans. A. C. Jacobs, in
Anthology of Modern Hebrew Poetry

❈❈

Who Has Lived?

"And Jacob lived" (Genesis 47:28). Of how few men, asks a famous modern Jewish preacher, can we repeat a phrase like, "And Jacob lived"? When many a man dies, a death-notice appears in the Press. In reality, it is a life-notice; because but for it, the world would never have known that that man had ever been alive. Only he who has been a force for human goodness, and abides in hearts and souls made better by his presence during his pilgrimage on earth, can be said to have lived, only such a one is heir to immortality.

—Joseph H. Hertz in
Light from Jewish Lamps

❈❈

I Know I Won't Come This Way Again

I know I won't come this way again. Now
I'll press the palm of my hand on the tree's bark. Maybe
someone else will come here before it rains and press
his palm on the bark and unknowing
add one touch of air to another.

Then the rain will come. And all the touching will glide
   down with it
to the base of the tree and sink reaching down to the roots
   and rise

in the trunk and the branches to fill the leaves with new
greenness. Where will I be when the green and short breath
of my hands and the one who comes after me join in a flow
of breathing eternally green.

—Amir Gilboa, trans. Shirley Kaufman
The Light of Lost Suns

※※

Part of Life

Death, preparation for death, and mourning are all worked into
the fabric of day-to-day life.

—Rabbi Adin Steinsaltz
The Strife of the Spirit

※※

Hold On and Let Go

Hold on and let go
On the surface of things contradictory counsel.
But one does not negate the other.
The two are complementary,
   two sides of one coin.

Hold on—for death is not the final word
The grave is not oblivion.
Hold on— Kaddish, yahrzeit, yizkor.
No gesture, no kindness, no smile evaporates—
Every embrace
has an afterlife
   in our minds, our hearts, our hands.

Hold on—and let go.
Sever the fringes of the *talit* and
the knots that bind us to the past.
Free the enslaving memory that sells the future
   to the past

Free the fetters of memory that turn us passive,
listless, resigned.
Release us for new life.
Lower the casket, the closure meant
to open again the world
of new possibilities.

Return the dust to the earth
not to bury hope
but to resurrect the will to live.

We who remember are artists, aerialists
on a swinging trapeze
   letting go one ring to catch another.
Hold on and let go
   a subtle duality
   that endows our life
   with meaning—
Neither denying the past
   nor foreclosing the future.
We are part of the flow of life
   the divine process,
   which gives and takes
creates and retains.
We, too, must give and take, seize hold and release.

The Lord giveth and the Lord taketh.
   Blessed be the Name of His Sovereign Glory.

—Rabbi Harold M. Schulweis
"Immortality Through Goodness and Activism"
What Happens After I Die?

❋

There Is Nothing New Beneath the Sun

The words of Koheleth son of David, king in Jerusalem.

Utter futility!—said Koheleth—
Utter futility! All is futile!

What real value is there for a man
In all the gains he makes beneath the sun?

One generation goes, another comes,
But the earth remains the same forever.
The sun rises, and the sun sets—
And glides back to where it rises.
Southward blowing,
Turning northward,
Ever turning blows the wind;
On its rounds the wind returns.
All streams flow into the sea,
Yet the sea is never full;
To the place [from] which they flow
The streams flow back again.
All such things are wearisome:
No man can ever state them;
The eye never has enough of seeing,
Nor the ear enough of hearing.
Only that shall happen
Which has happened,
Only that occur
Which has occurred;
There is nothing new
Beneath the sun!

—Ecclesiastes 1:1–9

✳✳

Grief

Grief is defined within, as it were, concentric ripples of diminishing intensity. The ripple on the first day of death is the strongest and most critical. Also powerful, but somewhat less so, is the first week of mourning. The succeeding periods are the first thirty days and the first twelve months, getting less and less grievous.

—Rabbi Adin Steinsaltz
The Strife of the Spirit

✳✳

A Parable

There is a simple folk parable about man's belief in the world to come that brings new insight to the mourner, and it may start him in resolving his feelings of injustice, and his unspoken intellectual doubts about life after death. It is an imaginative and telling analogy that conveys the hope and confidence in the afterlife, even though this hope must be refracted through the prism of death. It was created by a contemporary Israeli rabbi, the late Rabbi Y. Tuckachinsky.

Imagine twins growing peacefully in the warmth of the womb. Their mouths are closed, and they are being fed via the navel. Their lives are serene. The whole world, to these brothers, is the interior of the womb. Who could conceive anything larger, better, more comfortable? They begin to wonder: "We are getting lower and lower. Surely if it continues, we will exit one day. What will happen after we exit?"

Now the first infant is a believer. He is heir to a religious tradition which tells him that there will be a "new life" after this wet and warm existence of the womb. It is a strange belief, seemingly without foundation, but one to which he holds fast. The second infant is a thorough-going skeptic. Mere stories do not deceive him. He believes only in that which can be demonstrated. He is enlightened, and tolerates no idle conjecture. What is not within one's experience can have no basis in one's imagination.

Says the faithful brother: "After our 'death' here, there will be a great new world. We will eat through the mouth! We will see great distances, and we will hear through the ears on the sides of our heads. Why, our feet will be straightened! And our heads—up and free, rather than down and boxed in."

Replies the skeptic: "Nonsense. You're straining your imagination again. There is no foundation for this belief. It is only your survival instinct, an elaborate defense mechanism, a historically conditioned subterfuge. You are looking for something to calm your fear of 'death.' There is only this world. There is no world-to-come!"

"Well then," asks the first. "what do you say it will be like?" The second brother snappily replies with all the assurance of the slightly knowledgeable: "We will go with a bang. Our world will collapse and we will sink into oblivion. No more. Nothing. Black void. An end to consciousness. Forgotten. This may not be a comforting thought, but it is a logical one."

Suddenly the water inside the womb bursts. The womb convulses. Upheaval. Turmoil. Writhing. Everything lets loose. Then a mysterious pounding—a crushing, staccato pounding. Faster, faster, lower, lower.

The believing brother exits. Tearing himself from the womb, he falls outward. The second brother shrieks—startled by the "accident" befallen his brother. He bewails and bemoans the tragedy—the death of a perfectly fine fellow. Why? Why? Why didn't he take better care? Why did he fall into that terrible abyss?

As he thus laments, he hears a head-splitting cry, a great tumult from the black abyss, and he trembles: "Oh my! What a horrible end! As I predicted!"

Meanwhile, as the skeptic brother mourns, his "dead" brother has been born into the "new" world. The headsplitting cry is a sign of health and vigor, and the tumult is really a chorus of Mazel Tovs sounded by the waiting family thanking God for the birth of a healthy son.

Indeed, in the words of a contemporary thinker, man comes from the darkness of the "not yet," and proceeds to the darkness of the "no more." While it is difficult to imagine the "not yet," it is more difficult to picture the "no more."

As we separate and "die" from the womb, only to be born to life, so we separate and die from our world, only to be reborn to life eternal. The exit from the womb is the birth of the body. The exit from the body is the birth of the soul. As the womb requires a gestation period of nine months, the world requires a residence of seventy or eighty years. As the womb is a *prozdor*, an anteroom preparatory to life, so our present existence is a *prozdor* to the world beyond.

—Rabbi Maurice Lamm in
Understanding Bereavement and Grief

✳

Burial Kaddish

Mourners: May His great name be magnified and sanctified in the world that is to be created anew, where He will revive the dead and raise them up unto life eternal; will rebuild the city of Jerusalem, and establish His Temple in the midst thereof; and will uproot all alien worship from the earth and restore the worship of the true God. O may the Holy One, blessed be He, reign in His sovereignty and glory during your life and during your days, and during the life of all the house of Israel, even speedily and at a near time, and say ye, Amen.

Congregation and mourners: Let His great name be blessed forever and to all eternity.

Mourners: Blessed, praised and glorified, exalted, extolled and honored, magnified and lauded be the name of the Holy One, blessed be He; though He be high above all blessings and hymns, praises and consolations which are uttered in the world, and say ye, Amen.

Congregation: Let the name of the Lord be blessed from this time forth and forevermore.

Mourners: May there be abundant peace from heaven, and life for us and for all Israel, and say ye, Amen.

Congregation: My help is from the Lord, who made heaven and earth.

Mourners: He who maketh peace in His high places, may He make peace for us and for all Israel, and say ye, Amen.

✳❂✳

Evening Service

Thou, O God, art our light, our strength, and our portion for ever. In the darkest hours of life, we are sustained when we feel Thy presence with us. Thy love is a healing balm unto the stricken heart: and falls like a ray of light through the clouds of suffering and the mists of tears.

Grant that in those hours of trial when the vanity of earthly things is so apparent, life's higher meaning may become more real to us. May our sympathies be so quickened that we may seek opportunities to soothe the sorrow of others, and to lighten the loads of other burden-bearers.

May the thought of death not cast us into utter sadness and leave us desolate. O help us to believe that nothing that is evil can come from Thy hand, though we do not comprehend Thy ways, that death itself can only be a messenger of peace, leading to everlasting life. Praised, therefore, be Thy name, O God, Sovereign of life and of death, Source of our hope, and Comforter for ever. Amen.

—Israel Goldstein
Mourners' Devotions

✳❂✳

3

✖✖✖✖✖✖✖✖✖✖✖✖✖✖✖✖✖✖✖✖✖✖✖✖✖✖✖✖✖✖✖✖✖

Shivah: *The First Three Days after Burial*

The traditional mourning process begins with the first three days immediately after burial. Upon returning home from the cemetery, the mourners wash their hands before entering the house in which *shivah* will be observed, although there is also custom for mourners to wash their hands before leaving the cemetery.

Upon entering the house, the mourners remove their shoes. In some homes, mirrors have been covered. A tall *shivah* candle to last for seven days is lighted for the mourners, and cardboard boxes or low wood stools are provided for sitting.

The *mitzvah* of preparing the *seudat havraah*, meal of condolence, is performed by friends and neighbors as an act of consolation. It is customary for mourners to eat a shelled hard-boiled egg, symbolic of life and, in traditional Judaism, of resurrection at the time of the Messiah.

Traditionally, during *shivah*, *Shacharit* (Morning Services), *Minchah* (Afternoon Services), and *Maariv* (Evening Services) are held in the house of mourning.

Shivah had begun. "Avelut, the process of mourning, begins immediately after the deceased is interred and the casket is completely covered with earth" (Rabbi Maurice Lamm, *The Jewish Way in Death and Mourning*). The *shivah* is a "unique institution," writes Rabbi Tzvi Rabinowicz in *A Guide to Life*. "For seven days, the mourners, irrespective of status or disposition, are united in their common sorrow. Daily routine and work cease. Death, with its awesome majesty, casts its shadow on the mourners."

Unlike the drive from the funeral parlor to the cemetery, during which time I stared out of the limousine window at scenes that made me believe

99

they had been created by God's "Divine kiss," the relatively short drive from the cemetery to my home was uneventful. We were even more subdued than we were after leaving the funeral parlor. My father's body would never be with us again.

Although the limousine provided time for thinking and meditation, there are sounds to silence. My sounds were pleas for direction. I cannot help but think that the rabbi should have been with us in that limousine, perhaps if only to talk to us about the days of *shivah* to follow. What guidance did my sister and I have? The last time there was *shivah* in our home was 22 years before, when our maternal grandfather had died. And since then, although aunts and uncles and family friends had died, we were only visitors in the house of mourning, not the mourners we were now. But the rabbi was not with us and we would face *shivah*—as we did our father's death—unprepared and with only our mother to give us counsel.

"The second stage of mourning," Rabbi Lamm writes, "consists of the first three days following burial, days devoted to weeping and lamentation. During this time, the mourner does not even respond to greetings, and remains in his home (except under special circumstances). It is a time when even visiting the mourner is usually somewhat discouraged, for it is too early to comfort the mourner when the wound is so fresh." "We have to remember," gerontologist Carol P. Hausman writes, "that we not only cannot, but we should not, remove the sadness of the loss."

> What we really want out of a shiva call is to be helpful at a time of helplessness, to be responsive to the feelings of the bereaved, and to be intimate at a time when our friend is feeling bereft. Using Jewish guidelines, we can act in ways that are truly helpful, responsive and intimate, and which leave both the caller and bereaved feeling touched and fulfilled.
>
> —Carol P. Hausman
> "First You Mourn"
> *Moment*

Shivah had begun.

On one of the steps leading to the front door of our home was a white porcelain water pitcher and a white towel, both having been left by our neighbor Sheryl who had forgone accompanying us to the cemetery to prepare for our return home. Although mourners sometimes wash their hands before leaving the cemetery, the custom in my family had been to do so upon arrival at the home where *shivah* would be observed.

I have written earlier that some years before, after having attended the funeral of my father's aunt, and my great-aunt, Sally, I told my wife that after 120 years, when my parents had died, I wanted a pitcher of water prepared for the washing of my hands to be ready for us at our home and shelled, hard-boiled eggs for the mourners to eat upon entering our home. The actions would link me to the generations of my ancestors who had performed the same rituals, rituals I knew I would find life affirming.

"And what other goal for religion could there be? to see the Holy Ancient One face to face. Or through Scripture to reimagine the story and thus be reminded of its ever-present possibility. Or through ritual, whose sacred script compels us to act as if we were dreaming, or relive it" (Rabbi Lawrence Kushner, *The River of Light*).

But my father had died long before 120 years. No wonder that I shuddered at the sight of the white porcelain pitcher standing like a sentinel on the gray concrete step, beckoning me to remember, not allowing me to pass if I did not.

I washed my hands first, tilting the pitcher first over one hand and then over the other, conscious of others watching me as I performed the ancient rite. My mother followed, then my sister and my aunt and, finally, others who had returned with us from the cemetery who had their own needs as mourners.

"The cup of water is not transferred directly from one person to another. This is a symbolic expression of hope that the tragedy should not continue from person to person, but should end where it unfortunately began" (Lamm). We had observed the same custom at the cemetery when filling my father's grave with earth, avoiding transferring the shovel from one person to another, and for the same reason. Rushing water, too, has its own symbolism, as does the falling earth.

"'He maketh death to vanish in life eternal; and the Lord God wipeth away tears from off all faces; and the reproach of His people shall He take away from off all the earth: for the Lord hath spoken it' [Mishnah *Makkot* 3:5]" (Rabinowicz).

Rabbi Lawrence Kushner, in *The River of Light*, writes of the exodus from Egypt as a "story of the transformation of consciousness." He explains, "Above all we remember that at the beginning of the story there were slaves. And at the end of the story, when the children of Israel sang the Song at the Sea (Exod. 15), there were only free people." In a very real sense, after the burial of my father, after hearing the (falling) earth from the shovel as the "thunder of mortality," I had been transformed. Not only had I become an "orphaned adult" (*The Orphaned Adult*, by Rabbi Marc Angel), in a new relationship with my mother—not to mention my sister and my wife and children—but I had also become more aware in a way I had never before of the distant thunder of my own mortality. Washing my hands became perhaps another, and final, stage in the transformation. I would be reentering the familiarity of my own home, my world, for the first time without my father, as an orphan. And the washing of my hands at the entrance to my home became another symbol of that transformation.

Rabbi Lawrence Kushner continues to interpret the story of the exodus and the water symbol, the "river of light," of transformation, enlightenment.

> And this is the final stage. The passing through the waters. Like Jacob, our father, before us, who as the final act of return to his brother Esau, chose to be alone, by the edge of the waters of the river Jabok (which probably served as the boundary of the Land of Israel), and who wrestled there with the angel-person until the breaking of dawn and who, on account of his survival, was granted the name Israel, thus the children of Israel, and we, their grandchildren, are permitted to pass through the water and become new beings. For this reason, all acts of personal purification and conversion in traditional Judaism require immersion in the *mikveh,* the ritual bath. Completely naked, we come up out of the water new beings.
>
> —Rabbi Lawrence Kushner
> *The River of Light*

One of the origins of this custom of washing one's hands after a burial is it is a "symbolic cleansing from the impurity associated with death. This impurity, which is in the spiritual-legal category and has no relation to physical or hygienic cleanliness, underscores Judaism's constant emphasis on life and the value of living" (Lamm).

I had not felt unclean after my father's burial and so I did not feel I was cleansing myself after washing my hands upon my return home. Rather, in the rush of water over my hands, I felt a purity of spirit and history in having joined with my father in observance of a ritual act of our people: my father had washed his hands after he buried his father and his mother, and they had washed their hands after they buried their fathers and mothers, and their fathers and mothers after burying theirs. In performing rituals a generation apart, my father and I had become one, as we had at my *bar mitzvah* and my wedding and at every Passover seder and Sukkot party and Hanukkah celebration. The Jewish way in death and mourning, as the Jewish way in birth and celebration, made me one with my fathers and mothers, one with my people.

Shivah had begun.

Once inside our home, we saw that our neighbor Sheryl along with her husband, Marc, who had accompanied us to the cemetery, had also performed the *mitzvah* of preparing the *seudat havraah* (meal of condolence). "This meal is invariably provided by friends and neighbors," advises Rabbi Rabinowicz, "in obedience to the talmudic injunction, 'A mourner is forbidden to eat of his own food at the first meal after the burial' [*Moed Katan* 27b; *Yoreh De'ah* 378.1]."

Rabbi Rabinowicz also informs us that reference to this custom is made by both Jeremiah and Ezekiel: "Neither shall men break bread for them in mourning, to comfort for the dead; neither shall men give them the cup of consolation to drink for their father or for their mother" (Jeremiah 16:7). Ezekiel was told by God, "Sigh in silence; make no mourning for the dead, bind thy headtire upon thee, and put thy shoes upon thy feet, and cover not thine upper lip, and eat not the bread of men" (Ezekiel 24:17).

"Ezekiel was forbidden to observe the practices of mourning," Rabbi Rabinowicz explains. "We see, therefore, that one of the rites of mourning was not to eat of one's own food but to allow others to provide food. This custom gives friends and neighbors the opportunity to express in a practical form their solicitude and sympathy."

Rabbi Lamm refers to this meal of condolence as a "beautiful custom, which may appear strange to some American Jews [but which] possesses profound psychological insights."

> Another aspect of the meal of condolence is that it is the second formal expression of consolation. The first . . . is the parallel rows of friends through which the bereaved walk as they depart from the gravesite. That is a silent tribute, with only a Hebrew formula of condolence, but it is eloquent testimony that we share the pangs of our neighbor's anguish. The second stage of condolence takes us one step closer to the mourner in his state of misery; we move from the role of spectator to participant, from sentiment to service. We bring the mourner the sustenance of life, figuratively and literally, the "bread" of his existence.

> —Rabbi Maurice Lamm
> *The Jewish Way in Death and Mourning*

Once inside our home, I felt my body sag. Did I take off my shoes immediately? Did my mother? ". . . the observances [of *Shivah*] commence as soon as the mourners demonstrate final acceptance of mourning by removing their shoes and sitting on a low bench or stool" (Lamm). I could not sit for a long time after entering our home, nor could I eat anything but the shelled hard-boiled egg my wife had prepared in advance, the egg that Rabbi Rabinowicz reminds us was, in ancient times, "regarded as a symbol of life and resurrection" and about which I have written earlier.

A current of emotion shocked my sighing spirit as I realized my father's absence. I was a flurry of activity, moving from one visitor to another, in my hands an open album of photographs taken of my father during his illness, on my lips words of endearment and disbelief. The photographs included those taken of our family *seder* in my Aunt Dubby and Uncle Irving's Ft. Lauderdale condominium less than two weeks before my father died.

I felt a fever of excitement during those first few hours after returning from the cemetery. I could not stop to eat or to sit on one of the cardboard boxes the driver of our limousine had left in our living room. Like the tall *shivah* candle standing on a table in the corner of the living room, also provided by the funeral parlor, the cardboard boxes were astonishing reminders that ours was a home unlike others on our street that day and unlike anything it had ever been before.

In retrospect, my unrest may have been an acting out of denial: "Here's my father on the terrace of his condominium," I would proudly proclaim, pointing to one of the photographs in the album, and "Here he is reading from the *Haggadah* at the *seder* table. Sick, yes, but alive!" Whatever the reason for my behavior, I didn't stop to wonder; I allowed for it and was comforted by it.

My father was committed to the fullness of life and had lived a full life: in work and play, in fathering and grandfathering, in husbandly devotion. Why then should I not—even after his death—talk about how full was his living. But the stark reminders of his dying—*shivah* candle, cardboard box, and torn black ribbon pinned to my suit jacket—framed every photograph with a bittersweet sigh. "To have had a full life does not always reconcile one to death," Rabbi David J. Wolpe writes in *The Healer of Shattered Hearts*, "not to the death of a loved one, not to one's own death. In the icy inevitability of death, resented no matter the nature of one's life, is the most immediate argument for the need of a personal God."

I have written that I came to my father's dying with my own belief in a personal God, strengthened during the 4 months my father was ill by my father himself, who never abandoned hope, and by my mother, who never abandoned my father, and by a God, who never abandoned either. I have to believe that for them as well a personal God existed. "There is some comfort to be had," suggests Rabbi Wolpe, "in the certainty of memory, the fullness of God's understanding." I believed then, as I do now, in my God, who gave me memory to rebuild and whose understanding of my need to mourn was an acceptance of how I chose to mourn.

The *shivah* visitation, Rabbi Lamm tells us, is the "time that is ripe for the beginning of the mourner's verbalization of his feeling of loss. Here, too, the rabbis urge the visitors to sit in silence until the bereaved himself desires to speak. Even then," Rabbi Lamm adds, "the rabbis advise visitors to speak only on the subject of the death in the family."

But I had already spoken of death all too often during my father's illness; at least during those first few hours after his burial, in my own home, where my father and I had shared countless hours, I wanted to speak not of his death but of his life.

After the funeral, I followed the ritual of shivah, an intense seven days of mourning. People came and brought food, they cooked and cleaned up so that all my energy was devoted to grieving. Visitors told stories about my father; their anecdotes helped me make sense of my father's life and my life with him.

—Phyllis Toback
"Kaddish"
Invisible Thread

"It is customary to light a seven-day candle on returning from the cemetery as a memorial to the deceased, symbolic of the light brought by the deceased to the mourners during life" (Rabbi Simeon J. Maslin, *Gates of Mitzvah*).

My wife had set the *shivah* candle on the table in our living room, a "conspicuous place so that it may be seen, especially during shivah services" (Maslin). "The human spirit is the lamp of God," we said at the lighting of the candle. "Blessed is the Eternal One, who has implanted within us eternal life."

The flame of the *shivah* candle was a reminder during the *shivah*, not only of his death, which we were mourning, but that my father's presence in our lives would never be extinguished as long as we kept his memory alive in word and deed.

It is customary to cover mirrors or to turn them to the wall in the house of mourning. This custom is not mentioned in medieval sources. Some hold that this is done to prevent the soul of the departed from being reflected in the glass; others say that it is done simply to prevent the mourner from seeing his own sad countenance, thus adding to his grief. Another view is that mirrors, so often associated with vanity, are out of place at such a time. The most rational explanation is the rule that forbids prayer in front of a mirror, since the reflection distracts the attention of worshippers, and prayers are normally recited in the house of the mourner.

—Rabbi Tzvi Rabinowicz
A Guide to Life

Rabbi Lamm adds:

Judaism has taken great care to promote a relationship of kindness, concern, courtesy, and even physical desire between a man and his wife. Nevertheless, with the death of a child or a parent or sibling, this intimate relationship must be suspended. One commentator thus states that the ancient custom observed during shiva, of kfi'at hamitah, the overturning of the bed or couch, served as a means of discouraging marital relations. When the cloud of death settles on a household, the mirror—happy symbol of secure and intimate family living—must be covered, and the mourner must concentrate on the painful loss.

—Rabbi Maurice Lamm
The Jewish Way in Death and Mourning

The mirrors remained uncovered in our home during *shivah*. Perhaps because there had already been 4 months of grief, my mother did not think an uncovered mirror would have her grieve any less. But more so, the covered mirror frightened her. A covered mirror would "close upon me," and my mother wanted the "space" an uncovered mirror provided, space to "see" beyond herself. It was not her own face in the mirror that she desired to see but rather my father's. And so she asked that the mirrors remain uncovered. There was no mirror in our living room, where we prayed during *shivah*, and so that posed no distraction.

The first few hours of *shivah* passed; I had spoken with all those who had accompanied my family and me to our home, and, finally, in exhaustion, I found my cardboard box and sat down. Almost immediately there was a plate of food in my hands.

It is an ancient Jewish tradition that mourners, during shiva, do not sit upon chairs of normal height. Until modern times it was the custom to be seated on the earth itself, a procedure which demonstrated the departure from normalcy during the early stages of bereavement. Thus expression was given to the sense of loneliness and depression one felt after one's relative was interred in the very earth on which he sat. The Bible tells us that when Job suffered a succession of disasters he was comforted by friends who sat with him "to the earth." It is, almost in a literal sense, a physical adjustment to one's emotional state, a lowering of the body to the level of one's feelings, a symbolic enactment of remorse and desolation.

—Rabbi Maurice Lamm
The Jewish Way in Death and Mourning

When Job's three friends heard about all these calamities that had befallen him, each came from his home—Eliphaz the Temanite, Bildad the Shuhite, and Zophar the Naamathite. They met together to go and console him and comfort him. When they saw him from a distance, they could not recognize him, and they broke into loud weeping; each one tore his robe and and threw dust into the air onto his head. They sat with him on the ground seven days and seven nights. None spoke a word to him for they saw how very great was his suffering.

—Job 2:11–13

And when King David learned of his son Amnon's death, "David rent his garment and lay down on the ground, and all his courtiers stood by with their clothes rent" (2 Samuel 13:31).

And I sat, as I would for seven days, on a cardboard box, on a level lower than that of normal seating height. (Sleeping on a bed of normal height is permitted.) In my hands was a plate of food, my meal of condolence that would satisfy a hunger but not a yearning.

Minimally, [the meal of condolence] should include bread or rolls—the staff of life. It should also include hardboiled eggs, symbolic of the cyclical or continuous nature of life. Some explain that the egg is the only food that hardens the longer it is cooled, and man must learn to steel himself when death occurs. The meal of condolence may also include cooked vegetables or lentils, and a beverage such as coffee or tea. Some custom has it that wine should also be served. It is obvious that this occasion of drinking should not induce lightheartedness or a surfeit of conviviality.

—Rabbi Maurice Lamm
The Jewish Way in Death and Mourning

Bread is the staple food, Rabbi Rabinowicz reminds us: ". . . bread that sustains man's life" (Psalm 104:15) is "the bread of mourners" (Hosea 9:4). The egg, Rabbi Rabinowicz explains, is completely sealed inside its shell and serves as a "reminder to the mourners to remain silent and refrain from casual talk." The lentils, the rabbis said, were "made into a broth by Jacob to comfort his father when Abraham died [*Bava Batra* 16b; *Yoreh De'ah* 378:9]." Further, "Our sages gave us an additional reason: 'Lentils are round like a wheel, and mourning is a revolving wheel that touches everyone sooner or later.' " Also, Rabbi Rabinowicz informs, "just as lentils have no mouths, so too must mourners 'have no mouth,' for they are forbidden to greet people [*Midrash Genesis Rabbah* 63:14]."

I pushed the food around in my plate and ate reluctantly, hearing the murmur of voices around me but not listening to any of it.

Those who had accompanied us to our home from the cemetery were family and close friends, all of whom came to offer comfort but surely came to be comforted as well for they, too, suffered the heartwound of my father's death. I heard only talk of my father; especially vocal were those who had not spoken to my mother or to my sister or to me since my father's death, or even since my sister and I and our families had returned from visiting with our parents during Passover, less than two weeks before. They wanted to know everything about my father's last month, last week, last day. And, as I recall, they wanted to know everything. While they were certainly in our home to share our sorrow, they were also there to express their own individual sadness.

In Jewish mysticism the very emphasis on the community is at the same time an insistence on the infinite worth of the individual . . . If one person is missing, then the whole community is incomplete and its full coming together with the Divine Presence is impossible . . . Job, sunk in the miseries of loss and despair, suffers a profound crisis of faith. When others try to comfort him, Job . . . replies that it is none of their concern. But they insist; his fate is theirs, and they too will be held guilty.

—Rabbi Dr. Jonathan Sacks
"Practical Implications of Infinity"
To Touch the Divine

"My groaning serves as my bread: My roaring pours forth as water./For what I feared has overtaken me;/What I dreaded has come upon me./I had no repose, no quiet, no rest,/And trouble came" (Job 3:24–26).

. . . . Do not reject the discipline of the Almighty.
He injures, but He binds up;
He wounds, but His hands heal.
He will deliver you from six troubles;
In seven no harm will reach you:
In famine He will redeem you from death,
In war, from the sword.
You will be sheltered from the scourging tongue;
You will have no fear when violence comes.

—Job 5:17–21

Eliphaz speaks of Job, but not of Job; he speaks of the individual, but also of the community of humankind. Job's anguish is everyman's anguish. My father's death touched each of us and all of us.

During *Shivah*, *Shacharit* (Morning Services), *Minchah* (Afternoon Services), and *Maariv* (Evening Services) are held in the home; therefore, so is the *Kaddish* recited, a prayer that is part of every Jewish worship service and undoubtedly one of the best known prayers in the Hebrew liturgy.

When death stalks our homes it brings an end to physical life. The current is cut off. That is all. But the spirit is mightier than the grave. The thoughts and emotions, the ideals and attitudes of the heirs attest to the undying influence of the dead. The recitation of the Kaddish is a public demonstration that a parent's life was not lived without furthering, in some sense, the cause of the good. It is no exaggeration to say that the spiritual handclasp of the Kaddish has helped assure the continued survival of the Jewish people, the Jewish religion, the synagogue and its major institutions.

—Rabbi Maurice Lamm
The Jewish Way in Death and Mourning

Sometime after dinner, when the lights in our home were muted and the curtains were drawn over the windows and over my heart, they started coming: family and friends, neighbors and fellow congregants of Temple Emanu-el, the community of Israel. "Religion is community. It is the way people learn to relate to each other and to belong to each other in truly human ways" (Rabbi Harold Kushner, *Who Needs God*).

I remember some of the faces; tears shielded me from seeing them all. I felt some of the bodies crowded around me, and I felt refuge in their presence. Others came together in our living room and in our kitchen, in our hallway, and even on the outside steps. Our rabbi entered with representatives of the congregation's ritual committee, and while the committee members distributed copies of *Gates of Prayer for the House of Mourning*, we spoke with the rabbi about the turmoil of the first day of *shivah*.

It was time for *Maariv*, Evening Services, and words I had heard before in some distant past with my father standing next to me.

> The greatness of The Eternal One surpasses our understanding and yet at times we feel His nearness. Overwhelmed by awe and wonder as we behold the signs of His presence, still we feel within us a kinship with the divine. And so we turn to You, O God, looking at the world about us and inward to the world within us, there to find You, and from Your presence gain life and strength.

I stood between Jo and my mother; my sister next to her husband; my aunt next to her daughter, my cousin, Bettiann. When I was a child, I was asked to leave the sanctuary when it was time for my parents—and my grandparents—to recite the *Kaddish*, as I was asked to leave before *Yizkor*. And the words themselves—*Kaddish* and *Yizkor*—came to frighten me. If I had remained in the sanctuary when my grandparents and then my parents recited the *Kaddish*, I could be imposing a death sentence on them, so much a part of their own upbringing was this belief that they had carried it to America from Eastern Europe.

When my wife first stood to recite the *Kaddish* for her father more than a score of years earlier, I chose to stand with her, so she would not stand alone. And so began a custom in our family. But I didn't even whisper the words because then they were not mine to say. Even when, in our Reform congregation, we were encouraged to recite the *Kaddish* for the Six Million who perished in the Holocaust or for the thousands who have died in defense of Israel, my voice was still.

> We are assembled with our friends in the shadow that has fallen on their home. We raise our voices together in prayer to the Source of Life, asking for comfort and strength.
>
> We need light when gloom darkens our home; to whom shall we look, but to the Creator of light? We need fortitude and courage when pain and loss assail us; where shall we find them, if not in the thought of Him who preserves all that is good from destruction?
>
> Who among us has not passed through trials and bereavement? Some bear fresh wounds in their hearts, and therefore feel more keenly the kinship of sorrow. Others, whose days of mourning are more remote, still recall the comfort that sympathy brought to their sorrowing hearts.
>
> All things pass; all that lives must die. All that we prize is but lent to us; and the time comes when we must surrender it. We are travellers on the same road that leads to the same end.

The time was coming. *Kaddish* would be recited. And it would be mine.

We read Psalm 121, "I lift up my eyes to the mountains: what is the source of my help?"

O Lord, God of the spirits of all flesh, You are close to the hearts of the sorrowing, to strengthen and console them with the warmth of Your love, and with the assurance that the human spirit is enduring and indestructible. Even as we pray for perfect peace for those whose lives have ended, so do we ask You to give comfort and courage to the living.

There seemed only room to shift my weight from one leg to another, not any room to move about. I was embraced by my family and by my community.

The rabbi read *El Malay Rachamin*: "O God full of compassion, Eternal Spirit of the universe, grant perfect rest under the wings of Your Presence to our loved one who has entered eternity."

O Lord, Healer of the broken-hearted, Binder of their wounds, grant consolation to those who mourn. Give them strength and courage in the time of their grief, and restore to them a sense of life's goodness.

Fill them with reverence and love for You, that they may serve You with a whole heart, and let them soon know peace. Amen.

We read Psalm 23 in one voice: "The Lord is my shepherd, I shall not want." And followed that reading with *Aleinu*.

When cherished ties are broken, and the chain of love is shattered, only trust and the strength of faith can lighten the heaviness of the heart. At times, the pain of separation seems more than we can bear, but if we dwell too long on our loss we embitter our hearts and harm ourselves and those about us.

The Psalmist said that in his affliction he learned the law of God. And in truth, grief is a great teacher, when it sends us back to serve and bless the living. We learn how to counsel and comfort those who, like ourselves, are bowed with sorrow. We learn when to keep silence in their presence, and when a word will assure them of our love and concern.

Thus, even when they are gone, the departed are with us, moving us to live as, in their higher moments, they themselves wished to live. We remember them now; they live in our hearts; they are an abiding blessing.

Yitgadal veyitkadash. . . .

The *Kaddish*. I heard the murmurs of the congregation, not their words; I felt my lips move, but I did not hear the sounds escaping from them. I don't know if I recited anything at all from the *Kaddish* that first evening of *shivah*, but I do know though my heart was broken, I had become one with my people.

"May the Source of peace send peace to all who mourn and comfort to all who are bereaved. Amen."

Amen.

※※

Readings

✳✳✳✳✳✳✳✳✳✳✳✳✳✳

Pierced within Me

My heart is pierced within me.

—Psalm 109:22

✳✳

A Season for Everything

A season is set for everything, a time for every experience under heaven:
A time for silence and a time for speaking.

—Ecclesiastes 3:1, 7

✳✳

Silence

Silence is the mother tongue of awe.

—Rabbi David J. Wolpe
The Healer of Shattered Hearts

✳✳

The Death of Abraham

And Abraham breathed his last, dying at a good ripe age, old and contented; and he was gathered to his kin. His sons Isaac and Ishmael buried him in the cave of Machpelah, in the field of Ephron son of Zohar the Hittite, facing Mamre, the field that Abraham had bought from the Hittites; there Abraham was buried, and Sarah his wife. After the death of Abraham, God blessed his son Isaac.

—Genesis 25:8–11

※

Surviving the Loss of a Spouse

This is a brittle, cold and quiet period.

—Anne Brenner in
Journal of Jewish Communal Service

※

My Eyes Are Spent with Tears

My eyes are spent with tears,
My heart is in tumult,
My being melts away . . .

—Lamentations 2:11

※

I Know Not Your Ways

I know not your ways—
A sunset is for me
A Godset.
Where are you going,
God?

Take me along,
if, in the "along,"
it is light,
God.

I am afraid of the dark.

—Malka Heifetz Tussman, trans. from the Yiddish by Marcia Falk, in
Shirim: A Jewish Poetry Journal

❊

Life Cycle

It is a bittersweet truth, this breathing out and breathing in. But we acknowledge and understand it. Even as we stake our lives and the lives of our children on it. Like fallen leaves enriching the soil, it is true. This return of the genes and the generations must occur if new ones are to set out.

—Rabbi Lawrence Kushner
The River of Light

❊

On Returning Home after a Funeral

Out of the depths I cry unto You, Lord; hear my supplication. A heavy burden has fallen upon me and sorrow has bowed my head. Days of anguish have been my lot; days and nights of weeping. And now I turn to You, the Source of good, for comfort and help. Give me the eyes to see that pain is not Your will, that somewhere there weeps with me One who feels my trouble and knows the suffering of my soul! O divine Spirit in whose image my own spirit is cast, I seek the Light that will dispel the darkness that has overtaken me. Let me find You in the love of family and friends, in the sources of healing that are implanted within all the living, in the mind that conquers all infirmity and trouble. Grant me the strength to endure what cannot be escaped, and the courage to go on without bitterness or despair, basing my life on the abiding foundations of Your law. Amen.

—*Gates of the House*

❊

Mirrors

Mirrors at the time of death. Culture's greatest creation for pondering the mysteries of self-reference is, of course, the mirror. And it is just this invention found everywhere in the world that—according to Jewish folk tradition, on the occasion of death—must be covered up. Is it not perhaps a way of saying that the ultimate outcome of self-reflection is death? Or perhaps even a way of saying that, when the frail gauze separating this world of life and the other world of death has been momentarily torn, we must be especially careful to keep the portal of the mirror closed, lest there be additional passages going this way and that, between life and death. Let us instead cover the mirrors, doing the best we can to endure the mystery and pain.

—Rabbi Lawrence Kushner
The River of Light

❊❊

Moed Katan

Formerly, they used to bring food to the house of mourning, rich people in baskets of silver and gold, poor people in baskets of willow twigs; and the poor felt ashamed. Therefore, a law was passed that everybody should use baskets of willow twigs, out of deference to the poor. . . .

Formerly, they used to serve drinks in a house of mourning, the rich serving in white glasses and the poor in colored glasses [which were much less expensive]; and the poor felt ashamed. Therefore, a law was passed that everybody should serve drinks in colored glasses in deference to the poor. . . .

Formerly, they used to bring out the deceased for burial, the rich on a tall bed, ornamented with rich covers, the poor on a plain box; and the poor felt ashamed. Therefore, a law was passed that all should be brought out on a plain box, in deference to the poor. . . .

Formerly, the expense of burying the dead was harder for a family to bear than the death itself, so that sometimes family members fled to escape the expense. This was so until Rabban Gamaliel ordered that he be buried in a plain linen shroud instead of expensive garments. And since then people have buried their dead in simple shrouds. . . .

—Babylonian Talmud, tractate
Moed Katan, pages 27a-27b
Francine Klagsbrun
Voices of Wisdom

※

Ben

Uncle Ben died before I was three. That I remember. And I remember he was my favorite uncle, because I was never old enough to know him any other way than the uncle whose knees I always bounced on, and who would call me kind Yiddish names, and could afford to love me well, maybe because he was sick and wanted to leave someone on this earth who would remember him forever—enough to tell about him, and write and rewrite about him, and proclaim his kindness and honesty and softspokenness, no matter what was happening to Humanity.

And he died before I could ever find out he wasn't what I thought he was. A while ago, as I mused over how the world is really Tough and Realistic, I became suspicious, and certain that people aren't just good and simple. They're always hiding something that comes out sometime, even if you never see it. Even though they were always kind to you.

So I chanced it, and asked my parents, "Was Uncle Ben really like I knew he was?"—with the possibility that I would lose it all once I heard that he used to shout at my Aunt Anna or Cousin Phyllis, something I feared terribly as a growing child and more as an adult. But I still had to know, because Truth was replacing Fun in Life, and I thought, "If Ben were still the same. . . ."—then maybe I still had time to reconsider the shapes and textures of people.

And so he was. Not just because he died at forty-eight before he could get down to being the *momzer* everyone is supposed to be in the final analysis. As all parents tell their children certain essences, my own revealed to me that he was, indeed, a simple, hard-working linotypist, kind, honest, and devoted. His first child was Aliza, who died at thirteen of pneumonia, because she was susceptible to it, because she was hydrocephalic, and had a big head, and was ugly to look at, and completely helpless. And my uncle and aunt always took care of her, never leaving her alone for a minute, carrying her up and down the stairs, washing her, loving her, showing her with pride to everyone who asked. Never, never, never thinking to put her away, though she was helpless. Despite the endless rounds of doctors insisting there was nothing they could do.

They kept her alive for thirteen years, not as an experiment, nor because they were masochists, but because they loved her.

Ben raised her and buried her and was buried, in turn, by Anna and Phyllis, who snatched from those years the best tears and laughter. They are the ones who love you for what you are, with no excuses, no tricks—no matter what your idiosyncrasies or errors.

Ben was like clouds to me.

I shall never think of him as anything other than alive, waiting at the Messiah's right hand, ready to walk with him when it is time to redeem the Jews from any kind of wrong and unkindness thrust upon them.

He was like the big statue of Lincoln in the memorial in Washington: grand, but not terrifying.

You could think of his lap and curl up in bed fifteen years later, and thousands of miles from his home or grave, and think. "Ah, Life!"— and that is as far as you ever got, because you are asleep long, and quiet, and warm as you would ever want to be.

He was better than God. Ben was. If God treated His creatures as well as Ben treated Aliza, there would never be any suffering or need for the Messiah. If God would pay five minutes' attention to my aunt at Ben's and Aliza's grave, and gather a tear here and there when she goes to weep. . . . If He would just sit there on His God Almighty Throne, holding the tears in the palm of His hand, everything would be just fine.

He could learn a lot from Ben and Anna and Aliza, who never asked a thing from Him, never whined for a moment, never questioned Him when Ben died prematurely.

Any age was premature for Ben.

He should have lived forever.

—Danny Siegel
Between Dust and Dance

Summation of Faith

Kaddish is the summation of Israel's faith.

—Rabbi Leo Trepp
The Complete Book of Jewish Observance

✵

Kaddish

Jews have learned not to be afraid of mourning, perhaps because Jewish history is a continuous cycle of grief and rebirth, death and renewal. The Kaddish prayer helps us to understand this cycle.

Saying Kaddish helps me reconcile being a fatherless child with being a human who strives for a spiritual relationship with God. Sometimes when I'm daavening, I'll squeeze the leather tefillin strap in my left hand. I feel like I'm squeezing God's hand. God is there with me and I'm not alone.

—Phyllis Toback
Invisible Thread

✵

Henrietta Szold's Letter to Haym Peretz

It is impossible for me to find words in which to tell you how deeply I was touched by your offer to act as *"Kaddish"* for my dear mother. I cannot even thank you—it is something that goes beyond thanks. It is beautiful, what you have offered to do—I shall never forget it.

You will wonder, then, that I cannot accept your offer. Perhaps it would be best for me not to try to explain to you in writing, but to wait until I see you to tell you why it is so. I know well, and appreciate what you say about, the Jewish custom; and Jewish custom is very dear and sacred to me. And yet I cannot ask you to say *Kaddish* after my mother. The *Kaddish* means to me that the survivor publicly and markedly manifests his wish and intention to assume the relation to the Jewish community which his parent had, and that so the chain of tradition remains unbroken from generation to generation, each adding its own link. You can do that for the generations of your family, I must do that for the generations of my family.

I believe that the elimination of women from such duties was never intended by our law and custom—women were freed from positive duties when they could not perform them, but not when they could. It was never intended that, if they could perform them, their performance of them should not be considered as valuable and valid as when one of the male sex performed them. And of the *Kaddish* I feel sure this is particularly true.

My mother had eight daughters and no son; and yet never did I hear a word of regret pass the lips of either my mother or my father that one of us was not a son. When my father died, my mother would not permit others to take her daughters' place in saying the *Kaddish*, and so I am sure I am acting in her spirit when I am moved to decline your offer. But beautiful your offer remains nevertheless, and, I repeat, I know full well that it is much more in consonance with the generally accepted Jewish tradition than is my or my family's tradition. You understand me, don't you?

> —Henrietta Szold (1860-1945),
> founder of Hadassah,
> from a letter to Haym Peretz,
> September 16, 1916, in
> Marvin Lowenthal
> *Henrietta Szold: Life and Letters*

❋

The Rebbe's Visit

I heard a distant shout. All around me startled faces looked about, debate faltered. I heard the shout repeated, the words indistinct. It was outside somewhere, on the street, then on the walk, then on the porch. A strange and tangible whispering began to move through the air, like the trembling breaths of a hundred simultaneous astonishments. There was a sudden stirring and a concurrent movement of chairs. Everyone around me rose, and I rose, too, and stood looking at the crowd that jammed the hallway and blocked the door to the house. Silence invaded the house, and stillness, as though sound and motion had suddenly abandoned the world. In the hallway the crowd began abruptly to part, in silence, with a barely audible shuffling of feet, and through the divided crowd walked two tall dark-bearded men in dark coats and hats. Behind them, walking slowly with majestic stateliness and supported on his left arm by a third tall dark-bearded man, came the Rebbe. Behind the Rebbe walked a fourth man, very tall, his eyes glancing left and right. The Rebbe wore a dark coat and suit and an ordinary dark hat. His beard was stark white, his face pale. His eyes, gray and piercing, gazed out from the shadow cast by the brim of his hat. The tall men walked slowly through the crowd and passed close to where I stood, and I could smell the moisture of the still-damp air on their coats, see the wariness and determination on their faces and the fingers grasping gently but firmly the Rebbe's left arm, see the Rebbe scanning faces as if searching for a face he knew. Then I felt his eyes upon my face. He stopped for the briefest of moments, his eyes upon my face, and he nodded, once, and moved on—and everyone in the room saw that nod. A quiver of subdued motion passed through those around me. I sensed the nod as a palpable movement across my face: a hand had brushed my cheek. Over the heads of those near the front of the room I saw my father, his face showing clearly his surprise at the appearance of the Rebbe. My Cousin Yonkel stood dry and rigid, his mouth open. Cousin Nahum looked ecstatic. Instantly an easy chair was placed beside my father. The Rebbe carefully sat down. All took their seats. The Afternoon Service began, led by Cousin Nahum.

The Rebbe sat very still in his chair, praying. The sounds of the brief service filled the living room and seemed to echo on the porch outside. Those on the porch were praying, too. The Rebbe stood for the Silent Devotion and the Kedushoh and the final prayer. The Mourner's Kaddish was recited. A psalm was said, and the Kaddish was repeated. Cousin Nahum returned to his stool.

Everyone sat in silence, waiting, eyes upon the Rebbe.

The Rebbe turned to my father and nodded briefly. Someone brought my father a tractate of the Talmud. He opened the huge volume and began to teach a passage of Mishnah from the tractate Sanhedrin.

" 'All Israel have a portion in the world to come,' " my father intoned. " 'For it is written, "Thy people are all righteous; they shall inherit the land forever, the branch of My planting, the work of My hands, that I may be glorified." But the following have no portion therein. . . .' "

All eyes were turned upon my father. He spoke in a softly melodious tone, the traditional resonances for the teaching of a Talmudic text. I sensed the focused attention of the crowd and, at the same time, became gradually aware of a subtle dwindling in the light of the room, as though a vaguely discernible blurring shadow had settled across the chandelier in the center of the ceiling. The shadow slid slowly along the ceiling to the corner behind my father's stool. There it settled, gathering its edges into itself, becoming the thinnest of clouds. I saw the cloud gather depth and color and take on form, and it was my Uncle Yitzchok, and he stepped from the cloud and came toward me.

" ' . . . He who maintains that resurrection is not a biblical doctrine,' " my father went on. " 'And he who maintains that the Torah was not divinely revealed; and an epikoros.' "

My uncle moved slowly and effortlessly through the crowd and into the hallway and up the stairs. I heard my father continue reading from the Mishnah.

My uncle moved soundlessly through the second-floor hallway and through the door into his study. He turned on the lights and sat in the recliner.

" 'Three kings and four commoners have no portion in the world to come,' " my father said.

My uncle sat in the recliner, gazing at the paintings on the walls. On his white-bearded features was a look of awe; he seemed in the presence of mysteries of creation he knew he could never fathom. Surely the Master of the Universe was at the heart of this mystery! But what if not? What if at its core was the befouling sediment of the pagan, the menacing allure of centaurs and satyrs, garlanded and gamboling naiads and dryads, or, worse yet, the stark demoniacal world of the sitra achra, the Other Side, the Destroyer? Clearly such works did not emanate from the world of Torah. All the more fascinating, then, their allure! All the more blissful the gazing upon them, the slaking of one's thirst with their colors and forms! One could think of them at one moment as creations of the Master of the Universe, and at another moment as monstrous birthings from the realm of darkness. Two sides of the same coin? Yes. Dancing and flickering lights and shadows. Is that why there are no mezuzahs on those doorposts, Uncle Yitzchok? Because you're in rooms that are weighty with the possibilities of reverence and corruption *simultaneously?* How calmly he sits in his recliner, my Uncle Yitzchok. How he drinks in the paintings. God is everywhere, even in a Renoir. Or is He?

My uncle rises from the recliner and turns off the lights. The paintings vanish. I am in the living room. The Evening Service is at an end. I hear the final Mourner's Kaddish being recited by Cousin Nahum and Cousin Yonkel.

Inside the living room everyone was seated. Those in the hallway strained forward, watching. My aunt and her two daughters slipped silently into the room and sat down on their stools.

The Rebbe rose. Immediately, everyone in the living room, except the mourners, stood.

The Rebbe walked the few steps to my aunt and cousins.

"May God comfort you together with all the mourners of Zion and Jerusalem." His voice was soft, tremulous. "He was a good soul, a good man. I loved him as one loves a brother. I give you my blessing for strength in this time of darkness. Soon, soon the redemption will come, and there will be an end to our exile and suffering. Soon . . . "

He turned away and, together with his tall dark-bearded retinue, went slowly through the living room and the hallway and then through the front door and out of the house.

A silence followed. People stood about or moved slowly, as though fearful a sudden flurry of sound or action would tear apart the fabric of sanctity brought to my uncle's home by the Rebbe.

The house slowly emptied.

—Chaim Potok
The Gift of Asher Lev

✳✳

Consolation in Grief

When the son of Rabbi Yohanan ben Zakkai died the master's disciples came to console him.

First came Rabbi Eliezer ben Hyrkanos. Wishing to distract the bereaved father, he asked, "Would you like to listen to my discourse, Rabbi?"

"Speak!" Rabbi Yohanan assented.

So Rabbi Eliezer began: "Adam had a son and he died. Nonetheless, Adam allowed himself to be comforted. We construe this from the fact that Adam and Eve reconciled themselves to their loss and fulfilled their alloted tasks on earth. So you too, Master, must find solace in your bereavement."

"Not enough that I have my own sorrows," cried Rabbi Yohanan reproachfully, "must you remind me of the sorrows of Adam?"

Rabbi Joshua then entered and said, "Will you allow me, Rabbi, to discourse on Holy Lore?"

"Speak," said Rabbi Yohanan.

Rabbi Joshua began: "Job had sons and daughters, but they all died in one day. Nonetheless, he found solace. How do we know that? From the fact that he said: 'God gave and God took, blessed be the name of the Lord!' You too must find comfort."

"Not enough that I have my own grief, must you remind me of Job's grief?" Rabbi Yohanan cried reproachfully.

Rabbi Yose then entered.

"Permit me to say words of comfort to you," he asked.

"Speak," said Rabbi Yohanan.

Rabbi Yose began: "Aaron had two grown sons and both died on the same day. Nonetheless, Aaron allowed himself to be comforted. How do we know that? It is written in the Torah: ' Aaron was silent.' When a man who mourns falls silent it means he has ceased to lament and is consoled. And so, Rabbi, I say: you too must accept solace in your bereavement."

"Not enough that I have my own sorrows," cried Rabbi Yohanan reproachfully, "must you come and remind me of the sorrows of Aaron?"

After Rabbi Yose had left Rabbi Simeon entered.

"Will you allow me, Rabbi, to discourse on Holy Lore?" he asked.

"Speak," said Rabbi Yohanan.

Rabbi Simeon began: "King David had a son and he died. Nonetheless, he permitted himself to be comforted. And how do we know that? It is written in Scripture that he solaced himself with his wife Bathsheba and that she bore him a son whom they named Solomon. Like David, you too must find comfort."

"Not enough that I have my own grief, must you remind me of David's?" cried Rabbi Yohanan.

The last to go in to him was Rabbi Eleazar ben Arak.

"Will you allow me, Rabbi, to say words of comfort to you?" he asked.

"Speak," said Rabbi Yohanan.

Rabbi Eleazar began: "Let me tell you a fitting parable. A King had given one of his vassals a valuable object to hold for him. Each day this man would lament: 'Woe is me! When will the King come and take back his possession so that I won't be burdened with such a great responsibility?' The same holds true of you, Rabbi. You had a son who was accomplished and a fine scholar. He left the world unstained, pure from sin. Therefore, you must find comfort in the thought that you have returned unsullied the possession entrusted to your care by the King of Kings."

"You have comforted me, Eleazar, my son!" cried Yohanan.
And he arose and put grief aside.

—Nathan Ausubel
A Treasury of Jewish Folklore

✳

Ruth's Story

Now Naomi had a kinsman on her husband's side, a man of substance, of the family of Elimelech, whose name was Boaz.

Ruth the Moabite said to Naomi, "I would like to go to the fields and glean among the ears of grain, behind someone who may show me kindness." "Yes, daughter, go," she replied; and off she went. She came and gleaned in a field, behind the reapers; and, as luck would have it, it was the piece of land belonging to Boaz, who was of Elimelech's family.

Presently Boaz arrived from Bethlehem. He greeted the reapers, "The Lord be with you!" And they responded, "The Lord bless you!" Boaz said to the servant who was in charge of the reapers, "Whose girl is that?" The servant in charge of the reapers replied, "She is a Moabite girl who came back with Naomi from the country of Moab. She said, 'Please let me glean and gather among the sheaves behind the reapers.' She had been on her feet ever since she came this morning. She has rested but little in the hut."

Boaz said to Ruth, "Listen to me, daughter. Don't go to glean in another field. Don't go elsewhere, but stay here close to my girls. Keep your eyes on the field they are reaping, and follow them. I have ordered the men not to molest you. And when you are thirsty, go to the jars and drink some of [the water] that the men have drawn."

She prostrated herself with her face to the ground, and said to him, "Why are you so kind as to single me out, when I am a foreigner?"

Boaz said in reply, "I have been told of all that you did for your mother-in-law after the death of your husband, how you left your father and mother and the land of your birth and came to a people you had not known before. May the Lord reward your deeds. May you have a full recompense from the Lord, the God of Israel, under whose wings you have sought refuge!"

She answered, "You are most kind, my lord, to comfort me and to speak gently to your maidservant—though I am not so much as one of your maidservants."

At mealtime, Boaz said to her, "Come over here and partake of the meal, and dip your morsel in the vinegar." So she sat down beside the reapers. He handed her roasted grain, and she ate her fill and had some left over.

When she got up again to glean, Boaz gave orders to his workers, "You are not only to let her glean among the sheaves, without interference, but you must also pull some [stalks] out of the heaps and leave them for her to glean, and not scold her."

She gleaned in the field until evening. Then she beat out what she had gleaned—it was about an *ephah* of barley—and carried it back with her to the town. When her mother-in-law saw what she had gleaned, and when she also took out and gave her what she had left over after eating her fill, her mother-in-law asked her, "Where did you glean today? Where did you work? Blessed be he who took such generous notice of you!" So she told her mother-in-law whom she had worked with, saying, "The name of the man with whom I worked today is Boaz."

Naomi said to her daughter-in-law, "Blessed be he of the Lord, who has not failed in His kindness to the living or to the dead! For," Naomi explained to her daughter-in-law, "the man is related to us; he is one of our redeeming kinsmen." Ruth the Moabite said, "He even told me, 'Stay close by my workers until all my harvest is finished.' " And Naomi answered her daughter-in-law Ruth, "It is best, daughter, that you go out with his girls, and not be annoyed in some other field." So she stayed close to the maidservants of Boaz, and gleaned until the barley harvest and the wheat harvest were finished. Then she stayed at home with her mother-in-law.

—Ruth 2

✳

Mourner's Kaddish
קדיש יתום

יִתְגַּדַּל וְיִתְקַדַּשׁ שְׁמֵהּ רַבָּא בְּעָלְמָא דִּי־בְרָא כִרְעוּתֵהּ,
Yit•ga•dal ve•yit•ka•dash she•mei ra•ba be•al•ma di•ve•ra
chi•re•u•tei,

וְיַמְלִיךְ מַלְכוּתֵהּ בְּחַיֵּיכוֹן וּבְיוֹמֵיכוֹן וּבְחַיֵּי דְכָל־בֵּית
ve•yam•lich mal•chu•tei be•cha•yei•chon u•ve•yo•mei•chon
u•ve•cha•yei de•chol beit

יִשְׂרָאֵל, בַּעֲגָלָא וּבִזְמַן קָרִיב, וְאִמְרוּ: אָמֵן.

Yis•ra•eil, ba•a•ga•la u•vi•ze•man ka•riv, ve•i•me•ru: a•mein.

יְהֵא שְׁמֵהּ רַבָּא מְבָרַךְ לְעָלַם וּלְעָלְמֵי עָלְמַיָּא.

Ye•hei• she•mei ra•ba me•va•rach le•a•lam u•le•al•mei al•ma•ya.

יִתְבָּרַךְ וְיִשְׁתַּבַּח, וְיִתְפָּאַר וְיִתְרוֹמַם וְיִתְהַדָּר

Yit•ba•rach ve•yish•ta•bach, ve•yit•pa•ar ve•yit•ro•mam
ve•yit•na•sei, ve•yit•ha•dar

וְיִתְעַלֶּה וְיִתְהַלָּל שְׁמֵהּ דְּקוּדְשָׁא, בְּרִיךְ הוּא, לְעֵלָּא מִן־כָּל

ve•yit•a•leh ve•yit•ha•lal she•mei de•ku•de•sha, be•rich hu, le•ei•la
min kol

בִּרְכָתָא וְשִׁירָתָא, תֻּשְׁבְּחָתָא וְנֶחֱמָתָא דַּאֲמִירָן בְּעָלְמָא,

bi•re•cha•ta ve•shi•ra•ta, tush•be•cha•ta ve•ne•che•ma•ta,
da•a•mi•ran be•al•ma,

וְאִמְרוּ: אָמֵן.

ve•i•me•ru: a•mein.

יְהֵא שְׁלָמָא רַבָּא מִן־שְׁמַיָּא וְחַיִּים עָלֵינוּ וְעַל־כָּל־יִשְׂרָאֵל,

Ye•hei she•la•ma ra•ba min she•ma•ya ve•cha•yim a•lei•nu ve•al kol
Yis•ra•eil,

וְאִמְרוּ: אָמֵן.

ve•i•me•ru: a•mein.

עֹשֶׂה שָׁלוֹם בִּמְרוֹמָיו, הוּא יַעֲשֶׂה שָׁלוֹם עָלֵינוּ וְעַל־כָּל־

O•seh sha•lom bi•me•ro•mav, hu ya•a•seh sha•lom a•lei•nu ve•al kol

יִשְׂרָאֵל, וְאִמְרוּ: אָמֵן.

Yis•ra•eil, ve•i•me•ru: a•mein.

Let the glory of God be extolled, let His great name be hallowed, in the world whose creation He willed. May His kingdom soon prevail, in our own day, our own lives, and the life of all Israel, and let us say: Amen.

Let His great name be blessed for ever and ever.

Let the name of the Holy One, blessed is He, be glorified, exalted, and honored, though He is beyond all the praises, songs, and adorations that we can utter, and let us say: Amen.

For us and for all Israel, may the blessing of peace and the promise of life come true, and let us say: Amen.

May He who causes peace to reign in the high heavens, let peace descend on us, on all Israel, and all the world, and let us say: Amen.

May the Source of peace send peace to all who mourn, and comfort to all who are bereaved. Amen.

❈

I Am Weary with Groaning

I am weary with groaning;
   every night I drench my bed,
   I melt my couch in tears.

                              —Psalm 6:7

※

4

✖✖✖✖✖✖✖✖✖✖✖✖✖✖✖✖✖✖✖✖✖✖✖✖✖✖✖✖✖

Shivah:
The Concluding Days of the Week

After the first three days following burial, "the mourner emerges from the stage of intense grief to a new state of mind in which he is prepared to talk about his loss and to accept comfort from friends and neighbors" (Rabbi Maurice Lamm, *The Jewish Way in Death and Mourning*).

The traditional observances of the first three days of *shivah* continue: wearing the rent garment; sitting on the low stool; wearing slippers instead of shoes; for men, not shaving; for men and women, not grooming themselves; and for all mourners, reciting the *Kaddish*.

Friends and neighbors continue to visit, and conversation begins to include subjects of life outside the house of mourning.

During this time, as well, the mourners may begin to consider the monument for the grave of the deceased. "There is every reason," Rabbi Lamm writes, "to arrange for the tombstone to be built as soon after shiva as possible . . . Especially in order to honor the deceased, one should erect the tombstone immediately after shiva."

"No amount of tears, no number of teardrops," was how I described the depth of my mother's pain during the last days of my fathers's illness. The journal I had kept during my father's 4-month struggle with lymphoma steadied my hand and, with the photographs I had taken during that time, gave me direction and perspective, not only during those distressful and bewildering days, but during *shivah* as well. "The aim throughout the ages is the same: for each generation to be both anthologist and author; to preserve what was, and to create anew" (Rabbi David J. Wolpe, *The Healer of Shattered Hearts*).

My father was a writer. In his monthly column for the bulletin of Criers

Lodge, one of many in the international fraternal organization Knights of Pythias, he was both anthologist and author, preserving those too often ignored moments that make for the history of a people: beginnings and endings reflected in birth notices and death reminiscences; life cycle events joyously realized in birthday, *b'nei mitzvah*, and wedding celebrations, and middle passages characterized by journeys to all destinations. But his dreams of being a professional writer had been swept away by Miami hurricanes in the forms of wind and rain and anti-Semitism and the death of his father when my father was 12.

My father was born January 4, 1916, on the kitchen table in his parents' apartment on Saratoga Avenue in Brownsville, Brooklyn, New York. Later, when he and his parents returned to Miami, where his grandparents lived, he learned his father was born a Kukowsky but lived as a Kay in a community inhospitable to Jews; he learned of the devastation wrought by wind and rain and what the loss of a family business could do to dreams; he learned what the death of a 34-year-old father could do to the ambitions of a boy of 12 with two younger sisters and a mother to support; and much later, when he was a young father himself, he learned what hell could be raised by a Hitler and what he had to do to stop that madman.

But my father continued to write throughout high school, and later, in the evenings after work, writing first in longhand and then on a shiny black sixty-dollar Royal typewriter he bought in 1938 for five dollars down and five dollars a month.

It was a dull cold morning this Tuesday morning. The trees along the Parkway danced crazily with the chilling wind and the sun fought to break through the grey clouds.

I was walking along the Parkway with my hands deep in my overcoat pocket.
I was on my way to visit a friend of mine who lived in my old neighborhood.

And so began one of my father's stories. Most of his stories were about the "old neighborhoods" in Brownsville. His characters were almost always young men like himself and young women like the one he would soon meet and marry. They were gentle folk whose compliments were the simple words "Gee, you look swell," and whose expectations were no more demanding than "We'll be happy. I promise you. I always wanted to make you happy, ever since I first saw you."

One year before my father died, I collected his stories as a gift for his seventy-second birthday under the title *Saratoga Avenue Stories*. They were his stories of the 1920s and '30s and '40s, most of them written after my father's return to Saratoga Avenue in Brooklyn with his mother and sisters and before he and my mother began raising a family on East New York Avenue several blocks away.

My father wrote a letter to me after receiving his gift book.

Saratoga Avenue Stories indeed. What memories. I remembered some of the stories and titles, most just vaguely, but when I saw the words leap up at me, memory began to emerge. Nostalgic and kind of sad, you know, rejection slips and such. But it is great. I don't want to forget. I suppose they are not that good, but I thought they were and did my best. One was almost sold. The final reader sent me a letter and said something, I don't remember, but to keep sending in stories.

There were some things in your introduction I was not aware, I mean your wanting to use the typewriter. I just didn't realize that thought. You know you have a novel in that introduction. I have read it 6 times and find it better each time. Who knows, maybe sometime a book. I think of endings and beginnings but set nothing down.

That old Royal. The keys stick a little, it needs a cleaning. The ribbon does not move right. I think I'd have it overhauled. You know, of course, that it will be yours. It cost me $60 in 1938. I paid $5 down and the balance at $5 a month. You have no idea how I sweated to get up that $5 each month. I was taking a writing course with Thomas H. Uzzell, the one who wrote ''Narrative Technique,'' and that cost $20. I really had to watch my pennies but somehow I did it.

Anyway, I loved it all and it was great of you to do this. It made me very happy.

The night before his funeral, I placed my father's book and his letter to me on a small table next to the couch in our living room. During those first few hours after returning from the cemetery the following day, when I could not stop to eat or to sit, when I moved from one visitor to another sharing photographs of my father, I pointed to his book and urged family and friends to read his words, to hear his voice, to be reminded of his dreams; to be reminded that he was an accountant by vocation but a dreamer and writer by avocation and a college graduate at 69. "But it is great," my father wrote, "I don't want to forget." I don't want to forget either and I think I was a little afraid, during that awful first week while still in the shock of his death, of forgetting how he lived, and so I could not stop showing off my father in pictures and words. "We have lost what we have had," Rabbi Sidney Greenberg reminds the mourner. "For those years of love and comradeship there is no adequate compensation. Impoverished as we are by the passing of our beloved, we should be poorer by far if we had never tasted the joy and richness of that union. Sadder than losing a loved one is never having had a loved one to lose." (Rabbi Sidney Greenberg, *Words to Live By*). At night, I realized how grateful I should be that I had given my father the gift of his stories when I did. If I had waited only one more year, he might have been too ill to have cared to remember.

My family and I left for Ft. Lauderdale, Florida, the evening of April 18, 1989, to share Passover with my father and mother. My sister and her family had already arrived at my parents' apartment, having made the long drive from their home in Westchester several days earlier. Our families would be united with my parents for Passover, the quintessential Jewish family celebration.

"More than the story [Passover] tells," writes Rabbi Earl A. Grollman, "are the people who tell the story. They have been telling the same story for two thousand seven hundred years—always in the same setting. We gather in our home; we plug into Jewish eternity. We think of the untold generations in every corner of the globe year after year, century after century, who have continued to tell the same story about the very same people, and a tingle goes down our spine." But with all its joy, Rabbi Grollman reminds us that Passover is also a "time of tears."

> Perhaps at no other time do we feel the absence of our loved ones more than at the time of Passover. As we gather around the Passover table, we cannot help but recall those who were so dear to us in life and who are with us here no more. We recall them in friendship and in love, for Passover is the time of family service.
>
> —Rabbi Earl A. Grollman
> "Passover"
> *Bereavement*

I know my Passovers will never be the same without my father, but I also know that my father's Passovers had never been the same without his mother and father; that my mother's Passovers had never been the same without her mother and father—never the same yet always the same because my father had become his father and grandfathers at his *seder* table as I would become my father and grandfathers at ours.

What a remarkable Passover was that Passover of 1989. The *seder* was held at the home of my mother's sister, Dubby, and her husband, Irving. My father could not walk the short block from his apartment to theirs, so he sat in a wheelchair and I wheeled him to their building, Jo and my sister, Barbara, walking with my mother alongside. It was a cool evening, and my father was wearing a blue baseball cap and a blue Members Only brand jacket. His hands rested in his lap. I talked with him as we made our way. He tried to respond but found it tiring. But he kept his head high and turned to me occasionally to let me know he was listening. I felt pride in his dignity and in being his son. But my world could not have been more upside down. How many years earlier had my father wheeled me in a carriage on a cool Passover evening.

My father sat at the Passover table wearing a silk *Yarmulke*, courtesy of one of his grandchildren's *bar* or *bat mitzvah,* and sharing with my mother the *Haggadah* my sister had designed. But could his mind have been on Moses in Egypt?

What I will remember most vividly about that *seder* is my father singing "*Dayenu*" and clapping his hands as he did. I believe my father knew then— I believe we all knew then—that my father was grateful to have been able to share this *seder* with his wife and children and grandchildren, with his niece, Risë and with his sister-in-law and brother-in-law, with whom he had been as close as siblings. "*Dayenu.*" It would have to be enough. There would not be much more to come.

> But even as we mourn their loss, we understand that the life of the dead is now placed in the memory of the living. Grant but memory to us and we can lose nothing but death. For these memories have become part of our souls and they are eternally dear to us. The beauty of their lives continues with us as we sit around the Passover table.
>
> —Rabbi Earl A. Grollman
> "Passover"
> *Bereavement*

"Every aspect of life can be sacred," writes Rabbi Wolpe, "and each instant, no matter the activity, can be holy. Upon the death of his master, Menachem Mendle of Kotzk was asked what had been most important to the teacher whom he had just lost. He thought briefly and replied, 'Whatever he was doing at the moment.' " Such was the moment of my father's handclapping and of his singing of "*Dayenu.*"

"The type of inner discipline, piety, and spiritual devotion that surrounds our simplest and most commonplace acts, toward ourselves and toward one another, will create our experience in the world to come" (Edward Hoffman, *The Way of Splendor*). In my father's simple and commonplace, yet courageous, act at our *seder* table, he created for us an experience in the world that is; and we will hear his handclapping at our every *seder*. Only God knows if we will be fortunate enough to carry it with us in the world to come.

The first seven days after burial (which includes the first three days) is the period of *shivah*.

> During this time the mourner emerges from the stage of intense grief to a new state of mind in which he is prepared to talk about his loss and to accept comfort from friends and neighbors. The world now enlarges for the mourner. While he remains within the house, expressing his grief through the observances of avelut—the wearing of the rent garment, the sitting on the low stool, the wearing of slippers, the refraining from shaving and grooming, the recital of the Kaddish—his acquaintances come to his home to express sympathy in his

distress. The inner freezing that came with the death of his relative now begins
to thaw. The isolation from the world of people and the retreat inward now
relaxes somewhat, and normalcy begins to return.

—Rabbi Maurice Lamm
The Jewish Way in Death and Mourning

Rabbi Rabinowicz offers insight into why seven days has been chosen as the
period of mourning. The sources and interpretations are many.

One teacher, commenting on the verse "I will turn your feasts into mourning"
(Amos 8:10), says, "Just as the days of the Feasts (Passover and Tabernacles) are
seven, so are the days of mourning" [*Moed Katan* 20a; *Moed Katan* 3:5].
Another teacher traces it back to the verse:"Let her not, I pray, be as one
dead . . . And Miriam was shut up without the camp seven days" (Numbers
12:12,15); the days of isolation (for leprosy) are seven (Leviticus 13:31); finally,
the Zohar gives a mystical reason: "For seven days the soul goes to and fro,
from the house to the grave and from the grave to the house, mourning for the
body" [*Vayyechi* 26a].

—Rabbi Tzvi Rabinowicz
A Guide to Life

"And it came to pass after the seven days, that the waters of the flood were
upon the earth" (Genesis 7:10). The Talmud, Rabbi Rabinowicz reminds us,
asks, "What was the nature of these seven days? [*Sanhedrin* 108b]. These were
the days of mourning for Methuselah, thus teaching that the lamentation for
the righteous postpones retribution." Rabbi Joshua ben Levi, a third-century
amora, or interpreter (and the name given to rabbinic authorities responsible
for the *Gemara*), says, "God Himself mourned seven days for the destruction
of the world." According to the Jerusalem Talmud, it was Moses who
appointed seven days of mourning (*Ketubbot* 1:1). The Apocrypha is very
explicit on this point. Ben Sira declares, "Seven days are the days of mourning
for the dead" (Ben Sira 22:12) (Rabinowicz).

"[Joseph] made a mourning for his father seven days" (Genesis 50:10).
And so did we for our father.

For the first several mornings during *shivah*, I would awake with a start,
although I don't recall having spent restless nights. For me, the days of *shivah*
were far more restless than the nights: the days were full of dreams and the
fear of the night to come, but the nights were full of empty sleep. I didn't
dream. At least not then. Perhaps I didn't dream because I never went to be
bed alone with my grief. Jo was always with me. But my mother went to bed
alone. And she did dream.

Before my mother returned to Florida at the end of *shloshim*, the first thirty
days after burial, she shared a dream with us, one I recorded in my journal.

My mother was riding in a car with my father, who was driving. Soon, the car slowed and stopped. My father told my mother to get out of the car and to wait for him while he looked for a parking space. The car and my father disappeared. Suddenly, my mother found herself alone in an unfamiliar neighborhood. A tall man approached her with either a pipe or stick in his hand and he began to menace her. My mother was frightened. From nowhere, another man arrived. My mother didn't recognize him, but he came between her and the tall man. My mother believed it was my father. "Dad wants me to know," my mother told us, "that although he's gone, I will be protected, just as he protected me when he was here with me."

My father has entered my dreams only twice since his death, on two successive nights during Sukkot, more than one year after his death. In the first dream, I was young and unmarried and he and my mother and my sister were in our apartment reassuring each other of our mutual support during an unidentified crisis. In the second dream, I was married, and my father visited Jo and me in our first apartment. In the second dream, in the story itself, there was no apparent reason for his presence. In the act of dreaming itself, there was every reason for his presence. I accepted his appearance, as my mother had in her dream, as a sign of my father's eternal presence in our lives. "When prophets were no more," writes psychologist and scholar Edward Hoffman, "their place was taken by the Sages, who, in a sense, even excelled the prophets; and, in the absence of Sages, things to come are revealed in dreams."

I had been wary of dreaming about my father because I thought if I saw him, I would reach out to him, actually feel his body, and believe he was alive and that his dying and death had been a cruel hoax.

> It is a dream,
> and I am going to awake,
> and you are going to be here
> as you always were:
> Nothing has changed,
> nothing is going to change.
> You are my father,
> and I am your child,
> and we go on living
> forever and ever
> without interruption,
> as we did in the past
> before this terrible dream,
> this nightmare, this illusion
> happened.
>
> —Seymour Freedman
> "It Is a Dream"
> *Mourning for My Father*

Perhaps it was only coincidental that my father appeared in my dreams on Sukkot, but that was a holiday my father—and my mother—enjoyed celebrating with us in our *sukkah* and I was comforted by his visits, if only in dreams, during a time when his visit would always mean so much to me. "Far from simply seeing them as ethereal, inexplicable experiences, [kabbalistic thinkers] regarded most dreams as reflections of our daily frame of mind. That is, whatever we most usually think about as we go about our daily activities— that is what will typically occupy our dreams as well" (Hoffman).

Each breakfast during the first several mornings of *shivah* seemed to stretch until noon; each afternoon drifted lazily into early evening. Dinners were prepared by friends: Joann and Allen, Hope and Dan, Carol and Bud, Dot and Ed, Eileen and Sandy, Jerry and Linda, Bunny and Roy, Fran and Al, Arlene and Stu, Myra and Mel. We ate with no little self-reproach that while we were nourishing ourselves, my father would never again share a meal with us.

> I dare not go deep in memory,
> yet the pain comes.
> I need to talk with you.
> I see you in my mind
> and know
> I will never hear you again
> in this world
> I dare not go deep in memory,
> and yet the pain comes.

> —Seymour Freedman
> "I Dare Not Go Deep in Memory"
> *Mourning for My Father*

Although there were periods of silence, there was also much to say about my father and our lives with him and how vacant would be our lives without him. But it was my mother's words and weeping that reminded us that death had deprived her of a future we could only imagine. And when Jo spoke, I was reminded how bereft was her mother, Agnes, after her husband died at 51, before Jo and I were married. Jo had spoken so much during our lives together about how painful was her father's absence in her own life that I realized very clearly that as my father's child, I would be deprived of a future as well. And when our children spoke, while I listened to their words, I was also mindful that as they learned from Jo how to live without a father, they were learning from all of us how to mourn and yet how to go on living. When the sounds of silence became too loud to bear, or the words too sad to listen to, we found privacy hospitable. When we needed someone to comfort us, there were endearments in word and touch. We were living through that "awful first week" wondering how we could ever survive our loss.

Death can only take from us what might have been. It cannot take from us what has already been. It cannot rob us of our past. The days and years we shared, the common adventures and joys, the "little nameless acts of kindness and of love"—all these are part of the ineradicable record. Death has no dominion over them.

—Rabbi Sidney Greenberg
Words to Live By

My mother read through Rabbi Lamm's *The Jewish Way in Death and Mourning* in just a few days. It was one of the books our friends Arlene and Stu had brought when they visited the second night of *shivah*. My mother was hungry to learn about Jewish mourning practices and how to manage her grief. With all my religious education and teaching, I did not know what else to share with my mother, who was a zealous reader, as my father had been.

I recall vividly one moment when my mother called me to her, Rabbi Lamm's book closed in her lap, a finger serving as a page marker, her glasses held limply in her other hand. "And Rachel died and was buried on the way to Ephrath, which is Bethlehem. And Jacob erected a tombstone on Rachel's grave" (Genesis 35:19–20).

After *shivah*, my mother told me, she wanted to select a monument for my father's grave. "I don't want his grave to be unmarked," she said and opened Rabbi Lamm's book.

There is every reason, based on major commentaries and numerous sources and long tradition, to arrange for the tombstone to be built as soon after shiva as possible. . . . Especially in order to honor the deceased, one should erect the tombstone immediately after shiva. The sages considered this so important that in certain cases, they even permitted the mourner to leave the house of mourning during shiva to make the necessary arrangements. This was considered an integral part of the burial arrangements.

The reason usually given for waiting 12 months is that the tombstone serves as a reminder, and that for the first 12 months the deceased is remembered in any case, by the recitation of Kaddish and the avoidance of joyous occasions. Despite the rationale, however, the honoring of the dead should take priority over his being remembered and arrangements for the stone should be made immediately.

—Rabbi Maurice Lamm
The Jewish Way in Death and Mourning

My mother was quite certain that immediately after *shivah*, she would select a stone for my father's grave. I realized that even without Rabbi Lamm's encouragement, whatever my mother's requests regarding the care of my father's grave, they would have been honored. She was not only working through her grief but also tentatively beginning to manage life without my father. Deciding on this course of action was the first major decision she made following my father's death. It was reasonable, psychologically healthy, and emotionally revealing of how she intended to survive the enormity of my father's absence in her life. "The essence of mourning," writes Rabbi Adin Steinsaltz, "is not sorrow for the deceased, but rather compassion for the surviving relatives in their loneliness." But what if Rabbi Lamm's book were not available during a time when, for many mourners, there was a hunger to learn as much as possible about Jewish mourning practices? Who would be the teacher during the first seven days? The rabbi came to lead the *minyan* service and offer consolation, but then he left; who would talk about tombstones? For some mourners, it would have been too soon, but for others—perhaps many—like my mother, it was soon enough, part of her own grief management.

As I have written earlier I think it is in large measure the rabbi's responsibility to sense the condition of the mourner and offer the wisdom of our people whether from Job or Lamentations or Rabbi Lamm. Mourners may seem lost in their sorrow, and, indeed, there are those who are, and they may not be able on their own to find their way out of that sorrow so that they may go on with their lives. If not the rabbi, then family members or friends must take the lead, with the wisdom of our people as their guide.

There are many references to behavior during mourning in our tradition. In the Bible, it is explained that here is a time that must be set aside for the expression of grief. Aaron, the High Priest, is dazed by the death of his two sons at the height of their careers.

> Now Aaron's sons Nadab and Abihu each took his fire pan, put fire in it, and laid incense on it; and they offered before the Lord alien fire, which He had not enjoined upon them. And fire came forth from the Lord and consumed them; thus they died at the instance of the Lord. . . .

> And Moses spoke to Aaron and to his remaining sons, Eleazar and Ithamar: Take the meal offering that is left over from the Lord's offerings by fire and eat it unleavened beside the altar, for it is most holy. You shall eat it in the sacred precinct, inasmuch as it is your due, and that of your children, from the Lord's offerings by fire; for so I have been commanded. But the breast of wave offering and the thigh of leave offering you, and your sons and daughters with you, may eat in any clean place, for they have been assigned as a due to you and your children from the Israelites' sacrifices of well-being. Together with the fat of fire-offering, they must present the thigh of heave offering and the breast of wave offering, which are to be your due and that of your children with you for all time—as the Lord has commanded.

> Then Moses inquired about the goat of sin offering, and it had already been burned! He was angry with Eleazar and Ithamar, Aaron's remaining sons, and

said, "Why did you not eat the sin offering in the sacred area? For it is most holy, and He has given it to you to remove the guilt of the community and to make expiation for them before the Lord. Since its blood was not brought inside the sanctuary, you should certainly have eaten it in the sanctuary, as I commanded." And Aaron spoke to Moses, "See, this day they brought their sin offering as their burnt offering before the Lord, and such things have befallen me! Had I eaten sin offering today, would the Lord have approved?" And when Moses heard this, he approved.

—Leviticus 10:1–2, 12–20

Aaron explained that the time of mourning is not an occasion for feasting before the Lord. It is for the expression of grief.

The prophet Amos also refers to a special time for mourning. He prohesies the disastrous consequences of injustice and immorality and declares, "And I will turn your festivals into mourning/And all your songs into lamentations;/I will bring sackcloth upon all loins/And baldness upon every head./I will make it as the mourning for an only son/And the end thereof as a bitter day" (Amos 8:10).

After the revelation on Mt. Sinai, Rabbi Lamm explains, Moses established the seven days of mourning by special decree declaring as formal doctrine that which had been practiced only as custom.

He enacted, the sages asserted, the seven days of mourning as he enacted the biblical seven days of rejoicing of major holidays. The connection between the two opposites is hinted at in the verse from Amos . . . "And I will turn your feasts into mourning." Just as feasts were observed for seven days, so mourning was to last for one week.

From the earliest moments of recorded Jewish history, the Jewish people have observed shiva for deceased relatives as "days of bitterness." The occasional disregard of shiva in some quarters of the Jewish community, or the casual decision, without rabbinic authorization, to observe an arbitrary number of days of mourning to suit one's own needs, or to coincide with a weekend, amount, in fact, to a noxious disregard of generations of sacred observance.

—Maurice Lamm
The Jewish Way in Death and Mourning

Rabbi Simeon J. Maslin, in *Gates of Mitzvah: A Guide to the Jewish Life Cycle,* produced by the Committee on Reform Jewish Practice of the Central Conference of American Rabbis, advises that the "first three days of the shivah period are considered the most intense and in Reform Congregations are considered the minimum mourning period." Families that choose to observe *shivah* for three, four, or five days, do so with the authorization of their rabbis and in observance of the customs of their communities and their own families. We chose to observe *shivah* in the traditional way for seven days.

Grief, write Rabbi William B. Silverman and psychologist Kenneth M. Cinnamon, is a "journey into the self to search for meaning." (*When Mourning Comes*). *Shivah* is a comfort station on that journey, and the congregation of friends and relatives, Jewish and lay professionals, and the many writings of our tradition share in offering that comfort.

For seven days our community came and for seven days we recited the *Kaddish*.

By requiring that the Kaddish be recited with a quorum of worshippers, Judaism renders the mourner a profound service. A minyan almost invariably includes other mourners and thus brings home the realization that we alone have not been singled out.

The burning question: "Why did God do this to me?" loses much of its sting when others also rise to recite the Kaddish. We are not lonely travelers in the valley of the shadow. We thus see death for what it is—not a malevolent act of a vindictive God, but part of the incomprehensible mystery of human existence in which light and dark, joy and sadness, birth and death are interwoven and inseparable.

—Rabbi Sidney Greenberg
Words to Live By

❊❊

Readings

✖✖✖✖✖✖✖✖✖✖✖✖✖✖

Do Not Abandon Me, O Lord

Do not abandon me, O Lord;
my God, be not far from me;
hasten to my aid,
O Lord, my deliverance.

—Psalm 38:22–23

✖✖

Job's Story

There was a man in the land of Uz named Job. That man was blameless
and upright; he feared God and shunned evil. Seven sons and three
daughters were born to him; his possessions were seven thousand
sheep, three thousand camels, five hundred yoke of oxen and five
hundred she-asses, and a very large household. That man was wealthier
than anyone in the East.

It was the custom of his sons to hold feasts, each on his set day in his
own home. They would invite their three sisters to eat and drink with
them. When a round of feast days was over, Job would send word to
them to sanctify themselves, and, rising early in the morning, he would
make burnt offerings, one for each of them; for Job thought, "Perhaps

my children have sinned and blasphemed God in their thoughts." This is what Job always used to do.

One day the divine beings presented themselves before the Lord, and the Adversary came along with them. The Lord said to the Adversary, "Where have you been?" The Adversary answered the Lord, "I have been roaming all over the earth." The Lord said to the Adversary, "Have you noticed My servant Job? There is no one like him on earth, a blameless and upright man who fears God and shuns evil!" The Adversary answered the Lord, "Does Job not have good reason to fear God? Why, it is You who have fenced him around, him and his household and all that he has. You have blessed his efforts so that his possessions spread out in the land. But lay Your hand upon all that he has and he will surely blaspheme You to Your face." The Lord replied to the Adversary, "See, all that he has is in your power; only do not lay a hand on him." The Adversary departed from the presence of the Lord.

One day, as his sons and daughters were eating and drinking wine in the house of their eldest brother, a messenger came to Job and said, "The Oxen were plowing and the she-asses were grazing alongside them when Sabeans attacked them and carried them off, and put the boys to the sword; I alone have escaped to tell you." This one was still speaking when another came and said, "God's fire fell from heaven, took hold of the sheep and the boys, and burned them up; I alone have escaped to tell you." This one was still speaking when another came and said, "A Chaldean formation of three columns made a raid on the camels and carried them off and put the boys to the sword; I alone have escaped to tell you." This one was still speaking when another came and said, "Your sons and daughters were eating and drinking wine in the house of their eldest brother when suddenly a mighty wind came from the wilderness. It struck the four corners of the house so that it collapsed upon the young people and they died; I alone have escaped to tell you."

Then Job arose, tore his robe, cut off his hair, and threw himself on the ground and worshiped. He said, "Naked came I out of my mother's womb, and naked shall I return there; the Lord has given, and the Lord has taken away; blessed be the name of the Lord."

For all that, Job did not sin nor did he cast reproach on God. One Day the divine beings presented themselves before the Lord. The Adversary came along with them to present himself before the Lord. The Lord said to the Adversary, "Where have you been?" The Adversary answered the Lord, "I have been roaming all over the earth." The Lord said to the Adversary, "Have you noticed My servant Job? There is no one like him on earth, a blameless and upright man who fears God and shuns evil. He still keeps his integrity; so you have incited Me against him to destroy him for no good reason." The Adversary answered the Lord, "Skin for skin—all that a man has he will give up for his life. But lay a hand on his bones and his flesh, and he will surely blaspheme You to Your face." So the Lord said to the Adversary, "See, he is in your power; only spare his life." The Adversary departed from the presence of the Lord and inflicted a severe inflammation on Job from the sole of his foot to the crown of his head. He took a potsherd to scratch himself as he sat in ashes. His wife said to him, "You still keep your integrity! Blaspheme God and die!" But he said to her, "You talk as any shameless woman might talk! Should we accept only good from God and not accept evil?" For all that, Job said nothing sinful.

When Job's three friends heard about all these calamities that had befallen him, each came from his home—Eliphaz the Temanite, Bildad the Shuhite, and Zophar the Naamathite. They met together to go and console and comfort him. When they saw him from a distance, they could not recognize him, and they broke into loud weeping; each one tore his robe and threw dust into the air onto his head. They sat with him on the ground seven days and seven nights. None spoke a word to him for they saw how very great was his suffering.

Afterward, Job began to speak and cursed the day of his birth. Job spoke up and said:

Perish the day on which I was born,
And the night it was announced,
"A male has been conceived!"
May that day be darkness;
May God above have no concern for it;
May light not shine on it;
May darkness and deep gloom reclaim it;
May a pall lie over it;
May what blackens the day terrify it.
May obscurity carry off that night;
May it not be counted among the days of the year;
May it not appear in any of its months;
May that night be desolate;
May no sound of joy be heard in it;
May those who cast spells upon the day damn it,
Those prepared to disable Leviathan;

May its twilight stars remain dark;
May it hope for light and have none;
May it not see the glimmerings of the dawn—
Because it did not block my mother's womb,
And hide trouble from my eyes.
Why did I not die at birth,
Expire as I came forth from the womb?
Why were there knees to receive me,
Or breasts for me to suck?
For now would I be lying in repose, asleep and at rest,
With the world's kings and counselors who rebuild ruins
    for themselves,
Or with nobles who possess gold and who fill their
    houses with silver.
Or why was I not like a buried stillbirth,
Like babies who never saw the light?
There the wicked cease from troubling;
There rest those whose strength is spent.
Prisoners are wholly at ease;
They do not hear the taskmaster's voice.
Small and great alike are there,
And the slave is free of his master.

Why does He give light to the sufferer
And life to the bitter in spirit;
To those who wait for death but it does not come,
Who search for it more than for treasure,
Who rejoice to exultation,
And are glad to reach the grave;
To the man who has lost his way,
Whom God has hedged about?

My groaning serves as my bread;
My roaring pours forth as water.
For what I feared has overtaken me;
What I dreaded has come upon me.
I had no repose, no quiet, no rest,
And trouble came.

—Job 1—3

Losses

Gone.

It's sliding away.
New stages, new ties,
new names and losses.
Time for plants turning
and gazings at universal miracles
over the edge of sky,
the meanings of color,
wonderings I used to cherish and baby.
Gone. Torn to hell.
Surrendered for maturity
and just right thinking:
a straight-life jacket.

My sainted aunt used to say,
"The way you cut your farfel,
that's the way you have to eat it."
"So don't complain.
At least not here, now,"
she added with love
I needed just then, there.
She would let me say it all,
then, and again,
if I wanted.
But someday she'd die,
and I couldn't be sad in her presence
any more,
and I would be alone.

Dry.

—Danny Siegel
Between Dust and Dance

How Long Have We Forgotten How to Listen

Before they spring forth I tell you of them.

—Isaiah 42:9

How long have we forgotten how to listen!
He planted us once to listen
Planted us like lyme grass by the eternal sea,
We wanted to grow on fat pastures,
To stand like lettuce in the kitchen garden.

Although we have business
That leads us far
From His light,
Although we drink tap water,
And only as it dies it reaches
Our eternally thirsting mouths—
Although we walk down a street
Beneath which earth has been silenced
By a pavement,
We must not sell our ears,
Oh, we must not sell our ears.
Even in the market,
In the computation of dust,
Many had made a quick leap
Onto the tightrope of longing,
Because they heard something,
And leapt out of the dust
And sated their ears.
Press, oh press on the day of destruction
The listening ear to the earth,
And you will hear, through your sleep
You will hear
How in death
Life begins.

—Nelly Sachs in
Shirim: A Jewish Poetry Journal

Passover

Grant but memory to us and we can lose nothing but death.

—Rabbi Earl A. Grollman in
Bereavement

❈

Light a Candle

Light a candle.
Drink wine.
Softly the Sabbath has plucked
the sinking sun.
Slowly the Sabbath descends,
the rose of heaven in her hand.

How can the Sabbath
plant a huge and shining flower
in a blind and narrow heart?
How can the Sabbath
plant the bud of angels
in a heart of raving flesh?
Can the rose of eternity grow
in an age enslaved
to destruction,
an age enslaved
to death?

Light a candle!
Drink wine!
Slowly the Sabbath descends
and in her hand
the flower,
and in her hand
the sinking sun.

Zelda, trans. from the Hebrew by Marcia Falk, in
Shirim: A Jewish Poetry Journal

❈

Sorrow Can Enlarge the Domain of Our Life

Our sorrow can bring understanding as well as pain, breadth as well as the contraction that comes with pain. Out of love and sorrow can come a compassion that endures. The needs of others hitherto unnoticed, the anxieties of neighbors never before realized, now come into the ken of our experience, for our sorrow has opened our life to the needs of others. A bereavement that brings us into the lives of our fellowmen writes a fitting epilogue to a love that had taught us kindliness, and forbearance and had given us so much joy.

Sorrow can enlarge the domain of our life, so that we may now understand the triviality of the things many pursue. We have in our hands a noble and refined measure for judging the events and objects we daily see. What is important is not luxury but love; not wealth but wisdom; not gold but goodness.

And our sorrow may so clear our vision that we may, more brightly, see the God, of Whom it was said, "The Lord is nigh unto them, that are of a broken heart." Beyond the hurry and turmoil of life rises the Eternal. There is God in a world in which love like ours could bloom. There is God in a world in which human beings could experience tenderness. There is a God in a world in which two lives can be bound together by a tie stronger than death.

Out of that vision will come a sense of obligation. A duty, solemn, sacred and significant, rests upon us. To spread the love we have known to others. To share the joy which has been ours. To ease the pains which man's thoughtlessness or malice inflicts. We have a task to perform. There is work to be done and in work there is consolation.

Out of love may come sorrow. But out of sorrow can come light for others who dwell in darkness. And out of the light we bring to others will come light for ourselves—the light of solace, of strength, of transfiguring and consecrating purpose.

—Morris Adler in
Light from Jewish Lamps

✳✳

The Fraternity of Mourners

Recently I entered into one of the world's oldest fraternities, the mourners' minyan. From time immemorial this institution has perse-

vered in every age and every land in which Jews have found themselves—it ranks ever renewed as the swift hand of Death descends to
bereave a household in Israel.

The fraternity functions in the synagogues and temples, meeting
twice daily to participate in the traditional services. Belonging means
rising early because morning prayer begins promptly at seven fifteen.

There are no rites or ceremonies of induction. You enter the chapel
and take your place at one of the benches. The little group knows why
you are there. The sorrow which is still sharply etched on your features
is familiar to all of them. They know how difficult is your hour of trial.
Little is said. A brief murmur and a heartfelt handshake is enough to
make you welcome.

The first few days you follow the service in a mechanical, almost
uncomprehending way. The *shames* hovers at your elbow ready to be of
help—to point out the page, to assist in your inexpert reading of the
Kaddish, to show you how to place the *tefillin* on your forehead and
how to wind it upon your arm.

There isn't much time for conversation. Morning services chanted at
a rapid pace take better than thirty minutes, and on Monday and
Thursday when the reading of the Torah takes place, it takes more. Then
the little group breaks up quickly to make its way to its daily
occupations.

You soon gain a familiarity with the service. You are no longer the
latest initiate. Another mourner has joined, and then another. You
know each of the others now, exchanging greetings each day with
Charles and Moe and Gabe and Nat and Sam. You have become familiar
with the little mannerisms that mark each one. This one bows stiffly
from the waist as he intones the Kaddish, that one sways as he recites
the Amidah, another one delivers the Alenu with the gusto of a
cheerleader's chant, while another punctiliously folds his tallit with
loving care.

Why are these men there day after day? One day the rabbi spoke to
us about this loyalty which we associate with the passing of a loved one
which leads us to undertake this exacting pattern for the next eleven
months of our lives. He said that there is nothing else quite like it, quite
so universal in its observance, except perhaps the ceremony of the Bar
Mitzvah. These two, the mourner's Kaddish, and the Bar Mitzvah,
have so profound a place in our religious attitude that Jews who give
little if any thought to the rest of the observances of our faith
nevertheless observe these two functions with the most steadfast
faithfulness.

And thinking about this I came to a realization of why they are similar and why they are significant. In the first instance, for the Bar Mitzvah, the parent leads the young boy to the synagogue. There he undergoes the period of instruction—so incomprehensible—such strange, difficult material to study, to pore over in endless repetition until it is letter-perfect.

You were a mere boy. You never did get to understand what the religious service was all about, what the endless prayers meant. It was so ancient and so remote and so unrelated to what really interested you. It cut into your time for ball games and for playing with your friends. But you had gone through with it because your parents expected it of you. You had to do it so they could be proud of you on your Bar Mitzvah day.

When it was over you left the synagogue at the earliest opportunity, not to return to it again except on infrequent occasions. There has been the hiatus of the years. How they have flown by! Enough years for you to have been Bar Mitzvah a second and a third time.

Now you have been brought back to the synagogue. Strange, actually brought back by the same parents who brought you to the synagogue the first time. Except that the parents are not there this time to hover over you practicing the chanting, not there to wonder if you are going to do them proud.

But wait. Maybe the parents are there, in spirit, hovering over you as you renew your acquaintance with the ancient letters, repeating them over and over until you develop a facility in uttering them. You are there in the little minyan group because you know that the parents are proud of the son who rises for the Kaddish which sanctifies the Holy Name of God.

Your parents have brought you back to the synagogue for the second time. This time you are no longer the impatient, harried boy you were, but a mature man, tested and tried by the trials of life, brought back to the synagogue for a second time, for a second chance.

What will it mean this time? Will it be another period of incomprehension, of relief when it is over, again a going away?

Or this time, will you seek the meaning of the prayers? Will you follow the cycle of the Torah? Will you catch an understanding of what is implicit in the words? Will you grasp what your forebears have written in the ancient text with their tears and their anguish, with their wisdom and their insight, with their humanity and their humility, with their reverence and their love?

By their going, your parents have brought you back to the synagogue a second time, for a second chance. Will it be different this time?

—Joseph Zashin in
Jewish Reflections on Death

❃❃❃

We Do Not Stand Alone

It is an early weekday morn. A quiet residential street of the dynamic city is still enveloped in a drowsy stillness. Soon life will awake in its silent and comfortable houses, and noisy children, after a hasty breakfast, will leap through doors, schoolward bound. Men can be seen entering one of the houses. Their bearing is marked by reverence and solemnity. Sorrow has recently visited one of the homes on the street, and friends are gathering for the morning service. Within the residence, candles are lit, *tefillin* and *tallit* are quietly donned, and the voice of prayer is heard in the hushed atmosphere.

Long ago a people developed this practice so rich in meaning that neither the passing of centuries nor the roaring life of a metropolitan center has been able to render it obsolete. The friends are no longer individuals come to express sympathy, each in his particular way, with the feeling that the degree of his own friendship with the mourners dictates. They have coalesced into an *edah,* a community. Though this community is small in numbers, it represents in every religious detail the larger *klal yisrael* of which each identified Jew is part. Thus does a community symbolically and actually share in the sorrow of one of its members. The grief of the individual reechoes in the life of the group. No Jew stands alone in his bereavement, while his personal anguish stands as a wall between him and all those upon whose way in life the dark shadow has not fallen. A people closes ranks and encircles its stricken member with the warmth of brotherly sympathy.

The religious service of this little group, representing the larger community, takes place in the home. It is a tribute to the central position of the home. Where a family lives and loves and fashions the most intimate bonds to link persons one to the other, there you have a sanctuary no less than the synagogue. Its holiness is of no lesser kind than that with which the formal house of prayer of the entire community is invested. The poignancy and sanctity of grief are best expressed in the intimate sanctuary of the home. the sanctuary of the home can never be replaced by synagogue or temple, however large or magnificent.

The prayer is concluded. The imperatives of modern living compel the minyan to dissolve once again into its component individuals who hurry through streets, now filled with romping and laughing children and speeding automobiles, to offices, shops, and plants. The mourners remain. They are, however, no longer completely alone. In the atmosphere of their home the prayers linger and bespeak the solace of a tradition and the brotherhood of a community.

—Rabbi Morris Adler in
Jewish Reflections on Death

✻❀✻

Finally Answering the Call

We hardly knew each other. He and his wife had left the city, as we had, relocating to this small town in upstate New York with the idea of finding cleaner air and less noise and russet-colored dogs in russet-colored leaves. I had two young sons, he had three, and we shared the conviction that this small, clean, safe part of the world would insure our children "a better way of life." We shared as well a religion, and so we would sometimes encounter each other at the little synagogue which, for Jews in these parts, was the only game in town.

It was a very little synagogue indeed. Its littleness was integral to its identity, like the little house on the prairie or the little engine that could. Established 76 years ago as the diminutive beacon of a Jewish farming collective, it had endured lean years when the old Jewish farmers had either died or moved to Florida, and found new lifeblood in the expatriate yuppies, rife with *thirtysomething* ambivalence and spiritual confusion.

It was my wife who had led us to the little synagogue in the first place. It had been years since I had been part of a congregation. As a child I had been taken on Saturdays to a great and gloomy temple in Manhattan, where I felt bored and strange and itchy in the gray flannel pants I was made to wear. I rebelled years before I would have been *bar mitzvahed,* and had no reservoir of fond memories when it came to religion, but I agreed that our sons should at least be given the opportunity to come to their own decisions on the issue. And so, for appearance' sake, I put in an appearance, now and again, at the little synagogue.

On these occasions, it was my intention to linger in the shadows, but there weren't sufficient shadows. In fact, on one occasion, I was called upon to wrap the Torah in its silk mantle, breastplate and crown for its return to the ark, and, not knowing what I was doing, felt all thumbs and strange all over again. For quite some time thereafter, I was disinclined to hurry back to the little synagogue, and so my fellow congregant and I saw each other only intermittently, in chance meetings around town. The overtures of friendship were there, but our lives, although continuing to run parallel, had few occasions for real intersection.

And then, at the end of the summer, I got a call. There had been a tragedy. His youngest son, 18 months old, had fallen into their swimming pool. It only takes a moment, and the moment was there, savaging that dream that had brought them here in the first place.

The baby held on for five days, during which time we exercised the human reflex to look for blame, but what blame was there? For the truth of the matter is that, in the grand scheme of things, there is accident and there is human error and there are the unknown exigencies of destiny and fate. He and his wife were travelling to a place where any of us might have visited, and part of the sorrow and the pain we felt for them had to do with the fact that they had made the journey, this time, for all of us.

Still, although I felt for him, I barely knew the guy. Would it be inappropriate to pay a condolence call? Did they want their privacy? These questions quickly became academic, as the call for minyan went out. A minyan is a kind of quorum. Ten Jewish males must be present in order to take the Torah from the Ark. This requirement applies as well during *shiva,* the period of mourning that lasts a week. If there's no minyan, there's no Torah, and if there was no Torah—the very backbone of the religion—then how were the baby and his parents to complete their journey? In this small rural community where Jewish males are nearly as scare as hen's teeth, I had been called upon.

Early then, the next morning, I arrived at their home. He and his wife sat on low wooden benches, as one is instructed to do during *shiva*, so as to deprive oneself of any comfort or pleasure. He had gone, for days now, without shaving, a gesture also dictated by custom, and he and his wife wore rent garments. His shirt, her dress—they were torn down the front—they were rent.

The service was held in the library. From the casement windows, you could see the pool cover draped over the pool, an aqua swag of mourning. I looked around me, and recognized some faces from the little synagogue. A man in his 80's. Two other men, my contemporaries, both cabinetmakers, one of whom had made the pine box for the baby. A boy, just past *bar mitzvah* age, stood among the men.

Some of the men wore *tefillin,* two black leather boxes containing Scripture passages, which are attached by leather straps to the forehead and left arm. The first time I had seen *tefillin,* at my wife's grandmother's *shiva,* I had felt repelled by them. they looked medieval, a torturous thing, like a hair shirt, I had thought at the time, but now I felt differently. I watched the boy as he was having trouble affixing the *tefillin* and I watched his father help him get it right.

As the service progressed, I floated in time. The present was rent garments, and a father, bereft, with unshaven cheeks, and a thin boy in jams and T-shirt wearing a black box on his forehead. In the past was myself and the itchy pants which my mother had lined to little effect and my refusal, accepted perhaps too easily, not to be *bar mitzvahed.* And then, too, there was the future: the *bar mitzvahs* of my own sons; the role I would be called upon to play on those occasions; the honors that would come to me because I was their father.

While I was lost in these thoughts, one of the cabinetmakers—the one who had planed the coffin—came over to me and asked me my Hebrew name. It took me a moment and then I replied *Ariel Lieb,* vaguely proud that I even knew it. But he waited for more. *Ben Chaim,"* I added, meaning "son of Chaim," which is my father's Hebrew name, and my grandfather's, and the Hebrew name of my second son.

He led me to the boy in the jams and T-shirt who was sitting in a chair holding the Torah. It was my job now to tie the Torah and wrap it in its mantle. As I took the tie in hand, I realized that it had been too long since the last time I had done this and I didn't know now what to do any more than I did then. But the cabinetmaker, sensing my inexperience, whispered for me to tie it so that the knot would face in. Ah, there must be a reason for that, I thought, as I followed his instructions.

"You're doing fine," he whispered, leaning into me, as I pulled the knot tight. Carefully, but now almost deftly, I placed the silk mantle on the Torah and, having performed my duty, joined the other men.

—Alan Gelb in
New York Times Magazine

Today Again My Complaint Is Bitter

Job said in reply:

Today again my complaint is bitter;
My strength is spent on account of my groaning.
Would that I knew how to reach Him,
How to get to His dwelling-place.
I would set out my case before Him
And fill my mouth with arguments.
I would learn what answers He had for me
And know how He would reply to me.
Would He contend with me overbearingly?
Surely He would not accuse me!
There the upright would be cleared by Him,
And I would escape forever from my judge.

But if I go East—He is not there;
West—I still do not perceive Him;
North—since He is concealed, I do not behold Him;
South—He is hidden, and I cannot see Him.
But He knows the way I take;
Would He assay me, I should emerge pure as gold.
I have followed in His tracks,
Kept His way without swerving,
I have not deviated from what His lips commanded;
I have treasured His words more than my daily bread.
He is one; who can dissuade Him?
Whatever He desires, He does.
For He will bring my term to an end,
But He has many more such at His disposal.
Therefore I am terrified at His presence;
When I consider, I dread Him.
God has made me fainthearted;
Shaddai has terrified me.

Yet I am not cut off by the darkness;
He has concealed the thick gloom from me.

—Job 23

Heal Me, O Lord, and Let Me Be Healed

Heal me, O Lord, and let me be healed;
Save me, and let me be saved;
For You are my glory.

—Jeremiah 17:14

※※

Where Does It End?

I look out upon the far horizon. Where does it end? The line drawn by my eye is only imaginary. It will recede as I come near it. Space, like time, is continuous, and there are no sharp interruptions to differentiate one thing from another.

And is it not likewise with my life? I look back into my past. I cannot tell where it began. I am familiar with some of my ancestors, but my life did not begin with them, it stretches far back into time beyond my reckoning. A long line of generations labored to produce me.

The peculiarity of my walk, of my smile, may go back to one, and the bent of my mind to another. The sound of my voice may carry an echo of some unknown benefactor who passed something of himself on to me. The seed that develops in me was planted in a far away past, and as I reap the harvest I know that other hands made it possible.

Equally long is the line of my spiritual ancestors. The love of life, and the sense of kinship I feel for my fellow man is but a simple expression of my spirit, but men achieved it after groping and suffering. The first man who rubbed two stones to produce fire is my ancestor, and so is the first man who discovered the glow of friendship in the clasp of two hands. The men who explored the seas and the mountains and who brought up the hidden riches of the earth are my ancestors. They enriched me with the fruit of their discoveries, as well as with the spirit of their daring.

I am what I am because of the first amoeba which developed into a more complex form, impelled by the divine imperative to grow. A thousand sunsets have shaped my sense of beauty; and a thousand soft voices have taught me to be kind. Waters from a thousand springs have quenched my thirst. I look out upon my world and act in it with all that is mine, with every past experience, and with everything that entered into it.

As I think of the long line stretching far into the past, I also cast my glance forward. The line into the future is just as unbroken. It moves through me into generations yet unborn. And as I think of this I am comforted. For I am a point in that line, and the course of existence travels through me. I have inherited from all the past and I will bequeath to all the future. In the movement of that line lies the secret of immortality and I am a part of it.

—Rabbi Ben Zion Bokser
The Gift of Life

❋❋

Beyond Judgment

Not to judge—but to understand.
Who knows the inner life of others
private pains
secret sufferings
clandestine ambitions.

Not to judge—but to understanding
to see beneath the coolness
an interior self
   too bashful to speak aloud of love
   too frightened to embrace the other with both arms.

Judgment is simple, crude, mechanical
Understanding complex, subtle, personal
Judgment is external
   a slavish following of
   the letter of the law
Understanding reads between the lines
   uncovering
   unadmitted dreams.

We would not be judged
by the eye of others
Our faults picked apart
our failings magnified

We would be heard with the third ear
open to the muted sobs
An ear attentive to the quiet grace
buried in the surface noise of activity.

Place an ear to the soul
to the spirit that is joined
    to an understanding God.

—Rabbi Harold M. Schulweis

❋❋

The Existence of God

Sensitive people need to believe in the existence of God, in order to understand the world. The purpose and order and beauty of creation leaves them with the over-powering conviction that some guiding Intelligence, of infinite power, wisdom and goodness, is behind it all. The void that would be created by the surrender of this conviction would make our world totally irrational.

But the belief in the existence of God fills another need for sensitive people. It helps them find meaning in their own existence. No one can meet the challenging demands of living without the sustaining faith that one's work serves some abiding purpose. But what purpose of mine can have abiding significance unless there is significance in the entire drama of life in which it plays a part? Unless this be so, every individual episode within it is doomed to frustration, regardless of outcome.

The individual passengers aboard a ship cannot be sailing towards a destination unless the ship itself is being steered by some captain's hand. Otherwise, the ship will only drift. It will battle against the waves, but it will find no haven.

—Rabbi Ben Zion Bokser
The Gift of Life

❋❋

It Is Never Too Late

The last word has not been spoken
the last sentence has not been written
the final verdict is not in
    It is never too late
    to change my mind
    my direction
      to say "no" to the past
      and "yes" to the future
      to offer remorse
      to ask and give forgiveness

It is never too late
to start over again
to feel again
    to love again
    to hope again

It is never too late
to overcome despair
to turn sorrow into resolve
    and pain into purpose

It is never too late to alter my world
not by magic incantations
or manipulations of the cards
or deciphering the stars

But by opening myself
to curative forces buried within
to hidden energies
the powers in my interior self.

In sickness and in dying, it is never too late
    Living, I teach
    Dying, I teach
how I face pain and fear
Others observe me, children, adults,
    students of life and death

Learn from my bearing, my posture,
  my philosophy.

It is never too late—
  Some word of mine,
  some touch, some caress may be remembered
  Some gesture may play a role beyond the last
  movement of my head and hand.

Write it on my epitaph
that my loved ones be consoled
It is never too late.

—Rabbi Harold M. Schulweis

※※

The Kaddish

Its origin is mysterious; angels are said to have brought it down from heaven and taught it to men. About this prayer the tenderest threads of filial feeling and human recollection are entwined; for it is the prayer of the orphans! When the father or mother dies, the surviving sons are to recite it twice daily, morning and evening, throughout the year of mourning, and then also on each recurring anniversary of the death—on the Yahrzeit.

It possesses wonderful power. Truly, if there is any bond strong and indissoluble enough to chain heaven to earth, it is this prayer. It keeps the living together, and forms the bridge to the mysterious realm of the dead. One might almost say that this prayer is the watchman and the guardian of the people by whom alone it is uttered; therein lies the warrant of its continuance. Can a people disappear and be annihilated so long as a child remembers its parents? It may sound strange: in the midst of the wildest dissipation has this prayer recalled to his better self many a dissolute character, so that he has bethought himself and for a time at least purified himself by honoring the memory of his parents.

Because this prayer is a resurrection in the spirit of the perishable in man, because it does not acknowledge death, because it permits the blossom which, withered, has fallen from the tree of mankind to flower and develop again in the human heart, therefore it possesses sanctifying power. To know that when thou diest, the earth falling on thy head will not cover thee entirely; to know that there remain behind, those who, wherever they may be on this wide earth, whether they may be poor or rich, will send this prayer after thee; to know that thou leavest them no house, no estate, no field by which they must remember thee, and that yet they will cherish thy memory as their dearest inheritance—what more satisfying knowledge canst thou ever hope for? And such is the knowledge bequeathed to us all by the Kaddish.

—L. Kompert
Mourners' Devotions

❊❊

Thoughts on the Kaddish

The short Kaddish prayer which I have repeated several times daily for nearly a whole year, and which I annually recite on the anniversary of the death of my parents, has become to me so dear that I consider it is a language of communication between the living and the dead through the interposition of God.

Where else should my kind, pious mother be sought for than near the throne of the Almighty to whom the Kaddish prayer ascends?

Parents and children, grandparents and grandchildren are bound by an eternal, never and nowhere ending strongly uniting bond! What a noble and beautiful belief! How capable it is of ensuring the perpetual existence, unlimited by time and space, of the Jewish people! And it is thou, O holy Kaddish, who art the medium of exhortation for this, the bearer and promoter of this word—encompassing thought! Thy few lines uttered by the mouths of innocent, pious children open a floodgate of memories of the dear departed, and they ensure the existence of the Jewish people unto endless eternity.

—Rabbi Jacob Hubscher
The Kaddish Prayer

❊❊

Rabbi Akiva's Compassion

Once, R'Akiva saw a bizarre man with a complexion black as coal. On his head, he was carrying a load heavy enough for ten men, and he was running swiftly as a horse. R'Akiva ordered him to stop.

"Why do you do such hard work?," the Tanna asked.

The apparition answered, "Do not detain me lest my supervisors be angry with me."

"What is this? What do you do?"

"I am a dead man," he replied. "Every day I am punished anew by being sent to chop wood for a fire in which I am consumed."

"What did you do in life, my son?" asked R'Akiva.

"I was a tax-collector. I would be lenient with the rich and oppress the poor."

R'Akiva persisted. "Have you heard if there is any way to save you?"

"I heard that if only I had left a son who would stand before the congregation and call out בָּרְכוּ אֶת ה׳ הַמְבֹרָךְ, *Bless Hashem, Who is to be blessed*—to which the people would respond בָּרוּךְ ה׳ הַמְבֹרָךְ לְעֹלָם וָעֶד, *Blessed is Hashem, Who is to be blessed, forever and ever!* And if only had I left a son who could proclaim to the congregation, יִתְגַּדַּל וְיִתְקַדַּשׁ שְׁמֵהּ רַבָּא, *May His great Name be exalted and sanctified*—to which the people would respond יְהֵא שְׁמֵהּ רַבָּא מְבָרַךְ . . . , *May His great Name be blessed!* If I had such a son I would be released from my punishment.

"But I left no son. . . When I died, my wife was pregnant, but even if she had a son, there would be no one to teach him."

That moment R'Akiva resolved to discover if a boy had been born and, if so, to teach him until he could lead the congregation in prayer. He went to Ludkia and inquired after the despised tax-collector. "May the bones of the wicked one be pulverized!" the people spat out. To R'Akiva's inquiries about the widow, they responded, "May her memory be obliterated from the earth!" And his child—"He is not even circumcised."

R'Akiva took the child, had him circumcised, and personally taught him Torah and the order of prayers. When he was ready, R'Akiva appointed him to lead the congregation in prayer.

"Bor'chu es HASHEM . . ." and the people blessed Him. "Yisgadal V'yiskadash shmei rabbah . . ." and the people responded, "Yehei shmei rabbah . . ."

Instantly the tortured soul was freed from its punishment. That very night, it appeared to R'Akiva in a dream and blessed him. "May it be God's will that your mind be at ease in Paradise, for you have rescued me from the judgment of Gehinnom."

R'Akiva cried out to God, "May You be known as HASHEM [the Attribute of Mercy] forever; HASHEM is Your appellation throughout the generations!"

—Rabbi Jacob Hubscher
The Kaddish Prayer

Job and the Lord

Then the Lord replied to Job out of the tempest and said:

Who is this who darkens counsel,
Speaking without knowledge?
Gird your loins like a man;
I will ask and you will inform Me.

Where were you when I laid the earth's foundations?
Speak if you have understanding.
Do you know who fixed its dimensions
Or who measured it with a line?
Onto what were its bases sunk?
Who set its cornerstone
When the morning stars sang together
And all the divine beings shouted for joy?

Who closed the sea behind doors
When it gushed forth out of the womb,
When I clothed it in clouds,
Swaddled it in dense clouds,
When I made breakers My limit for it,
And set up its bar and doors,
And said, "You may come so far and no farther;
Here your surging waves will stop"?

Have you ever commanded the day to break,
Assigned the dawn its place,
So that it seizes the corners of the earth
And shakes the wicked out of it?
It changes like clay under the seal
Till [its hues] are fixed like those of a garment.
Their light is withheld from the wicked,
And the upraised arm is broken.

Have you penetrated to the sources of the sea,
Or walked in the recesses of the deep?
Have the gates of death been disclosed to you?
Have you seen the gates of deep darkness?
Have you surveyed the expanses of the earth?
If you know of these—tell Me.

Which path leads to where light dwells,
And where is the place of darkness,
That you may take it to its domain
And know the way to its home?
Surely you know, for you were born then,
And the number of your years is many!

Have you penetrated the vaults of snow,
Seen the vaults of hail,
Which I have put aside for a time of adversity,
For a day of war and battle?
By what path is the west wind dispersed,
The east wind scattered over the earth?
Who cut a channel for the torrents
And a path for the thunderstorms,
To rain down on uninhabited land,
On the wilderness where no man is,
To saturate the desolate wasteland,
And make the crop of grass sprout forth?
Does the rain have a father?
Who begot the dewdrops?
From whose belly came forth the ice?
Who gave birth to the frost of heaven?
Water congeals like stone,
And the surface of the deep compacts.

Can you tie cords to Pleiades
Or undo the reins of Orion?
Can you lead out Mazzaroth in its season,
Conduct the Bear with her sons?
Do you know the laws of heaven
Or impose its authority on earth?

Can you send up an order to the clouds
For an abundance of water to cover you?
Can you dispatch the lightning on a mission
And have it answer you, "I am ready"?
Who put wisdom in the hidden parts?
Who gave understanding to the mind?
Who is wise enough to give an account of the heavens?
Who can tilt the bottles of the sky,
Whereupon the earth melts into a mass,
And its clods stick together.

Can you hunt prey for the lion,
And satisfy the appetite of the king of beasts?
They crouch in their dens,
Lie in ambush in their lairs.
Who provides food for the raven
When his young cry out to God
And wander about without food?

Do you know the season when the mountain goats give birth?
Can you mark the time when the hinds calve?
Can you count the months they must complete?
Do you know the season they give birth,
When they couch to bring forth their offspring,
To deliver their young?
Their young are healthy; they grow up in the open;
They leave and return no more.

Who sets the wild ass free?
Who loosens the bonds of the onager,
Whose home I have made the wilderness,
The salt land his dwelling-place?
He scoffs at the tumult of the city,
Does not hear the shouts of the driver.
He roams the hills for his pasture;
He searches for any green thing.

Would the wild ox agree to serve you?
Would he spend the night at your crib?
Can you hold the wild ox by ropes to the furrow?
Would he plow up the valleys behind you?
Would you rely on his great strength
And leave your toil to him?
Would you trust him to bring in the seed
And gather it in from your threshing floor?

The wing of the ostrich beats joyously;
Are her pinions and plumage like the stork's?
She leaves her eggs on the ground,
Letting them warm in the dirt,
Forgetting they may be crushed underfoot,
Or trampled by a wild beast.
Her young are cruelly abandoned as if they were not hers;
Her labor is in vain for lack of concern.

For God deprived her of wisdom,
Gave her no share of understanding,
Else she would soar on high,
Scoffing at the horse and its rider.

Do you give the horse his strength?
Do you clothe his neck with a mane?
Do you make him quiver like locusts,
His majestic snorting [spreading] terror?
He paws with force, he runs with vigor,
Charging into battle.
He scoffs at fear; he cannot be frightened;
He does not recoil from the sword.
A quiverful of arrows whizzes by him,
And the flashing spear and the javelin.
Trembling with excitement, he swallows the land;
He does not turn aside at the blast of the trumpet.
As the trumpet sounds, he says, "Aha!"
From afar he smells the battle,
The roaring and shouting of the officers.

Is it by your wisdom that the hawk grows pinions,
Spreads his wings to the south?
Does the eagle soar at your command,
Building his nest high,
Dwelling in the rock,
Lodging upon the fastness of a jutting rock?
From there he spies out his food;
From afar his eyes see it.
His young gulp blood;
Where the slain are, there is he.

The Lord said in reply to Job.

Shall one who should be disciplined complain against
   Shaddai?
He who arraigns God must respond.

Job said in reply to the Lord:

See, I am of small worth; what can I answer You?
I clap my hand to my mouth.
I have spoken once, and will not reply;
Twice, and will do so no more.

Then the Lord replied to Job out of the tempest and said:

> Gird your loins like a man;
> I will ask, and you will inform Me.
> Would you impugn My justice?
>
> Would you condemn Me that you may be right?
> Have you an arm like God's?
> Can you thunder with a voice like His?
> Deck yourself now with grandeur and eminence;
> Clothe yourself in glory and majesty.
> Scatter wide your raging anger;
> See every proud man and bring him low.
> See every proud man and humble him,
> And bring them down where they stand.
> Bury them all in the earth;
> Hide their faces in obscurity.
> Then even I would praise you
> For the triumph your right hand won you.
> Take now behemoth, whom I made as I did you;
> He eats grass, like the cattle.
> His strength is in his loins,
> His might in the muscles of his belly.
> He makes his tail stand up like a cedar;
> The sinews of his thighs are knit together.
> His bones are like tubes of bronze,
> His limbs like iron rods.
> He is the first of God's works;
> Only his Maker can draw the sword against him.
> The mountains yield him produce,
> Where all the beasts of the field play.
> He lies down beneath the lotuses,
> In the cover of the swamp reeds.
> The lotuses embower him with shade;
> The willows of the brook surround him.
> He can restrain the river from its rushing;
> He is confident the stream will gush at his command.
> Can he be taken by his eyes?
> Can his nose be pierced by hooks?
> Can you draw out Leviathan by a fishhook?
> Can you press down his tongue by a rope?
> Can you put a ring through his nose,

Or pierce his jaw with a barb?
Will he plead with you at length?
Will he speak soft words to you?
Will he make an agreement with you
To be taken as your lifelong slave?
Will you play with him like a bird,
And tie him down for your girls?
Shall traders traffic in him?
Will he be divided up among merchants?
Can you fill his skin with darts
Or his head with fish-spears?
Lay a hand on him,
And you will never think of battle again.

See, any hope [of capturing] him must be disappointed;
One is prostrated by the very sight of him.
There is no one so fierce as to rouse him;
Who then can stand up to Me?
Whoever confronts Me I will requite,
For everything under the heavens is Mine.
I will not be silent concerning him
Or the praise of his martial exploits.
Who can uncover his outer garment?
Who can penetrate the folds of his jowls?
Who can pry open the doors of his face?
His bared teeth strike terror.
His protective scales are his pride,
Locked with a binding seal.
One scale touches the other;
Not even a breath can enter between them.
Each clings to each;
They are interlocked so they cannot be parted.
His sneezings flash lightning,
And his eyes are like the glimmerings of dawn.
Firebrands stream from his mouth;
Fiery sparks escape.
Out of his nostrils comes smoke
As from a steaming, boiling cauldron.
His breath ignites coals;
Flames blaze from his mouth.
Strength resides in his neck;

Power leaps before him.
The layers of his flesh stick together;
He is as though cast hard; he does not totter.
His heart is cast hard as a stone,
Hard as the nether millstone.
Divine beings are in dread as he rears up;
As he crashes down, they cringe.
No sword that overtakes him can prevail,
Nor spear, nor missile, nor lance.
He regards iron as straw,
Bronze, as rotted wood.
No arrow can put him to flight;
Slingstones turn into stubble for him.
Clubs are regarded as stubble;
He scoffs at the quivering javelin.
His underpart is jagged shards;
It spreads a threshing-sledge on the mud.
He makes the depths seethe like a cauldron;
He makes the sea [boil] like an ointment-pot.
His wake is a luminous path;
He makes the deep seem white-haired.
There is no one on land who can dominate him,
Made as he is without fear.
He sees all that is haughty;
He is king over all proud beasts.

Job said in reply to the Lord:

I know that You can do everything,
That nothing you propose is impossible for You.
Who is this who obscures counsel without knowledge?
Indeed, I spoke without understanding
Of things beyond me, which I did not know.
Hear now, and I will speak;
I will ask, and You will inform me.
I had heard You with my ears,
But now I see You with my eyes;
Therefore, I recant and relent,
Being but dust and ashes.

After the Lord had spoken these words to Job, the Lord said to Eliphaz
the Temanite, "I am incensed at you and your two friends, for you have

not spoken the truth about Me as did My servant Job. Now take seven bulls and seven rams and go to My servant Job and sacrifice a burnt offering for yourselves. And let Job, My servant, pray for you; for to him I will show favor and not treat you vilely, since you have not spoken the truth about Me as did My servant Job.'' Eliphaz the Temanite and Bildad the Shuhite and Zophar the Naamathite went and did as the Lord had told them, and the Lord showed favor to Job. The Lord restored Job's fortunes when he prayed on behalf of his friends, and the Lord gave Job twice what he had before.

All his brothers and sisters and all his former friends came to him and had a meal with him in his house. They consoled and comforted him for all the misfortune that the Lord had brought upon him. Each gave him one *kesitah* and each one gold ring. Thus the Lord blessed the latter years of Job's life more than the former. He had fourteen thousand sheep, six thousand camels, one thousand yoke of oxen, and one thousand she-asses.

He also had seven sons and three daughters. The first he named Jemimah, the second Keziah, and the third Keren-happuch. Nowhere in the land were women as beautiful as Job's daughters to be found. Their father gave them estates together with their brothers. Afterward, Job lived one hundred and forty years to see four generations of sons and grandsons. So Job died old and contented.

—Job 38—42

5

✖✖✖✖✖✖✖✖✖✖✖✖✖✖✖✖✖✖✖✖✖✖✖

Shloshim:
The First Thirty Days after Burial

The thirty days following burial, which includes *shivah*, is the period of *shloshim*. It embodies the full mourning period for all relatives except for parents, for whom mourning ends after 12 Hebrew months.

"The mourner is encouraged to leave the house after shiva," Rabbi Maurice Lamm writes in *The Jewish Way in Death and Mourning*, "and to slowly rejoin society, always recognizing that enough time has not yet elapsed to assume full, normal social relations. The rent clothing may customarily still be worn for deceased parents, and haircutting for male mourners is still generally prohibited."

Rabbi Tzvi Rabinowicz adds that a "mourner must not take part in any festivity or attend a place of entertainment whether on the Sabbath, Festival, or a weekday. If he mourns a parent, this period of abstinence should continue to the full twelve months"(*A Guide to Life*).

Although mourners may greet another and respond to greetings of others, "*Shalom*" is not generally used. But the mourner returns to a normal work schedule, surrounded with people outside the immediate community of family and close friends. The mourner has begun to return order to his or her life. The monument may be purchased during this period.

I "got up" from sitting *shivah* for my father on the morning of the seventh day of *shivah*. I returned to my school later that day dressed in the black suit and tie I had worn at my father's funeral, the torn black ribbon, symbol of *keriah*, still pinned to the left lapel of my suit jacket near to my heart. I drifted mournfully through the day lost between two worlds.

The 30-day period of *shloshim* begins after interment. References to the 30 days are found in the Torah. The Israelites mourned Aaron's death for 30 days.

> Setting out from Kadesh, the Israelites arrived in a body at Mount Hor. At Mount Hor, on the boundary of the land of Edom, the Lord said to Moses and Aaron, "Let Aaron be gathered to his kin: he is not to enter the land that I have given to the Israelite people, because you disobeyed my command about the waters of Meribah. Take Aaron and his son Eleazar and bring them up on Mount Hor. Strip Aaron of his vestments and put them on his son Eleazar. There Aaron shall be gathered unto the dead."
>
> Moses did as the Lord had commanded. They ascended Mount Hor in the sight of the whole community. Moses stripped Aaron of his vestments and put them on his son Eleazar, and Aaron died there on the summit of the mountain. When Moses and Eleazar came down from the mountain, the whole community knew that Aaron had breathed his last. All the house of Israel bewailed Aaron thirty days.
>
> —Numbers 20:22–29

And for Moses, too, the children of Israel wept for 30 days.

> Moses went up from the steppes of Moab to Mount Nebo, to the summit of Pisgah, opposite Jericho, and the Lord showed him the whole land: Gilead as far as Dan; all Naphtali; the Land of Ephraim and Manasseh; the whole land of Judah as far as the Western Sea; the Negeb; and the Plain—the Valley of Jericho, the city of palm trees—as far as Zoar. And the Lord said to him, "This is the land of which I swore to Abraham, Isaac, and Jacob, 'I will give it to your offspring.' I have let you see it with your own eyes, but you shall not cross there."
>
> So Moses the servant of the Lord died there, in the land of Moab, at the command of the Lord. He buried him in the valley in the land of Moab, near Beth-peor; and no one knows his burial place to this day. Moses was a hundred and twenty years old when he died; his eyes were undimmed and his vigor unabated. And the Israelites bewailed Moses in the steppes of Moab for thirty days.
>
> —Deuteronomy 34:1–8

Rabbi Rabinowicz reminds us that "in mishnaic times, Rabbi Judah Hanasi, before he died, gave instructions that the 'assembly for study should be reconstituted after the lapse of thirty days from the day of his death' [*Ketubbot* 103b]." During *shloshim*, Rabbi Rabinowicz continues, "a mourner must not take part in any festivity or attend a place of entertainment whether on the Sabbath, Festival, or a weekday. If he mourns a parent, this period of abstinence should continue for the full twelve months [*Yoreh De'ah* 391:2].

He should not listen to instrumental music or play any musical instruments himself during the whole period of mourning."

Rabbi Rabinowicz informs us that it was custom at one time for mourners to wear black throughout *shloshim*, "since black was the symbol of death." Today, however, "Orthodox Jews do not wear black for mourning."

"The mourning period," Rabbi Simeon J. Maslin writes in *Gates of Mitzvah*, "is one of great personal vulnerability." On the day I "got up" from sitting *shivah* and returned to my school, I was particularly vulnerable, and self-consciously wore my black suit and rent ribbon as much to draw people to me as to keep them at a distance: these were the two worlds in which I found myself on that day, the world in which I sought sympathetic, even empathic comforters, to ease my pain, and the world in which I desired to be alone because no amount of comfort could ever lighten my painful burden.

"Some pains are too deep to salve," writes Rabbi David J. Wolpe in *The Healer of Shattered Hearts*, "and too inexplicably awful to pretend they have explanation." With my wife, Jo's, quiet empathic strength borne out of having lived without her father for more than half of her life, I left my home that morning assured that resuming my own life would not mean forgetting my father. Jo, too, returned to her school that day. Even though it was not her father who had died, my father was the only father she had known for 25 years, and she had been observing her own personal *shivah*. Our daughters, Corinne, Lisa, and Adina, returned to school, and with my mother visiting in my sister's home, our home was empty that day but for the echoes of weeping.

What might others have said to me that day I returned to my school? What might I have said to those who approached me? After *shivah*, Rabbi Lamm instructs, the mourners "may initiate the greeting and respond to it. Customarily, however, the mourner is not greeted with shalom for the full year of mourning in the case of a parent's death, and for the 30 days after the death of other relatives."

In school, some colleagues and students came close to me with whispers of "I'm sorry"; others approached, touched my arm, and retreated silently; still others, at a distance, nodded their heads in acknowledgment of my loss and turned away. I was still cloaked in the mourner's shadow that day and believed that if others did not see the beat of my heart, they heard it. I whispered thank-yous to the whispers I heard, and I bowed my head in recognition of the silent messages of condolence. In the very acts of "getting up" from sitting *shivah*, returning to work, and surrounding myself with people outside my immediate community of family and close friends, I was beginning to return order to my life and learning how to live without my father.

We received many cards and letters during that first month in which family and friends found they were able to share what they could not share face-to-face. "I know your loss is a loss in the profoundest sense," my colleague Michelle Schlein wrote to me. "[I have been] told of the depth of your relationship with your father and its importance in your life. I can only offer a little something from my own experience. There is hardly a day when something doesn't happen to bring my dad to mind with such sweetness and such clarity that his presence is always with me. I am very far removed from a spiritual life, but this never fails to move me. For those of us who have been lucky enough to make our peace with our parents and felt their positive influence in our lives, the gifts are enduring."

Every word and whisper, every card, whether printed or original, every touch, every visit, helps to build the bridge between the mourner's world and the world of normal relations that the mourner must reenter in order to resume a healthy life.

"I don't want his grave to be unmarked," my mother had said to me during *shivah*, after having read in Rabbi Lamm's book the chapter on erecting the *matzevah*, the monument. My mother wanted to select a stone for my father's grave immediately after *shivah* and I had agreed.

During the week following *shivah*, my mother and I visited the office and showroom of the monument maker from whom my mother and father had purchased the monuments for my paternal and maternal grandparents. I don't recall having talked with my mother in advance about the style of the monument or the inscription she desired. It was not until we entered the showroom—and with the expert, compassionate assistance of the owner—that she made her selection.

"Good taste, quiet dignity, and the avoidance of ostentation are the only guidelines for selecting the monument," Rabbi Lamm advises. "What is recommended is a short Hebrew descriptive phrase, in addition to the Hebrew name of the deceased and his father's Hebrew name, the full English name, and the Hebrew and English dates of birth and death. It may contain all of these or only the names. It is most appropriate, however, to include the Hebrew dates whenever Christian dates are inscribed."

Rabbi Lamm cautions against having the face of the deceased or figures of animals cut into the stone. Equally, photographs are inappropriate. "It does seem that a person should be remembered without having his portrait to stare at. If already erected, however, these tombstones should cause no disputes, and are better left to stand as they are."

My mother and I walked among the monuments in the showroom and, as we touched the cold stone and read the sample inscriptions, as we stepped back and imagined first one stone and then another at the head of my father's grave, we shared ideas about how my father's monument should look and what it should read. My mother chose a monument with two tablets and, as she touched my arm, assured me that setting a tablet aside for her was in no way a sign as to her own state of mind. "There's no question where I will be buried," she said, "and there is no reason I cannot make a choice of a monument for both of us."

In addition to my father's Hebrew name and the name of his father, and that he was a Levite, we wanted him to be remembered as

Beloved Husband
Devoted Father
Loving Grandfather
Dear Brother

And so those remembrances were to be carved on the tablet after his name. Not that my father would not be remembered without those inscriptions, but when the grave is visited, the inscriptions would be read aloud and, in part, would be a prayer to my father.

We decided on a carving of the eternal flame to separate the two tablets. I was comforted by that symbol that so often had drawn my attention in the sanctuary. In the upper right-hand corner, a *menorah* would be carved and in the upper left-hand corner, a pitcher, to represent my father's status as a Levite—and mine, as well.

My maternal grandfather, Samuel Ovshia Lubliner, was a *cohain*. According to Orthodox and Conservative Jews, a *cohain* is a descendant of Aaron, Moses' brother and the first high priest of the Temple in Jerusalem. During the Torah reading on the Sabbath and on festivals and whenever the Torah is read, a *cohain* is the first of the worshipers called upon to repeat the blessings and, later, to offer the priestly benediction.

The Levites are Jews who trace their ancestry to the Levites of biblical days. Then, in the time of the ancient Temple, the Levites were responsible for the physical care of the sanctuary. But they had another job as well.

Before my maternal grandfather would enter the sanctuary during the High Holy Days to offer the priestly benediction, my father and I would pour water from a pitcher over his hands. Perhaps more than any other ritual I performed in the presence of my father, this one linked me religiously to my father (and grandfather) and historically to my heritage. Here was the literal "passing down" from generation to generation of Jewish ritual: my father would pour water first, then hand the pitcher to me, and then together we would follow my grandfather into the sanctuary. Although I did not stand with my grandfather on the *bimah*, I was as much a part of him then as I was a part of my father, next to whom I proudly stood. In the sanctuary, when I was a boy I held my father's *tallit*; later I held his hand, and still later, I draped my arm around his shoulders. A pitcher of water, like the *tallit* each of us later wore, had made us inextricably linked to each other and to our heritage.

As my mother and I left the monument showroom, I told her the day would come when I would visit my father's grave with my grandchildren and they would ask about the pitcher of water. I would tell them not only of their great-grandfather as Beloved Husband, Devoted Father, Loving Grandfather, and Dear Brother but also of their great-grandfather as Affectionate Teacher.

✻✻

Readings

✸✸✸✸✸✸✸✸✸✸✸✸✸✸

Our Days Upon the Earth

Our days upon the earth are a shadow.

—Job 8:9

✸✸

Ecclesiastes Rabbah

As a man enters the world, so he departs.

He enters the world with a cry, and departs with a cry.

He enters the world weeping, and leaves it weeping.

He enters the world with love, and leaves it with love.

He enters the world with a sigh, and leaves it with a sigh.

He enters the world devoid of knowledge, and leaves it devoid of knowledge.

It has been taught in the name of Rabbi Meir:

When a person enters the world his hands are clenched as though to say, "The whole world is mine. I shall inherit it."

But when he leaves, his hands are spread open as though to say, "I have taken nothing from the world."

—*Ecclesiastes Rabbah*, chap. 5, sec. 14
Francine Klagsbrun
Voices of Wisdom

✸✸

Comfort Ye, Comfort Ye

Comfort ye, comfort ye, my people.
Saith your God.

—Isaiah 40:1

❈

He Will Cover Thee with His Pinions

He will cover thee with His pinions
And under His wings shalt thou take refuge;
His truth is a shield and a buckler.

—Psalm 91:4

❈

He Will Give His Angels Charge over Thee

He will give His angels charge over thee.
To keep thee in all thy ways.

—Psalm 91:11

❈

Man in Time

Man is really so deeply in time—
He is ruler over the sea and the land.
His frame is called to him with a fiery brand,
And with a swordsharp idea of meaning
He drives his lines to the stars.

But there are moments, under thick clouded bars,
Towards evening,
When he softens, discarding all plans,
For it is suddenly enough, towards evening, to nod
And to speak lyrical, old, wellworn words:
I feel so sad this evening, my God!

(And in this sadness is something that rejects going out
To seek a teller of fortunes at midnight,
To show her a hand with its secret of lines—)

Man is really as hard as the metal
Alloyed of passions as numerous as sands;
And he prides himself on the gift of his hands
In the midst of the din and the burst.

But there are times when he lifts the tips of his soul
To touch the tips of another poor soul,
To say but a word and to hear but a word—
Like a sip of live water in thirst.

Man is really so deeply in time:
His life streaming on into distances that roll,
His axe hewing the tangle of tomorrow's new goal,
But under his feet is that pole of old misery
Of the ancient, the naked, the red and the hairy,
And there is no trace of grass on the pole—

He is ready to roar: *Yah-veh!*
As once he roared.

> —Uri Zvi Greenberg, trans. Richard Flantz, in
> *Anthology of Modern Hebrew Poetry*

✳✳

A Terrible Inner Numbness

When a person suffers the loss of a beloved with whom there have been vital interpersonal relations, the immediate result is a terrible inner numbness and a loss of equilibrium; a feeling that one has no longer any conduct patterns to follow. The world is a dreary wasteland. Grief, loneliness, despair, possess his soul. Shall he give way to these passions, or eternally crush them down?

> —Rabbi Joshua Loth Liebman
> *Peace of Mind*

✳✳

Kaddish

When he was dead, when mourning was over,
Our mother got up from the mourner's bench
To write letters to her sons: one north, one south,
One to the other world.

All began the same way:
How our sick father called to her in the night,
Put his head on her shoulder
And, like a fallen bird, silently closed his black eyes.

She lifted his head from her shoulder
And put it back on the pillow. His skin was warm.
The hair she had always loved—it was not yet entirely gray—
Was curly, fine as silk, even after he was dead.

The letters ended in a different way.
The living—north, south—
Were told to cherish his name.
The one in the other world: Greet him in proper fashion!

That is how our mother wrote three letters to her sons.
One north, one south,
One in the real world.

The sons received them,
They bowed their heads,
And in the night, thought of their beloved father.

—Melech Rawitch, trans. Nathan Halper
A Treasury of Yiddish Poetry

※※

The Conquest of Grief

The melody that the loved one played upon the piano of our life will
never be played quite that way again, but we must not close the
keyboard and allow the instrument to gather dust. We must seek out
other artists of the spirit, new friends who gradually will help us to find
the road to life again, who will walk on that road with us. The

establishment of new patterns of interaction with other people, beginning with the interaction of language and moving on to new avenues of
creative expression is [a] law for the conquest of grief and the conquest
of death.

—Rabbi Joshua Loth Liebman
Peace of Mind

⁂

הוֹלֶכֶת אַתְּ מֵעִמִּי
You're Leaving Me

You're leaving me. Then go in peace. And let
Your wish alone be lamp to light your path,
And find tranquillity where'er you be.
I? Do not give it thought. I am not desolate.
While yet the sun in beauty rises and descends
And God's own stars unwearied beckon me
I have not altogether lost estate,
Nor is the fountain of my comfort wholly drained.
See, you I have no more, but much remains:
A world replete with all the green of spring,
The gold of summer, and the white of winter.
And I still own my heart, a shrine of dreams and visions,
My pain is there contained, the sacred sorrow,
An angel pure is with me, the semblance of your image,
That canopies my head with God's own grace
And whispers low a blessing, trembling and constrained,
So like a mother's secret tear o'er Sabbath lamp
In the quietude of peaceful holiness,
And like a winking star there far on high
That still with eye benign does gaze on me,
Its golden scepter in the dark extends to me.

And I, full well I know
There still will spread o'er all the earth,
Like dusky Ethiopian maids, the nights of summer
In hangings blue with gold embroidered,
Sweet fevered nights and strangely silent
With blackness overlaid and wreaths of stars,
Each star, each star a pomegranate of gold.

And sate with sinful thoughts, wearied with longing,
Couches the earth in bosom of the night.
And suddenly—a stillness great and vast.
A quiver of desire pervades the world,
And multitudes of stars are shaken out
And poured with all their fragments to the earth,
Like golden showers of falling leaves in autumn.
And parched with lust, devoured by longing,
Each man in hunger and in thirst goes forth,
Groping the walls as blind men hug a stone,
Flings himself to the earth, crawls on his belly
To gather up one golden particle, one crumb
From what his star has cast him from the height,
And find of love a handful, one grain of bliss.
In such an hour if longings seize upon you,
And your searching weary eye should stray
And wander hopeless in the darkness,
And your soul long for God and happiness,
Then lift your eyes as I do to the Heavens,
And from them teach your heart tranquility:
See, many stars each night are lost to heaven,
Yet the Heavens in their richness calmly stand,
And do not feel their loss, as though indeed
Naught were diminished of their store of gold.

                                        —Hayyim Nahman Bialik
                                        Selected Poems

                                ❋❋

The Rose Is Queen

The rose is queen among the flowers,
    None other is so fair;
The lily nodding on her stem,
    With fragrance fills the air.
But sweeter than the lily's breath,
    And than the rose more fair.
The tender love of human hearts.
    That springeth everywhere

The rose will fade and fall away,
    The lily too will die;

But love shall live for evermore
  Beyond the starry sky.
Then sweeter than the lily's breath
  And than the rose more fair,
The tender love of human heart.
  Upspringing everywhere

—Isaac Moses
The Sabbath-School Hymnal

⁂

God Kisses Moses' Soul

In the meanwhile Moses' time was at an end. A voice from heaven resounded, saying: "Why, Moses, dost thou strive in vain? Thy last second is at hand." Moses instantly stood up for prayer, and said: "Lord of the world! Be mindful of the day on which Thou didst reveal Thyself to me in the bush of thorns, and be mindful also of the day when I ascended into heaven and during forty days partook of neither food nor drink. Thou, Gracious and Merciful, deliver me not into the hand of Samael." God replied: "I have heard thy prayer. I Myself shall attend to thee and bury thee." Moses now sanctified himself as do the Seraphim that surround the Divine Majesty, whereupon God from the highest heavens revealed Himself to receive Moses' soul. When Moses beheld the Holy One, blessed be His Name, he fell upon his face and said; "Lord of the world! In love didst Thou create the world, and in love Thou guidest it. Treat me also with love, and deliver me not into the hands of the Angel of Death." A heavenly voice sounded and said: "Moses, be not afraid. 'Thy righteousness shall go before thee; the glory of the Lord shall be thy rearward.' "

With God descended from heaven three angels, Michael, Gabriel and Zagzagel. Gabriel arranged Moses' couch, Michael spread upon it a purple garment, and Zagzagel laid down a woolen pillow. God stationed Himself over Moses' head, Michael to his right, Gabriel to his left, and Zagzagel at his feet, whereupon God addressed Moses: "Cross thy feet," and Moses did so. He then said, "Fold thy hands and lay them upon thy breast," and Moses did so. Then God said, "Close thine eyes," and Moses did so. Then God spake to Moses soul: "My daughter, one hundred and twenty years had I decreed that thou shouldst dwell in this righteous man's body, but hesitate not now to leave it, for thy time is run." The soul replied: "I know that Thou are the God of spirits and of souls, and that in Thy hand are the souls of the living and of the dead. Thou didst create me and put me into the body of this righteous man. Is there anywhere in the world a body so pure and holy as this is? Never a fly rested upon it, never did leprosy show itself upon it. Therefore do I love it, and do not wish to leave it." God replied: "Hesitate not, my daughter! Thine end hath come. I Myself shall take thee to the highest heavens and let thee dwell under the Throne of My Glory, like the Seraphim, Ofannim, Cherubim, and other angels." But the soul replied: "Lord of the world! I desire to remain with this righteous man; for whereas the two angels Azza and Azazel when they descended from heaven to earth, corrupted their way of life and loved the daughters of the earth, so that in punishment Thou didst suspend them between heaven and earth, the son of Amram, a creature of flesh and blood, from the day upon which Thou didst reveal Thyself from the bush of thorns, has lived apart from his wife. Let me therefore remain where I am." When Moses saw that his soul refused to leave him, he said to her: "Is this because the Angel of Death wishes to show his power over thee?" The soul replied: "Nay, God doth not wish to deliver me into the hands of death." Moses: "Wilt thou, perchance, weep when the others will weep at my departure?" The soul: "The Lord 'hath delivered mine eyes from tears.'" Moses: "Wilt thou, perchance, go into Hell when I am dead?" The soul: "I will walk before the Lord in the land of the living." When Moses heard these words, he permitted his soul to leave him, saying to her: "Return unto thy rest, O my soul: for the Lord hath dealt bountifully with thee." God thereupon took Moses' soul by kissing him upon the mouth.

Moses activity did not, however, cease with his death, for in heaven he is one of the servants of the Lord. God buried Moses' body in a spot that remained unknown even to Moses himself. Only this is known concerning it, that a subterranean passage connects it with the graves of the Patriarchs. Although Moses' body lies dead in its grave, it is still as fresh as when he was alive.

—Louis Ginzberg
Legends of the Jews III

The Mourning for Moses

When Moses died, a voice resounded from heaven throughout all the camp of Israel, which measured twelve miles in length by twelve in width, and said, "Woe! Moses is dead. Woe! Moses is dead." All Israel who, throughout thirty days before Moses' decease, had wept his impending death now arranged a three months' time of mourning for him. But Israel were not the only mourners for Moses. God Himself wept for Moses, saying, "Who will rise up for Me against the evil-doers? Who will stand up for Me against the workers of iniquity?" Metatron appeared before God and said: "Moses was Thine when he lived, and he is thine in his death." God replied: "I weep not for Moses' sake, but for the loss Israel suffered through his death. How often had they angered Me, but he prayed for them and appeased My wrath." The angels wept with God, saying, "But where shall wisdom be found?" The heavens lamented: "The godly man is perished out of the earth." The earth wept: "And there is none upright among men." Stars, planets, sun, and moon wailed: "The righteous perisheth, and no man layeth it to heart," and God praised Moses' excellence in the words: "Thou hast said of Me, 'The Lord He is God: there is none else,' and therefore shall I say of thee, 'And there arose not a prophet in Israel like unto Moses.'"

Among mortals, it was particularly Jochebed, Moses' mother, and Joshua, his disciple, that deeply mourned Moses' death. They were not indeed certain if Moses were dead, hence they sought him everywhere. Jochebed went first to Egypt and said to that land, "Mizraim, Mizraim, hast thou perchance seen Moses?" But Mizraim replied, "As truly as thou livest, Jochebed, I have not seen him since the day when he slew all the firstborn here." Jochebed then betook herself to the Nile, saying, "Nile, Nile, hast thou perchance seen Moses?" But Nile replied, "As truly as thou livest, Jochebed, I have not seen Moses since the day when he turned my water to blood." Then Jochebed went to the sea and said, "Sea, sea, hast thou perchance seen Moses?" The sea replied, "As truly as thou livest, Jochebed, I have not seen him since the day when he led the twelve tribes through me." Jochebed thereupon went to the desert and said, "Desert, desert, hast thou perchance seen Moses?" The desert replied, "As truly as thou livest, Jochebed, I have not seen him since the day whereon he caused manna to rain down upon me." Then Jochebed went to Sinai, and said, "Sinai, Sinai, hast thou perchance seen Moses?" Sinai said, "As truly as thou livest, Jochebed, I have not seen him since the day whereon he descended from me with the two tables of the law." Jochebed finally went to the rock and said, "Rock, rock, hast thou perchance seen Moses?" The rock replied, "As truly as thou livest, I have not seen him since the day when with his staff he twice smote me."

Joshua, too, sought his teacher Moses in vain, and in his grief for Moses' disappearance he rent his garments, and crying aloud, called ceaselessly, "'My father, my father, the chariot of Israel and the horsemen thereof.' 'But where shall wisdom be found?'" But God said to Joshua: "How long wilt thou continue to seek Moses in vain? He is dead, but indeed it is I that have lost him, and not thou."

—Louis Ginzberg
Legends of the Jews III

❈

Healthy Grief

The discoveries of psychiatry—of how essential it is to express rather than to repress grief, to talk about one's loss with friends and companions, to move step by step from inactivity to activity again— remind us that the ancient teachers of Judaism often had an intuitive wisdom about human nature and its needs which our more sophisticated and liberal age has forgotten. Traditional Judaism, as a matter of fact, had the wisdom to devise almost all of the procedures for healthy-minded grief which the contemporary psychologist counsels, although Judaism naturally did not possess the tools for scientific experiment and systematic case study, nor did it always understand, as we now can, the underlying reasons for its procedures.

—Rabbi Joshua Loth Liebman
Peace of Mind

❈

Between

Where?
God is not in me
nor in you.
But between us.

God is not me or mine
nor you or yours
But ours.

God is known
not alone
but in relationship.

Not as a separate, lonely power
but revealed through our kinship, our
friendship
through our healing and binding
and raising up of each other.

To know God is to know others
to love God is to love others
to hear God is to hear others

More than meditations within
more than insights within
more than feeling within
Between us are
Claims, obligations, commandments
to act, to do, to behave our beliefs

I seek God
not as if He were a person alone,
He or She,
a process, a power, a being, a thing.
Nor as if I were alone
a thinker, a meditator, a discrete entity.
I seek God in connection
in the nexus of community.
I pray and celebrate the betweenness
that binds and holds together.

Even alone
I am sustained by my
memory of our betweenness
and the promise of our betweenness

God is not in me or in you or in Himself
but in betweenness
There we find the evidence of
God's reality and our own.

—Rabbi Harold M. Schulweis

※

Religious Rituals

Religious rituals at the time of death, no matter how much they may differ in form and in content, seek to perform two functions: to ferry the departed one safely across the waters of oblivion to the shores of eternity, and at the same time to build a bridge upon which the bereaved living can move from the numbness of sorrow toward a renewed acceptance of life.

—Rabbi Joshua Loth Liebman
Peace of Mind

※

The Meaning of the Kaddish

Have you ever stood at the open grave of a dear relative? Have you ever felt the dignity, the terror, and the beauty of death? Have you ever heard a wooden voice dead to all emotion, or the voice of a broken heart, of a soul that is crushed—have you heard them say, "*Yitgadal veyitkadash shmeh rabba*"? Have you ever stopped to wonder what these words might mean—whether they are a lamentation for the dead, or if perchance they may bring to you a message from that bourn whence none return?

Have you wondered why the most faithless Jew, he who has driven godliness from his life, who has spurned the Rock of the Ages and the traditions of his race—why even he will find the way back to the synagogue, will appease some secret longing in his heart by mixing with the old-fashioned folk who every day seek contact with their Maker? Do you feel there is some magic in the Kaddish, some mystic formula that will hold the heart, though one fails to grasp its meaning?

What was the life purpose of the Jew who believed in the Kaddish?

Why the anxiety of our parents to have a "Kaddish," someone to pronounce those strange Aramaic words when they have joined the ranks of the sleepers?

There is a term in Jewish lore and life which may be called peculiarly Jewish. It is quite unknown outside Jewish spheres of thought, and it fits the peculiar Jewish mentality. It is the phrase *kiddush hashem*. Where a Jew may be weak, because temptation is too alluring, this word will give him strength to resist. Where a Jew may be lacking courage to face a mob of bloodthirsty ruffians in a pogrom-swept land, or on any of the fields which have drunk Jewish blood; where a Jew may hesitate to bring a sacrifice too heavy for the everyday spirit of man, flash that word before his eyes and you will discover heroism and self-sacrifice and strength you would never have divined.

Kiddush hashem means "sanctification of the Divine Name." So close is the affection of the Jew for his God that he dreads doing anything that might offend His dignity, that might in any manner slight the veneration of the great Father of Israel. So ingrained is our love for God that we sink all our small objections and rise to the heights, wherever *kiddush hashem* is at stake.

To live so that our life may be a glory unto God, a source of added devotion among Jew and Gentile, that was the great ambition of true Jews. *Kiddush hashem* was not only the theme of some great occasion, the reaction of the Jew to some soul-stirring event; it was the motto of his life.

It often meant ascending the scaffold on which the tortured Jew breathed his last. It meant, in thousands of cases, weary wandering from shore to shore, going astray in the wilderness of life, with human beasts of prey howling their wild cries into panicky ears. It meant unceasing struggle against efforts to destroy our substance and our honor. It meant facing every terror that fiendish cruelty, that blind hatred could devise, every degradation of bigotry and hypocrisy. It was a white light of godliness among the murky flames of human perversity and inhuman folly.

As the Jew learned the duties of life, this was his greatest goal. As he founded his home, this became his undying light, his *ner tamid*. As he saw his years roll by, this was his greatest concern. As God blessed him with children, with sons to face the turmoil of life, with daughters to kindle a Sabbath lamp not to be dimmed during the week; as he saw the babes develop into boys and girls; as he felt his own powers grow weaker and their energies extend and increase; this was his main care— that they become bone of his bone, heart of his heart, soul of his soul;

that they take upon themselves the glory of his supreme duty to feel personally and continually responsible for the *kiddush hashem* of their days. As he felt his days numbered, his last moments were filled with torture if doubt beset his soul. Will my son remain a Jew, a good Jew? Not one who uses the name as a mere flag, or as an occasional outlet of excessive energy. But will they who have my name, my possessions, my work, my fruits, will they prove strong or weak, true sons of Israel, or mere pursuers after the idols of the multitude?

His last tears were as his first prayers, his last hopes as his first care: "May the Almighty bless my child, that happiness and health be his lot; may He give him joy of life and strength and plenty; but, above all, may He give him eyes to see, a heart to feel where glory lies, where duty is and honor. May He open his heart and strengthen his mind; may He help him and enable him to be and remain a Jew." With this wish he closed his eyes, commending his soul to God.

The father's heart beat no more. The kindly eye was closed forever. No more on this globe were they to meet—son and father. The son had stepped into the parent's shoes. He had undertaken the responsibilities for the honor of his house. And there at the open grave he did not wail and lament. There at the last terrible meeting with his beloved he did not engage in eulogies. There he stood in the presence of the whole congregation of friends and strangers, before those of the age passing and those who were to lead in the age after him, and there at the saddest moment of his life he recalled neither his sorrow nor his loss, but his duty. As a Jew he knew the holiness of the moment, and he framed his resolution in the words holiest to Jewish hearts; there he opened his lips to Jewish hearts; there he opened his lips and made a pledge, a holy promise: "*Yitgadal veyitkadash shmeh rabba*, Lord God, I do not murmur against Thy decree, I am a child of Jewry. Lord God, hear my voice at this moment. As my father lived for Thee, as his life was dedicated to Thy glory and Thy name, so do I declare *Yitgadal veyitkadash*, 'that Thy great Name may be magnified and sanctified' as the promise for my future. So do I undertake to remember his fidelity, and never to forget my own duty."

That was the meaning of Kaddish in the generations of our fathers. That is the meaning of the words today when said for mother and father. Not a prayer for the dead, but a pledge from the living; not a superstitious phrase, but a man's motto of life.

That is the meaning of *hazkarah*—that we continue where our parents ceased; that we do not allow the heritage of Israel to decay for want of men with the courage to bring sacrifices in a godless, thoughtless world.

Kaddish is the eternal appeal to the divine spark in every Jewish soul. It is the "river of light," the stream of idealism in which the elect bathe for their eternal rejuvenation. From its fire the historical body of our people draws the secret of its eternity. The Kaddish is the living consciousness of our obligation to add Jewish assets to those acquired by the generations before us—to save God for the world. It is the great "Remember!" of the Jew, sounding from the dawn of history, the *kazkarah* which calls out: "Our Father in heaven. We have remembered; we are conscious of Thy grace and our defection. We remember our task and our negligence; the glory of our mission and our deep failings. Do Thou remember, our God! Do Thou make an end to the terror and the grief, the slaughter of the innocent, the terrible night of Thy people!

"Give Thou unto us peace and strength.

"Banish Thou the shadows of the past, and let the glorious light of Thy grace illumine human darkness.

"*Yitgadal veyitkadash shmeh rabba*"—"Sanctified and magnified be Thy great name."

—Rabbi Leo Jung in
Jewish Reflections on Death

※※

A Day with My Mother and Aunt Phyllis, Her Sister

The azaleas were out, everywhere, surrounded by lush lawns, trees, bushes of a thousand kinds. We drove through New Jersey towns called Shrewsbury and Little Silver and Tinton Falls, admiring estates and stunning gardens bursting in purples and yellows, blues and greens. "I knew these houses," my mother explained. "I used to cover the garden parties and horse shows for the Asbury Park Press while your father was in medical school . . . and of course the reporters were always the first to edge towards the tables of food."

This was only one tone of the day—gentle reminiscences, a touch of sentimentality at unforeseen moments. I had sensed weeks back that our day together—my mother, my aunt, and me—would be an event of some importance, a focusing and point of reference for later on. I had decided not to take notes: I did not want the writer's urge to interfere with the pure living of the day. Only once, during lunchtime at the old seafood restaurant I remembered from my childhood (and they from theirs), did I jot down an idea or two, afraid to lose them in the onrush of words. I could tell from my preparations that we would all, indeed, drink fully of these few hours together, and the occasional exclamations of pleasure at the Springtime colors and smells were only small indications of the moment's grandeur.

Ostensibly the two sisters had wanted to go to my grandfather's town (their town, their childhood town) to see about selling a piece of land their father had bought more than a generation ago. They paid eight dollars in taxes annually on the land, and rumor had it that it was a swamp. As it turned out, the realtor had trouble finding it on her map, but there was more laughter about the property than concern. It had been worthless for years, they concluded, and would probably remain so, at least until the Messiah came. Unless, of course, some bureaucratic idiot decided it was time to put an interstate through a marsh.

But, really, for all that, the strip of mud Grandpa owned was only a pretext, a chance to be away, to remember things worthy of remembering, to enjoy company and recollections and a little sisterly love, in the presence of the next generation who could well guard their secrets and memories, and record their thoughts with the proper respect—a certain brightening of the eyes, a specific tone in the voice, a certain placing in time and space of the words to be said. We were determined to taste the delicious and rare taste of unadulterated joy for a few hours together.

As the day wore on and I watched the interplay of my mother and aunt, I began to see what fine stock they came from, the Silberblatts. I was shown a postcard from 1904 addressed to their Grandfather Louie. On it was an admonition that if he didn't have so-and-so's pants ready by such and such a date, the owner of said pants would have to terminate his relationship with my great-grandfather, the tailor, the pantspresser. It is likely that I earned more in the past three months than he ever made in a year (even counting inflated dollars), but a certain sense of values was being handed down, silently, underneath, as my mother and aunt spoke of the hardworking grandfather they remembered. It was a *Yerushah*, an inheritance, through him to his son, to the two daughters, and to me. It was a certain striving for uprightness, integrity, a touch of *Edelkeit*, a gentility impervious to corruption, proclaiming that beyond the struggles of labor was family, caring, life itself. The stories that emerged from the postcard bespoke an enthusiasm for living so precious to all it would be related in stories and warnings and glances throughout all our generations. All from a seemingly insignificant postcard about a pair of pants. It was a modest point of departure, to be sure, but indicative of the surging back and forth of the sisters' minds, from the mundane to the broadest, most universal thoughts of human sensitivities.

During the day we visited the cemetery. There, in a small Jewish graveyard, lie my grandfather and grandmother. Reviewing the dates on the marker, I recalled Pesach 1959, and the phone call (I was away), telling me that my grandmother had died. And the other phone call, nineteen years later, of the passing of the other grandparent. I left the sisters to their thoughts and their prayerbook words. They were entitled to some moments alone, in the presence of something they understood far better than I could grasp. Besides, they had told me that some great uncle of mine, was buried in the older part of the cemetery, in the corner, away from where they stood, and I wanted to see.

Yale Hirshowitz, my grandfather's brother, dead at fifty-one, unmarried. No one knew for certain where he lived. Aunt Phyllis said, "He died in Grandpa's store. I remember running upstairs to Grandma to tell her I couldn't wake him up." She must have been about eleven.

And Mom adds, "No one really understood him. Something was wrong—he was a spastic or something like that. Many people treated him like an outcast, but the family always supported him."

There are no pictures left of Uncle Yale. My mother and aunt had searched over the years. So we looked here and there for some stones and pebbles to leave on the grave, to show that, fifty years later, someone had visited and remembered.

It seems that everything we were to do that day was fraught with possibilities for second and third thoughts. My muffler fell out on the way down from New York. It happened no more than a hundred yards from a Plymouth dealer where my Grandpa used to buy his cars a half century and more ago. My mother asked about the descendants of the original owner (the "Old Man"), who now sold the cars. The patriarch is still alive, and must be nearly ninety, and here, again, was a flash of recognition.

Along the way I took pictures, to preserve the similarity of their faces, Mom and Phyllis, her kid sister, their mutual dignity, their demeanor that radiates gentleness, and yes, one might say without hesitation, holiness. I, bearing their dreams, their thoughts of a future, was charged with catching everything as it happened, even down to the earliest memories of their childhood. "Come on, Mom—how corny! Outhouses! My mother grew up in a house with outdoor plumbing?" Laughter, with no sadness for the passing of years. Pristine laughter. Children. The two of them sleeping in the attic, covered with *perenes*, the thick old feather blankets, heavy, warmer than the latest in fashionable quilted comforters. And the chickens Grandma used to hatch in the kitchen. More laughter, waves of laughter, their heads thrown back, talking in the air to laugh some more.

I kept asking as the emotions swung high then "normal," I kept wondering what was the final meaning of all this, a day together in family. Was it no more than a break from humdrum and casual daily goings on? Was the point that nostalgia is a great blessing, to be nurtured and embraced? Early on in the day I could see that this was but a minor part of the experience. More was happening than could be captured in a picture or a flashback to the nineteen-twenties and thirties, the Crash, the Hindenburg's flaming demise in Lakehurst, the Charlestons they danced in their youth. I felt, at moments, that I was as close to touching life as I had ever been, and these two extraordinary women were my teachers. People were revealing themselves to me as I had not known them before—not just my mother and my aunt, but People as human beings.

And so it became apparent at the final event of the day, a visit to our Cousin Joe Bennet.

Joe was a favorite when we were kids. Colonel Joe Bennet had played professional baseball (sometime in the '20's it must have been), which was like something higher than being a king. Joe is related somehow through Grandma (his mother and my mother's mother were sisters), and there he was now, pushing eighty, forgetting things, burdened with arthritis, diabetes, and some single or double form of cancer.

God, he was ramrod straight! He spoke slowly, slurred some words, but he was lucid enough to curse the hell out of the old folks living in his building complex, a neighborhood for the elderly. He doesn't really belong there, I don't believe. He should be on a hot line for people who feel lonely or feel that life is a waste, people who need to be reminded what glorious creatures God Almighty has put on this earth.

Most of the day Joe keeps the door open a little. He says, "So when I have to get to heaven, it will be easier to get there." Laughter, more of the wonderful laughter, Joe's dentures showing, making sounds. Doctors' considered diagnoses or not, Joe is here in full stature until his time comes. Tests and medical charts mean nothing. Living, that's the thing. Ah, Joe, I love you.

All of us know none of the family is perfect. Grandpa wasn't the best businessman in the world, and in past generations, as in ours, faults are evident everywhere. But you reminded me of something, Joe. It happened when I was in Tel Aviv—seeing one of Grandpa's friends, someone he had met in a hotel bar some years back. By chance. I was the first relative to see him since my grandfather had died, and all he could say, this stranger who had become an intimate through time and visits, all he could say was, "Ah, how I loved him." With pain for the loss of a friend, with loneliness, with the greatest love of one human being for another.

—Danny Siegel
Angels

❈❈

A Death in the Family

We must take with each other's feelings;
Words we speak now will be remembered for years to come.

—Helen Epstein in
New York

❈❈

6

✕✕✕✕✕✕✕✕✕✕✕✕✕✕✕✕✕✕✕✕✕✕✕✕✕✕✕✕✕

Yahrzeit: *The Yearly Anniversary of the Death (Mourning for a Parent)*

Yahrzeit is the day of commemoration of the death of a loved one and recognition of the enormity of loss. "It may be observed for any relative or friend, but it is meant primarily for parents" (Rabbi Maurice Lamm, *The Jewish Way in Death and Mourning*). The monument over the grave has been erected and the unveiling of the monument has occurred. A candle is lit. When the *yahrzeit* is for our parents, the day is also a reminder of the respect due them in death as well as in life.

Because it is a day when the death itself is recalled, some people fast, some study, and others give to charity or engage in other acts of kindness. The synagogue may become a safe haven for those who find the need to be comforted by being part of the community and its traditions.

In more traditional settings, writes Rabbi Lamm, on the Sabbath before *yahrzeit*, *El Malay Rachamin* is recited after the Torah reading at *Minchah*.

My mother returned alone to her condominium in Sunrise, Florida, a Ft. Lauderdale community, after the *shloshim*. It was the middle of June, almost seven weeks after my father's death. For the first time in the 11 years they had lived in Sunrise, for the first time in almost 49 years of marriage, my mother returned to her apartment alone. My mother told me before she left that she wanted the unveiling of my father's tombstone to be held in November, when she came up for her regular Thanksgiving visit. I told her I could think of no reason that could not be arranged.

My mother surprised us and joined the family again in late summer, at the same time we received notice that the tombstone had been erected. After visiting my father's grave then and seeing the monument, my mother, reassured that my father's grave was properly marked and therefore protected,

195

changed her mind about the time for the unveiling. We would schedule it for the following spring, sometime after Passover. It would be too cold in late November, she said, to hold an outdoor service.

My mother cried when she first saw the stone.

"It's a beautiful stone, Mom," I said.

What strength that block of granite provided me then—and now. It seemed to rise out of the earth as I approached it, dwarfing me in its presence; the family name, KAY, engraved in large, unadorned letters near the top of the stone, seemed, at first, a name I did not know. But as I walked along the path leading to the grave, my mind focused, my heart started racing, and the name became recognizable, not only as my father's family name but as my name as well. The monument then shrank in size, so I stood over it rather than let it stand over me. But its power to make my heart race has never diminished.

My mother walked closer to the stone to touch my father's first name, so prominently engraved at the top of one tablet. When she walked around the stone, her hand caressing the granite as she did, I brushed my fingers over the letters of my father's name, as though I were spelling his name for the first time. My mother and I said nothing to each other, but when she stopped for one last look, I stared at her lips, moving in personal reflection.

Before we left my father's grave, I picked up two small, smooth white pebbles lying at the foot of the grave and gave one to my mother. She placed it on top of the stone, and I placed mine next to hers. I rested my hand a moment next to the pebbles, as my father had so often rested his hand on my shoulder when I was a child, and I whispered, "I love you, Dad." My mother wept as she stepped back from the stone, and together we returned to my car.

"This custom [of placing pebbles on the tombstone]," Rabbi Lamm writes, "probably serves as a reminder of the family's presence. Also, it may hark back to biblical days when the monument was a heap of stones. Often, the elements or roving vandals dispersed them, and so visitors placed other additional stones to assure that the grave was marked.

"The service of commemoration or unveiling is a formal dedication of the monument. It is customary to hold the unveiling within the first year after death. It should be held at any time between the end of shiva and the yahrzeit."

As it would turn out, the Sunday in April after Passover the following year best suited for the unveiling arrived one week after my father's *yahrzeit*. Tombstones are not consecrated on *Chol Ha-Moed* (neither on Purim nor Tisha B'Av), which eliminated the Sunday during Passover. Since we wanted our rabbi to lead the service, we had to skip the first Sunday after Passover because he was involved with Yom Ha-Shoah observances. But by April, the monument had been in place seven months, guarding my father's grave and symbolizing our adherence to Jewish law and tradition. Therefore, we did not feel compelled to act immediately. We waited patiently for our day.

"The unveiling is the formal removal of a veil, a cloth, or handkerchief draped over the stone. It symbolizes the erection of the tombstone" (Lamm). Tombstone dedications or unveilings, Rabbi Maslin writes in *Gates of Mitzvah,* "are not required by Jewish tradition. However, it is praiseworthy for a family to go to the cemetery together at some time after the monument or marker is set in place for a consecration service."

On the day of my father's unveiling, 399 other families would be at the same cemetery participating in tombstone consecration services. Four hundred unveilings scheduled for one cemetery on one Sunday in April! While unveilings may not be law, custom often becomes law.

Sunday, April 29, the fourth of *Iyar* on the Hebrew calendar, was a bright, almost cloudless day, the light-blue sky a perfect backdrop to the ritual about to be performed because it offered no distractions. But then, it was also a windy day, and when we stood around the grave, the white veil tied around the granite stone like a kerchief around a silver-haired head rippled in the wind and struggled to free itself from the knots that held it in place. The wind roughed up our hair and forced us to button the collars to our coats.

And while we were huddled together, my mother, Jo, and I, my sister, Barbara, and her husband, our children, family, and friends, each one of us was in our own world. The tombstone was another stark reminder of my father's death and our loss. Our rabbi, Jay Rosenbaum, sensitive to and respectful of our feelings, spoke caringly yet firmly and occasionally touched my mother's shoulder during the service as she stood between the rabbi and the tombstone.

Psalm 1 is often read at a tombstone consecration service, offering an "appropriate theme for the service" (Lamm).

> Happy is the man who has not followed the counsel of the wicked,
> > or taken the path of sinners,
> > or joined the company of the insolent;
> > rather, the teaching of the Lord is his delight,
> > and he studies that teaching day and night.
> He is like a tree planted beside streams of water,
> which yields its fruit in season,
> whose foliage never fades,
> and whatever it produces thrives.
>
> Not so the wicked;
> > rather, they are like chaff that wind blows away.
> Therefore the wicked will not survive judgment,
> > nor will sinners, in the assembly of the righteous.
> For the Lord cherishes the way of the righteous,
> > but the way of the wicked is doomed.

—Psalm 1

Psalms 16 and 23, also read during the tombstone consecration service, are further affirmations of God as Protector. Rabbi Tzvi Rabinowicz adds that sometimes verses from Psalm 119 are read. Psalm 119 consists of 22 stanzas, corresponding to the number of letters in the Hebrew alphabet. Appropriate stanzas are chosen to correspond with the Hebrew name of the deceased. "It is also usual to pay a brief tribute to the departed and to recite a Hazkarah, and Kaddish is also recited" (*A Guide to Life*). In *Gates of the House: The New Union Home Prayerbook,* published by the Reform movement's Central Conference of American Rabbis, Psalms 8, 15, 103, and 121 are additionally suggested.

> To this sacred place I come, drawn by the eternal ties that bind my soul to the soul of my beloved. Death has separated us. You are no longer at my side to share the beauty of the passing moment. I cannot look to you to lighten my burdens, to lend me your strength, your wisdom, your faith. And yet what you mean to me does not whither or fade. For a time we touched hands and hearts; still your voice abides with me, still your tender glance remains a joy to me. For you are part of me for ever; something of you has become a deathless song upon my lips. And so beyond the ache that tells how much I miss you, a deeper thought compels: we were together. I hold you still in mind, and give thanks for life and love. The happiness that was, the memories that do not fade, are a gift that can not be lost. You continue to bless my days and years. I will always give thanks for you.
>
> *—Gates of the House*

The service concluded, we all stepped forward to place a pebble on the tombstone and touch it, one more time; run our fingers over the letters of my father's name, one more time; admire the strength and beauty of the granite stone that had become an inextricable part of our lives, one more time; and weep for our Beloved Husband, Devoted Father, Loving Grandfather, Dear Brother—and Cherished Friend, one more time.

We returned to our home for lunch after the late-morning service and talked more about my father than anything else. As it should be.

The date of my father's *yahrzeit* was ten days before the unveiling, the twenty-fifth of *Nisan* on the Hebrew calendar, one year after his death.

> Various reasons are given for the twelve-month period of mourning. According to the Zohar [*Vayeychi* 225a], the soul clings to the body for twelve months. The Talmud, on the other hand, says: "For twelve months the body is in existence and the soul ascends and descends; after twelve months the body ceases to exist and the soul ascends but descends no more [*Shabbat* 152b]." It was furthermore believed that purification in afterlife takes place in the first twelve months and that after a year the memory wanes.
>
> —Rabbi Tzvi Rabinowicz
> *A Guide to Life*

On that day, the twenty-fifth of *Nisan*, a Friday, before sundown, Jo and I lit our *yahrzeit* candles, she for her father, as she had done for more than half her life, and I for my father, for the first time. After nearly 24 years of marriage, we had something new to share.

> Tradition regards this day as commemorative of both the enormous tragedy of death and the abiding glory of the parental heritage. It was a day set aside to contemplate the quality and life-style of the deceased, and to dwell earnestly upon its lessons. It is a day when one relives the moment of doom, perhaps even fasts to symbolize the unforgettable despair. It is a day conditioned by the need to honor one's parent in death as in life, through study and charity and other deeds of kindness. It is also conditioned by the non-rational, but all-too-human feelings that it is the day itself which is tragic, one which might bring misfortune with every annual cycle, and for which reason one slows one's activities and spends a good part of the day safely in the synagogue.
>
> —Rabbi Maurice Lamm
> *The Jewish Way in Death and Mourning*

The first scriptural reference to *yahrzeit*, Rabbi Rabinowicz informs us, is found in Judges 11:40: "And it was the custom in Israel, that the daughters of Israel went yearly to lament the daughter of Jephthah, the Gileadite, four days in a year." Rabbi Rabinowicz also offers the following talmudic citations: *Nedarim* 12a; *Yevamot* 122a, and Rashi ad loc.; and *Shevuot* 20a. Further, the rabbi advises us, the term itself was first used by Rabbi Moses Minz, a fifteenth-century scholar, and among the Sephardim is called *nachalah meldado* or *Annos*.

"Fasting was closely associated with mourning in the Bible [*Nedarim* 12a] and also in the Apocrypha, where we read that Judith fasted every day except Friday and Saturday while she was in mourning. Also on yahrzeit, time should be set aside for study and money should be given to charity"; Rabbi Rabinowicz also reminds us, however, that most *hasidim*, following the tradition of Rabbi Dov Baer, the *Maggid* of Messeritz, "make a seudah, distribute money to charity, and say 'the soul should have an aliyah' ('May the soul of the deceased be raised to a still higher level of purity')."

According to Rabbi Rabinowicz, lighting the memorial candle to burn for 24 hours is a "well-established practice . . . although no authority for this is found in the Talmud or Midrash." Rabbi Lamm suggests that candles of wick and paraffin be used as the memorial light. "If these are not available at all, gas or electric lights are permitted. As the flame and wick symbolize soul and body, it does appear significant to use the candle, rather than a bulb, if at all possible."

Proverbs 20:27, "The soul of man is the lamp of the Lord" is one source cited by Rabbi Rabinowicz for the custom of burning a memorial candle. The mystics, he writes, "have pointed out that the numerical value of the letters of the Hebrew phrase ner daluk (a kindled light) and the Hebrew word Ha-Shechinah (the Divine Presence) add up to 390 [1 Samuel 31:13; 2 Samuel 1:12; Joel 1:17; Zechariah 7:4–7, 9]." The rabbi also cites Exodus 27:20 to 30:10, *Tetzaveh*, read during the week of the seventh of *Adar*, the traditional date for commemorating Moses' death, as another source for memorial candle lighting:

> You shall further instruct the Israelites to bring you clear oil of beaten olives for lighting, for kindling lamps regularly. Aaron and his sons shall set them up in the Tent of Meeting, outside the curtain which is over the Pact, [to burn] from evening to morning before the Lord. It shall be a due from the Israelites for all time, throughout the ages.
>
> —Exodus 27:20–21

On the stove-top in my grandparents' apartment and later in my parents' apartment, the *yahrzeit* candles would burn in small, textured glasses, the flames casting eerie shadows against the back wall and on the stove-top itself in the otherwise dark kitchen. As a child, I often wondered who saw the candles burn after we had gone to sleep for the night, and when I awoke in the morning to find much of the paraffin gone and the flame only a flicker, I believed those for whom the candles burned had, during the night, carried the wax away to some unknown place.

On that Friday in April, one year after my father's death, I lit a *yahrzeit* candle for the first time and set it on the stove-top next to the one my wife had lit, and I joined the generations of Jews, my parents and grandparents among them, who had kept alive this ancient custom.

Later, in the synagogue, my *Kaddish* prayer was recited with the understanding that a year had passed since I first said those words. Although I may have been undistinguished among the mourners in Zion, although generations of sons before me had become fatherless, I still felt as a child in the mourning process and my lips still could not form all the words in a prayer that the Kabbalists say "elevates the soul every year to a higher sphere in paradise [Isaac Luria]" (Rabinowicz).

In more traditional synagogue settings, Rabbi Lamm informs us, on the Sabbath before *yahrzeit*, the *El Malay Rachamin* memorial prayer is recited after the Torah reading at *Minchah*. "If possible, the mourner should chant the maftir portion and should lead the Saturday night ma'ariv service. He should, in any case, receive an aliyah, a Torah honor. This aliyah is considered a 'required' honor."

On the day of *yahrzeit* itself, Rabbi Lamm continues, the mourner should lead synagogue services. "Those who cannot, would do well to learn at least the minchah service, which is brief and simple. The rabbi will be delighted to teach the mourner, or direct him to the cantor or sexton or lay teacher. He should recite the Kaddish at every service. In addition, there is usually a Psalm added to the morning service so that the yahrzeit observer may recite at least one Kaddish without the accompaniment of other mourners.'' The mourner's *Kaddish*, Rabbi Rabinowicz writes, ''should be recited at every service during the day, a custom that is mentioned by Rabbi Isaac b. Moses of Vienna (c. 1250) in his ritual code Or Zarua.''

The third location of *yahrzeit* observance is the cemetery. Rabbi Rabinowicz quotes Rashi (*Yevamot* 122a): ''I have seen in the response [written replies to questions on all aspects of Jewish law] of the geonim that on the anniversary of the death people assemble around the grave and hold a discourse and offer a prayer.''

Because the unveiling of my father's tombstone had been scheduled for less than two weeks later, we did not visit the cemetery for the first *yahrzeit* of my father's death. The Psalms, traditionally read at unveilings, and the *El Malay Rachamim* are usually recited at the graveside on *yahrzeit* visitations. Rabbi Lamm tells us that Mishnah should also be studied at the graveside.

Rabbi Lamm concludes his discussion of *yahrzeit* with a detailed explanation of how to calculate the date of *yahrzeit*.

The English calendar date of my father's death came two weeks later, and the emptiness I had felt earlier seemed to grow even larger in anticipation of that date until the following day, when sweet memories filled me both with gratitude for the life he had shared with all of us and with the love his memory would always stir in our souls.

Like the Kaddish, the yahrzeit (anniversary of a death) is a powerful magnet, drawing a man back to the synagogue and back to his people with regular and incessant rhythm. Even those whose synagogue affiliations are slender make new contact on this memory-hallowed day. Even in small communities, where there is no regular minyan and where the house of prayer is closed the entire week, even there the doors of the synagogue are opened and arrangements are made for a service to take place when a Jew has a yahrzeit to observe. For the observance of the yahrzeit is one of the honors that a man can pay his departed parents, and it is a duty that his heart, mind, and conscience bid him pay with scrupulous care. As the strains of the yahrzeit reverberate through his soul, they reawaken with indescribable poignancy the faded memories of past years.

—Rabbi Tzvi Rabinowicz
A Guide to Life

Readings

※※※※※※※※※※※※※

The God of Springing Grass

The God of springing grass and the loving heart is with us.

—*Gates of Prayer*

※※

Personal Credo

I do not believe that sickness is a divine punishment
a warning malediction thrust down upon me from above
a chastisement meant to correct some transgression of mine
nor do I believe that sickness is some mysterious reward
strange compensation designed to test
or enable my character.

I believe what some of the rabbinic sages observed
"olam K'minhago noheg"
nature pursues its own course.
A course most often independent of my doing or will
an amoral course of events
indiscriminately affecting young and old, good and bad.

Flowers wither, leaves fall
the earth cracks open
Accidents occur not properly traced to a judging rod.

Where divinity enters
is in the curative forces
discovered within me and between us.
Healing powers that form scars
Life-sustaining powers within me
brought forth by trained men and women,
doctors, nurses, research people
social workers, aides.

Health-sustaining powers energized
by family and friends
who stand beside my bed,
and hold my hand, bless me with their prayers.

Curative powers I exercise consciously
following prescriptions, respecting counsel, willing strength
and unconscious forces I cannot identify, locate, control
but the surge within me
filling me with the will to recover, the will to struggle for health.

For these benevolent forces—within, without,
conscious and unconscious
I give thanks to the Source of healing, the Ground of
hope and courage, the faithful Physician, the Life of the universe.

—Rabbi Harold M. Schulweis

※☀※

As Much as Man Can Comfort

When the son of Rabban Johanan ben Zakkai died, his disciples came
to console him. Rabbi Eliezer came and sat before him and asked,
"Master, is it your wish that I say a word in your presence?" He
replied, "Speak." He said, "Adam, the first man, had a son who died
and he permitted himself to be comforted in his loss. Whence do we
know that? It is stated, *Adam knew his wife again* (Gen. 4:25). So should
you also be comforted." He retorted, "Is it not enough that I have my
own grief that you must also mention Adam's grief?" Then Rabbi
Joshua entered and asked, "My master, is it your wish that I say a word
in your presence?" He answered, "Speak." He said, "Job had sons and
daughters who all died in one day and he permitted himself to be
comforted; you too should find comfort. How do we know that Job

found comfort? It is written, The Lord has given, and the Lord has taken away; blessed be the name of the Lord (Job 1:21)." He retorted, "Is it not enough that I have my own grief, that you must also mention Job's grief?" Next Rabbi Jose entered and asked, "My Master, is it your wish that I say a word in your presence?" He replied, "Speak." He said, "Aaron had two grown sons and both died in one day, yet he allowed himself to be comforted, as it is said, And Aaron was silent (Lev. 10:3), signifying that he was comforted. Therefore, you too be comforted." He retorted, "Is it not enough that I have my own grief that you must mention Aaron's grief?" Rabbi Simon then came in and asked, "My master, is it your wish that I say a word in your presence?" He replied, "Speak." He said, "King David had a son who died, yet he allowed himself to be comforted; you too be comforted." How do we know that David was comforted? It is stated, David consoled his wife Bathsheba; he went to her and lay with her. She bore a son and she named him Solomon (2 Sam. 12:24)." He retorted, "Is it not enough that I have to bear my own grief that you have to mention King David's grief?" Finally Rabbi Eleazar ben Arakh entered. When Rabban Johanan saw him coming, he said to his attendant, "Take my clothes and follow me to the bathhouse because this man is so distinguished and I cannot appear before him as I am." Then Rabbi Eleazar came in and said, "Let me tell you a parable. To what is the matter like? To the example of a man with whom a king had deposited an article of value. Every day the man wept and cried out, 'Woe is me! When shall I be free of the responsibility of this trust?' You, too, my master, had a son versed in the Torah, who had studied the Pentateuch, Prophets, and Hagiographa, Mishnah, laws, and legends—and he departed from this world sinless. Surely you should derive comfort from having returned your trust intact!" Rabban Johanan said to him, "Eleazar, my son, you have comforted me as much as man can comfort."

—Judah Nadich
Jewish Legends of the Second Commonwealth

✺✺

Death and Fear of Death
Moed Katan 28a

Rav Nachman was dying.
That was certain.
He had no desire for miracles,

and his chest heaved.
Rava mouthed the final recitations
for his teacher, word-by-word.
so Nachman might pass easily, at peace,
to the Life-after-Death
his Talmudic belief had promised him.
These, then, were the last events:
The Shema was recited,
and Rava chanced a request
"Show yourself to me in a dream,
Rebbi."
Then no breath.
That night Rava saw his Master.
"Rebbi," he asked,
"did you suffer much pain?
Just how is Death, my master?"
"Rava, my comfort,
constant friend in all of Life,
there was no pain.
What was it like?
It was gentle,
like picking a hair
from a cup of milk.
So easy. So smooth.
I am dead, but not bruised.
I do not suffer.
And yet,
were God to say,
'You may go back to Life
as you once were,'
I would refuse,
for the Fear of Death
is crushing to the soul."

—Danny Siegel
Between Dust and Dance

Lord Make Me to Know Mine End

Lord make me to know mine end,
and the measure of my days, what it is;
let me know how short-lived I am.

—Psalm 39:5

✳✳

The Death of Adam

On the last day of Adam's life, Eve said to him, "Why should I go on living, when thou art no more? How long shall I have to linger on after thy death? Tell me this!" Adam assured her she would not tarry long. They would die together, and be buried together in the same place. He commanded her not to touch his corpse until an angel from God had made provision regarding it, and she was to begin at once to pray to God until his soul escaped from his body.

While Eve was on her knees in prayer, an angel came, and bade her rise. "Eve, arise from thy penance," he commanded. "Behold, thy husband hath left his mortal coil. Arise, and see his spirit go up to his Creator, to appear before Him." And, lo, she beheld a chariot of light, drawn by four shining eagles, and preceded by angels. In this chariot lay the soul of Adam, which the angels were taking to heaven. Arrived there, they burnt incense until the clouds of smoke enveloped the heavens. Then they prayed to God to have mercy upon His image and the work of His holy hands. In her awe and fright, Eve summoned Seth, and she bade him look upon the vision and explain the celestial sights beyond her understanding. She asked, "Who may the two Ethiopians be, who are adding their prayers to thy father's?" Seth told her, they were the sun and the moon, turned so black because they could not shine in the face of the Father of light. Scarcely had he spoken, when an angel blew a trumpet, and all the angels cried out with awful voices, "Blessed be the glory of the Lord by His creatures, for He has shown mercy unto Adam, the work of His hands!" A seraph then seized Adam, and carried him off to the river Acheron, washed him three times, and brought him before the presence of God, who sat upon His throne, and, stretching out His hand, lifted Adam up and gave him over to the archangel Michael, with the words, "Raise him to the Paradise of the third heaven, and there thou shalt leave him until the great and fearful day ordained by Me.'' Michael executed the Divine behest, and all the angels sang a song of praise, extolling God for the pardon He had accorded Adam.

Michael now entreated God to let him attend to the preparation of Adam's body for the grave. Permission being given, Michael repaired to earth, accompanied by all the angels. When they entered the terrestrial Paradise, all the trees blossomed forth, and the perfume wafted thence lulled all men into slumber except Seth alone. Then God said to Adam, as his body lay on the ground: ''If thou hadst kept My commandment, they would not rejoice who brought thee hither. But I tell thee, I will turn the joy of Satan and his consorts into sorrow, and thy sorrow shall be turned into joy. I will restore thee to thy dominion, and thou shalt sit upon the throne of thy seducer, while he shall be damned, with those who hearken unto him.''

Thereupon, at the bidding of God, the three great archangels covered the body of Adam with linen, and poured sweet-smelling oil upon it. With it they interred also the body of Abel, which had lain unburied since Cain had slain him, for all the murderer's efforts to hide it had been in vain. The corpse again and again sprang forth from the earth, and a voice issued thence, proclaiming, ''No creature shall rest in the earth until the first one of all has returned the dust to me of which it was formed.'' The angels carried the two bodies to Paradise, Adam's and Abel's—the latter had all this time been lying on a stone on which angels had placed it—and they buried them both on the spot whence God had taken the dust wherewith to make Adam.

God called unto the body of Adam, ''Adam! Adam!'' and it answered, ''Lord, here am I!'' Then God said: ''I told thee once, Dust thou art, and unto dust shalt thou return. Now I promise thee resurrection. I will awaken thee on the day of judgment , when all the generations of men that spring from thy loins shall arise from the grave.'' God then sealed up the grave, that none might do him harm during the six days to elapse until his rib should be restored to him through the death of Eve.

—Louis Ginzberg
The Legends of the Jews I

The Death of Eve

The interval between Adam's death and her own Eve spent in weeping. She was distressed in particular that she knew not what had become of Adam's body, for none except Seth had been awake while the angel interred it. When the hour of her death drew nigh, Eve supplicated to be buried in the selfsame spot in which the remains of her husband rested. She prayed to God: "Lord of all powers! Remove not Thy maid-servant from the body of Adam, from which Thou didst take me, from whose limbs Thou didst form me. Permit me, who am an unworthy and sinning woman, to enter into his habitation. As we were together in Paradise, neither separated from the other; as together we were tempted to transgress Thy law, neither separated from the other, so, O Lord, separate us not now." To the end of her prayer she added the petition, raising her eyes heavenward, "Lord of the world! Receive my spirit!" and she gave up her soul to God.

The archangel Michael came and taught Seth how to prepare Eve for burial, and three angels descended and interred her body in the grave with Adam and Abel. Then Michael spoke to Seth, "Thus shalt thou bury all men that die until the resurrection day." And again, having given him this command, he spoke: "Longer than six days ye shall not mourn. The repose of the seventh day is the token of the resurrection in the latter day, for on the seventh day the Lord rested from all the work which He had created and made."

—Louis Ginzberg
Legends of the Jews I

✳

Thy Sun Shall No More Go Down

Thy sun shall no more go down,
Neither shall Thy moon withdraw itself;
For the Lord shall be thine everlasting light,
And the days of thy mourning shall be ended.

—Isaiah 60:20

✳

Preparing Aaron for Impending Death

As a sign of especial favor God communicates to the pious the day of their death, that they may transmit their crowns to their sons. But God considered it particularly fitting to prepare Moses and Aaron for impending death, saying: "These two pious men throughout their lifetime did nothing without consulting Me, and I shall not therefore take them out of this world without previously informing them."

When, therefore, Aaron's time approached, God said to Moses: "My servant Moses, who has been 'faithful in all Mine house,' I have an important matter to communicate to thee, but it weighs heavily upon Me." Moses: "What is it?" God: "Aaron shall be gathered unto his people; for he shall not enter into the land which I have given unto the children of Israel, because ye rebelled against My word at the waters of Meribah." Moses replied: "Lord of the world! It is manifest and known before the Throne of Thy glory, that Thou art Lord of all the world and of Thy creatures that in this world Thou hast created, so that we are in Thy hand, and in Thy hand it lies to do with us as Thou wilt. I am not, however, fit to go to my brother, and repeat to him Thy commission, for he is older than I, and how then shall I presume to go up to my older brother and say, "Go up unto Mount Hor and die there!" God answered Moses: "Not with the lip shalt thou touch this matter, but 'take Aaron and Eleazar his son, and bring them up unto Mount Hor.' Ascend thou also with them, and there speak with thy brother sweet and gentle words, the burden of which will, however, prepare him for what awaits him. Later when ye shall all three be upon the mountain, 'strip Aaron of his garments, and put them upon Eleazar his son, and Aaron shall be gathered unto his people, and shall die there.' As a favor to Me prepare Aaron for his death, for I am ashamed to tell him of it Myself."

When Moses heard this, there was a tumult in his heart, and he knew not what to do. He wept so passionately that his grief for the impending loss of his brother brought him to the brink of death himself. As a faithful servant of God, however, nothing remained for him to do, but to execute his Master's command, hence he betook himself to Aaron to the Tabernacle, to inform him of his death.

Now it had been customary during the forty years' march through the desert for the people daily to gather, first before the seventy elders, then under their guidance before the princes of the tribes, then for all of them to appear before Eleazar and Aaron, and with these to go to Moses to present to him their morning greeting. On this day, however,

Moses made a change in this custom, and after having wept through the night, at the cock's crow summoned Eleazar before him and said to him: "Go and call to me the elders and the princes, for I have to convey to them a commission from the Lord." Accompanied by these men, Moses now betook himself to Aaron who, seeing Moses when he arose, asked: "Why hast thou made a change in the usual custom?" Moses: "God hath bidden me to make a communication to thee." Aaron: "Tell it to me." Moses: "Wait until we are out of doors." Aaron thereupon donned his eight priestly garments and both went out.

Now it had always been the custom for Moses whenever he went from his house to the Tabernacle to walk in the centre, with Aaron at his right, Eleazar at his left, then the elders, at both sides, and the people following in the rear. Upon arriving within the Tabernacle, Aaron would seat himself as the very nearest at Moses' right hand, Eleazar at his left, and the elders and princes in front. On this day, however, Moses changed this order: Aaron walked in the centre, Moses at his right hand, Eleazar at his left, the elders and princes at both sides, and the rest of the people following.

When the Israelites saw this, they rejoiced greatly, saying: "Aaron now has a higher degree of the Holy Spirit than Moses, and therefore does Moses yield to him the place of honor in the centre." The people loved Aaron better than Moses. For ever since Aaron had become aware that through the construction of the Golden Calf he had brought about the transgression of Israel, it was his endeavor through the following course of life to atone for his sin. He would go from house to house, and whenever he found one who did not know how to recite his Shema', he taught him the Shema'; if one did not know how to pray he taught him how to pray; and if he found one who was not capable of penetrating into the study of the Torah, he initiated him into it. He did not, however, consider his task restricted 'to establishing peace between God and man,' but strove to establish peace between the learned and the ignorant Israelites, among the scholars themselves, among the ignorant, and between man and wife. Hence the people loved him very dearly, and rejoiced when they believed he had now attained a higher rank than Moses.

Having arrived at the Tabernacle, Aaron now wanted to enter, but Moses held him back, saying: "We shall now go beyond the camp." When they were outside the camp, Aaron said to Moses: "Tell me the commission God hath given thee." Moses answered: "Wait until we reach the mountain." At the foot of the mountain Moses said to the people: "Stay here until we return to you; I, Aaron, and Eleazar will go to the top of the mount, and shall return when we shall have heard the Divine revelation." All three now ascended.

—Louis Ginzberg
Legends of the Jews III

✳✳

Aaron's Death

Moses wanted to inform his brother of his impending death, but knew not how to go about it. At length he said to him: "Aaron, my brother, hath God given anything into thy keeping?" "Yes," replied Aaron. "What, pray?" asked Moses. Aaron: "The altar and the table upon which is the shewbread hath He given into my charge." Moses: "It may be that He will now demand back from thee all that He hath given into thy keeping." Aaron: "What, pray?" Moses: "Hath He not entrusted a light to thee?" Aaron: "Not one light only but all seven of the candlestick that now burn in the sanctuary." Moses had, of course, intended to call Aaron's attention to the soul, "the light of the Lord," which God had given into his keeping and which He now demanded back. As Aaron, in his simplicity, did not notice the allusion, Moses did not go into further particulars, but remarked Aaron: "God hath with justice called thee an innocent, simple-hearted man."

While they were thus conversing, a cave opened up before them, whereupon Moses requested his brother to enter it, and Aaron instantly acquiesced. Moses was now in a sad predicament, for, to follow God's command, he had to strip Aaron of his garments and to put them upon Eleazar, but he knew not how to broach the subject to his brother. He finally said to Aaron: "My brother Aaron, it is not proper to enter the cave into which we now want to descend, invested in the priestly garments, for they might there become unclean; the cave is very beautiful, and it is therefore possible that there are old graves in it." Aaron replied, "Thou art right." Moses then stripped his brother of his priestly garments, and put them upon Aaron's son, Eleazar.

As it would have been improper if Aaron had been buried quite naked, God brought about the miracle that, as soon as Moses took off one of Aaron's garments, a corresponding celestial garment was spread over Aaron, and when Moses had stripped him of all his priestly garments, he found himself arrayed in eight celestial garments. A second miracle came to pass in the stripping of Aaron's garments, for Moses was enabled to take off the undermost garments before the upper. This was done in order to satisfy the law that priests may never use their upper garments as undergarments, a thing Eleazar would have had to do, had Moses stripped off Aaron's outer garments first and with these invested his son.

After Eleazar had put on the high priest's garments, Moses and Aaron said to him: "Wait for us here until we return out of the cave," and both entered it. At their entrance they beheld a couch spread, a table prepared, and a candle lighted, while ministering angels surrounded the couch. Aaron then said to Moses: "How long, O my brother, wilt thou still conceal the commission God hath entrusted to thee? Thou knowest that He Himself, when for the first time He addressed thee, with His own lips declared of me, 'When he seeth thee, he will be glad in his heart. Why, then, dost thou conceal the commission God hath entrusted to thee? Even if it were to refer to my death, I should take it upon myself with a cheerful countenance." Moses replied: "As thou thyself dost speak of death, I will acknowledge that God's words to me do concern thy death, but I was afraid to make it known to thee. But look now, thy death is not as that of the other creatures of flesh and blood; and not only is thy death a remarkable one, but see! The ministering angels have come to stand by thee in thy parting hour."

When he spoke of the remarkable death that awaited Aaron, Moses meant to allude to the fact that Aaron, like his sister Miriam and later Moses, was to die not through the Angel of Death, but by a kiss from God. Aaron, however, said: "Oh my brother Moses, why didst not thou make this communication to me in the presence of my mother, my wife, and my children?" Moses did not instantly reply to this question, but tried to speak words of comfort and encouragement to Aaron, saying: "Dost thou not know, my brother, that thou didst forty years ago deserve to meet thy death when thou didst fashion the Golden Calf, but then I stood before the Lord in prayer and exhortation, and saved thee from death. And now I pray that my death were as thine! For when thou diest, I bury thee, but when I shall die, I shall have no brother to bury me. When thou diest, thy sons will inherit thy position, but when I die, strangers will inherit my place." With these and similar words Moses encouraged his brother, until he finally looked forward to his end with equanimity.

Aaron lay down upon the adorned couch, and God received his soul. Moses then left the cave, which immediately vanished, so that none might know or understand how it had happened. When Eleazar saw

Moses return alone, he said to him: "O my teacher, where is my father?" Moses replied: "He has entered Paradise." Then both descended from the mountain into the camp. When the people saw Moses and Eleazar return without Aaron, they were not at all in the mood to lend faith to the communication of Aaron's death. They could not at all credit that a man who had overcome the Angel of Death was now overcome by him. Three opinions were then formed among the people concerning Aaron's absence. Some declared that Moses had killed Aaron because he was jealous of his popularity; some thought Eleazar had killed his father to become his successor as high priest; and there were also some who declared that he had been removed from earth to be translated to heaven. Satan had so incited the people against Moses and Eleazar that they wanted to stone them. Moses hereupon prayed to God, saying: "Deliver me and Eleazar from this unmerited suspicion, and also show to the people Aaron's bier, that they may not believe him to be still alive, for in their boundless admiration for Aaron they may even make a God of him." God then said to the angels: "Lift up on high the bier upon which lies My friend Aaron, so that Israel may know he is dead and may not lay hands upon Moses and Eleazar." The angels did as they were bidden, and Israel then saw Aaron's bier floating in the air, while God before it and the angels behind intoned a funeral song for Aaron. God lamented in the words, "He entereth into peace; they rest in their beds, each one that walketh in his uprightness," whereas the angels said: "The law of truth was in his mouth, and unrighteousness was not found in his lips: he walked with Me in peace and uprightness, and did turn many away from iniquity."

—Louis Ginzberg
Legends of the Jews III

❊❊

The Days of Our Years Are Three Score Years

The days of our years are three score years,
    or, even by reason of strength, fourscore years;
    yet is there pride but travail and vanity
For it is speedily gone and we fly away.

—Psalm 90:10

❊❊

A Herald of Death

When the day of the death of Abraham drew near, the Lord said to Michael, "Arise and go to Abraham and say to him, Thou shalt depart from life!" so that he might set his house in order before he died. And Michael went and came to Abraham and found him sitting before his oxen for ploughing. Abraham, seeing Michael, but not knowing who he was, saluted him and said to him, "Sit down a little while, and I will order a beast to be brought, and we will go to my house, that thou mayest rest with me, for it is toward evening, and arise in the morning and go whithersoever thou wilt." And Abraham called one of his servants, and said to him: "Go and bring me a beast, that the stranger may sit upon it, for he is wearied with his journey." But Michael said, "I abstain from ever sitting upon any fourfooted beast, let us walk therefore, till we reach the house."

On their way to the house they passed a huge tree, and Abraham heard a voice from its branches, singing, "Holy art thou, because thou hast kept the purpose for which thou wast sent." Abraham hid the mystery in his heart, thinking that the stranger did not hear it. Arrived at his house, he ordered the servants to prepare a meal, and while they were busy with their work, he called his son Isaac, and said to him, "Arise and put water in the vessel, that we may wash the feet of the stranger." And he brought it as he was commanded, and Abraham said, "I perceive that in this basin I shall never again wash the feet of any man coming to us as a guest." Hearing this, Isaac began to weep, and Abraham, seeing his son weep, also wept, and Michael, seeing them weep, wept also, and the tear of Michael fell into the water, and became precious stones.

Before sitting down to the table, Michael arose, went out for a moment, as if to ease nature, and ascended to heaven in the twinkling of an eye, and stood before the Lord, and said to Him: "Lord and Master, let Thy power know that I am unable to remind that righteous man of his death, for I have not seen upon the earth a man like him, compassionate, hospitable, righteous, truthful, devout, refraining from every evil deed." Then the Lord said to Michael, "Go down to My friend Abraham, and whatever he may say to thee, that do thou also, and whatever he may eat, eat thou also with him, and I will cast the thought of the death of Abraham into the heart of Isaac, his son, in a dream, and Isaac will relate the dream, and thou shalt interpret it, and he himself will know his end." And Michael said, "Lord, all the heavenly spirits are incorporeal, and neither eat nor drink, and this man has set before me a table with an abundance of all good things earthly and corruptible. Now, Lord, what shall I do?'' The Lord answered him, ''Go down to him and take no thought for this, for when thou sittest down with him, I will send upon thee a devouring spirit, and it will consume out of thy hands and through thy mouth all that is on the table.''

Then Michael went into the house of Abraham, and they ate and drank and were merry. And when the supper was ended, Abraham prayed after his custom, and Michael prayed with him, and each lay down to sleep upon his couch in one room, while Isaac went to his chamber, lest he be troublesome to the guest. About the seventh hour of the night, Isaac woke and came to the door of his father's chamber, crying out and saying, ''Open, father, that I may touch thee before they take thee away from me.'' And Abraham wept together with his son, and when Michael saw them weep, he wept likewise. And Sarah, hearing the weeping, called forth from her bedchamber, saying: ''My lord Abraham, why this weeping? Has the stranger told thee of thy brother's son Lot, that he is dead? or has aught befallen us?'' Michael answered, and said to her, ''Nay, my sister Sarah, it is not as thou sayest, but thy son Isaac, methinks, beheld a dream, and came to us weeping, and we, seeing him, were moved in our hearts and wept.'' Sarah, hearing Michael speak, knew straightway that it was an angel of the Lord, one of the three angels whom they had entertained in their house once before, and therefore she made a sign to Abraham to come out toward the door, to inform him of what she knew. Abraham said: ''Thou hast perceived well, for I, too, when I washed his feet, knew in my heart that they were the feet that I had washed at the oak of Mamre, and that went to save Lot.'' Abraham, returning to his chamber, made Isaac relate his dream, which Michael interpreted to them, saying: ''Thy son Isaac has spoken truth, for thou shalt go and be taken up into the heavens, but thy body shall remain on earth, until seven thousand ages are fulfilled, for then all flesh shall arise. Now, therefore, Abraham, set thy house in order, for thou hast heard what is decreed concerning thee.'' Abraham answered, ''Now I know thou art an angel of the Lord, and wast sent to take my soul, but I will not go with thee, but do thou whatever thou art commanded.'' Michael returned to heaven and told God of Abraham's refusal to obey his summons, and he was again commanded to go down and admonish Abraham not to rebel against God, who had bestowed many blessings upon him, and he reminded him that no one who has come from Adam and Eve can escape death, and that God in His great kindness toward him did not permit the sickle of death to meet him, but sent His chief captain, Michael, to him. "Wherefore, then," he ended "hast thou said to the chief captain, I will not go with thee?" When Michael delivered these exhortations to Abraham, he saw that it was futile to oppose the will of God, and he consented to die, but wished to have one desire of his fulfilled while still alive. He said to Michael: "I beseech thee, lord, if I must depart from my body, I desire to be taken up in my body, that I may see the creatures that the Lord has created in heaven and on earth." Michael went up into heaven, and spake before the Lord concerning Abraham, and the Lord answered Michael, "Go and take up Abraham in the body and show him all things, and whatever he shall say to thee, do to him as to My friend."

—Louis Ginzberg
Legends of the Jews I

✠

Abraham Views Earth and Heaven

The archangel Michael went down, and took Abraham upon a chariot of the cherubim, and lifted him up into the air of heaven, and led him upon the cloud, together with sixty angels, and Abraham ascended upon the chariot over all the earth, and saw all things that are below on the earth, both good and bad. Looking down upon the earth, he saw a man committing adultery with a wedded woman, and turning to Michael he said, "Send fire from heaven to consume them." Straightway there came down fire and consumed them, for God had commanded Michael to do whatsoever Abraham should ask him to do. He looked again, and he saw thieves digging through a house, and Abraham said, "Let wild beasts come out of the desert, and tear them in pieces," and immediately wild beasts came out of the desert and devoured them. Again he looked down, and he saw people preparing to commit murder, and he said, "Let the earth open and swallow them," and, as he spoke, the earth swallowed them alive. Then God spoke to Michael: "Turn away Abraham to his own house and let him not go round the whole earth, because he has no compassion on sinners, but I have compassion on sinners, that they may turn and live and repent of their sins, and be saved."

So Michael turned the chariot, and brought Abraham to the place of judgment of all souls. Here he saw two gates, the one broad and the other narrow, the narrow gate that of the just, which leads to life, they that enter through it go into Paradise. The broad gate is that of sinners, which leads to destruction and eternal punishment. Then Abraham wept, saying, "Woe is me, what shall I do? for I am a man big of body, and how shall I be able to enter by the narrow gate?" Michael answered, and said to Abraham, "Fear not, nor grieve, for thou shalt enter by it unhindered, and all they who are like thee." Abraham, perceiving that a soul was adjudged to be set in the midst, asked Michael the reason for it, and Michael answered, "Because the judge found its sins and its righteousness equal, he neither committed it to judgment nor to be saved." Abraham said to Michael, "Let us pray for this soul, and see whether God will hear us," and when they rose up from their prayer, Michael informed Abraham that the soul was saved by the prayer, and was taken by an angel and carried up to Paradise. Abraham said to Michael, "Let us yet call upon the Lord and supplicate His compassion and entreat His mercy for the souls of the sinners whom I formerly, in my anger, cursed and destroyed, whom the earth devoured, and the wild beasts tore in pieces, and the fire consumed, through my words. Now I know that I have sinned before the Lord our God."

After the joint prayer of the archangel and Abraham, there came a voice from heaven, saying, "Abraham, Abraham, I have hearkened to thy voice and thy prayer, and I forgive thee thy sin, and those whom thou thinkest that I destroyed, I have called up and brought them into life by My exceeding kindness, because for a season I have requited them in judgment, and those whom I destroy living upon earth, I will not requite in death."

When Michael brought Abraham back to his house, they found Sarah dead. Not seeing what had become of Abraham, she was consumed with grief and gave up her soul. Though Michael had fulfilled Abraham's wish, and had shown him all the earth and the judgment and recompense, he still refused to surrender his soul to Michael, and the archangel again ascended to heaven, and said unto the Lord: "Thus speaks Abraham, I will not go with thee, and I refrain from laying my hands on him, because from the beginning he was Thy friend, and he has done all things pleasing in Thy sight. There is no man like him on earth, not even Job, the wondrous man." But when the day of the death of Abraham drew nigh, God commanded Michael to adorn Death with great beauty and send him thus to Abraham, that he might see him with his eyes.

While sitting under the oak of Mamre, Abraham perceived a flashing of light and a smell of sweet odor,and turning around he saw Death coming toward him in great glory and beauty. And Death said unto Abraham: "Think not, Abraham, that this beauty is mine, or that I come thus to every man. Nay, but if any one is righteous like thee, I thus take a crown and come to him, but if he is a sinner, I come in great corruption, and out of their sins I make a crown for my head, and I shake them with great fear, so that they are dismayed." Abraham said to him, "And art thou, indeed, he that is called Death? He answered, and said, "I am the bitter name," but Abraham answered, "I will not go with thee." And Abraham said to Death, "Show us thy corruption." And Death revealed his corruption, showing two heads, the one had the face of a serpent, the other head was like a sword. All the servants of Abraham, looking at the fierce mien of Death, died, but Abraham prayed to the Lord, and he raised them up. As the looks of Death were not able to cause Abraham's soul to depart from him, God removed the soul of Abraham as in a dream, and the archangel Michael took it up into heaven. After great praise and glory had been given to the Lord by the angels who brought Abraham's soul, and after Abraham bowed down to worship, then came the voice of God, saying thus: "Take My friend Abraham into Paradise, where are the tabernacles of My righteous ones and the abodes of My saints Isaac and Jacob in his bosom, where there is no trouble, nor grief, nor sighing, but peace and rejoicing and life unending."

Abraham's activity did not cease with his death, and as he interceded in this world for the sinners, so will he intercede for them in the world to come. On the day of judgment he will sit at the gate of hell, and he will not suffer those who kept the law of circumcision to enter therein.

—Louis Ginzberg
Legends of the Jews I

✳✳

Into Thine Hand I Commit My Spirit

Into thine hand I commit my spirit;
Thou hast redeemed me, O Lord, Thou God of truth.

—Psalm 31:6

✳✳

The Death and Burial of Sarah

While Abraham was engaged in the sacrifice, Satan went to Sarah, and appeared to her in the figure of an old man, very humble and meek, and said to her: "Dost thou not know all that Abraham has done unto thine only son this day? He took Isaac; and built an altar, slaughtered him, and brought him up as a sacrifice. Isaac cried and wept before his father, but he looked not at him, neither did he have compassion upon him." After saying these words to Sarah, Satan went away from her, and she thought him to be an old man from amongst the sons of men who had been with her son. Sarah lifted up her voice, and cried bitterly, saying: "O my son, Isaac, my son, O that I had this day died instead of thee! It grieves me for thee! After that I have reared thee and have brought thee up, my joy is turned into mourning over thee. In my longing for a child, I cried and prayed, till I bore thee at ninety. Now hast thou served this day for the knife and the fire. But I console myself, it being the word of God, and thou didst perform the command of thy God, for who can transgress the word of our God, in whose hands is the soul of every living creature? Thou art just, O Lord our God, for all Thy works are good and righteous, for I also rejoice with the word which Thou didst command, and while mine eye weepeth bitterly, my heart rejoiceth." And Sarah laid her head upon the bosom of one of her handmaids, and she became as still as a stone.

She rose up afterward and went about making inquiries concerning her son, till she came to Hebron, and no one could tell her what had happened to her son. Her servants went to seek him in the house of Shem and Eber, and they could not find him, and they sought throughout the land, and he was not there. And, behold, Satan came to Sarah in the shape of an old man, and said unto her, "I spoke falsely unto thee, for Abraham did not kill his son, and he is not dead," and when she heard the word, her joy was so exceedingly violent that her soul went out through joy.

When Abraham with Isaac returned to Beer-sheba, they sought for Sarah and could not find her, and when they made inquiries concerning her, they were told that she had gone as far as Hebron to seek them. Abraham and Isaac went to her to Hebron, and when they found that she was dead, they cried bitterly over her, and Isaac said: "O my mother, my mother, how hast thou left me, and whither hast thou gone? O whither hast thou gone, and how hast thou left me?"

And Abraham and all his servants wept and mourned over her a great and heavy mourning, even that Abraham did not pray, but spent his time in mourning and weeping over Sarah. And, indeed, he had great reason to mourn his loss, for even in her old age Sarah had retained the beauty of her youth and the innocence of her childhood.

The death of Sarah was a loss not only for Abraham and his family, but for the whole country. So long as she was alive, all went well in the land. After her death confusion ensued. The weeping, lamenting, and wailing over her going hence was universal, and Abraham, instead of receiving consolation, had to offer consolation to others. He spoke to the mourning people, and said: "My children, take not the going hence of Sarah too much to heart. There is one event unto all, to the pious and the impious alike. I pray you now, give me a burying-place with you, not as a gift, but for money."

In these last few words Abraham's unassuming modesty was expressed. God had promised him the whole land, yet when he came to bury his dead, he had to pay for the grave, and it did not enter his heart to cast aspersions upon the ways of God. In all humility he spoke to the people of Hebron, saying, "I am a stranger and a sojourner with you." Therefore spake God to him, and said, " Thou didst bear thyself modestly. As thou livest, I will appoint thee lord and prince over them."

To the people themselves he appeared an angel, and they answered his words, saying: "Thou art a prince of God among us. In the choice of our sepulchres bury thy dead, among the rich if thou wilt, or among the poor if thou wilt."

Abraham first of all gave thanks to God for the friendly feeling shown to him by the children of Heth, and then he continued his negotiations for the Cave of Machpelah. He had long known the peculiar value of this spot. Adam had chosen it as a burial-place for himself. He had feared his body might be used for idolatrous purposes after his death; he therefore designated the Cave of Machpelah as the place of his burial, and in the depths his corpse was laid, so that none might find it. When he interred Eve there, he wanted to dig deeper, because he scented the sweet fragrance of Paradise, near the entrance to which it lay, but a heavenly voice called to him, Enough! Adam himself was buried there by Seth, and until the time of Abraham the place was guarded by angels, who kept a fire burning near it perpetually, so that none dared approach it and bury his dead therein. Now, it happened on the day when Abraham received the angels in his house, and he wanted to slaughter an ox for their entertainment, that the ox ran away, and in his pursuit of him Abraham entered the Cave of Machpelah. There he saw Adam and Eve stretched out upon couches, candles burning at the head of their resting-places, while a sweet scent pervaded the cave.

Therefore Abraham wished to acquire the Cave of Machpelah from the children of Heth, the inhabitants of the city of Jebus. They said to him. "We know that in time to come God will give these lands unto thy seed, and now do thou swear a covenant with us that Israel shall not wrest the city of Jebus from its inhabitants without their consent." Abraham agreed to the condition, and he acquired the field from Ephron, in whose possession it lay.

This happened the very day on which Ephron had been made the chief of the children of Heth, and he had been raised to the position so that Abraham might not have to have dealings with a man of low rank. It was of advantage to Abraham, too, for Ephron at first refused to sell his field, and only the threat of the children of Heth to depose him from his office, unless he fulfilled the desire of Abraham, could induce him to change his disposition.

Dissembling deceitfully, Ephron then offered to give Abraham the field without compensation, but when Abraham insisted upon paying for it, Ephron said: "My lord, hearken unto me. A piece of land worth four hundred shekels of silver, what is that betwixt me and thee?" showing only too well that the money was of the greatest consequence to him. Abraham understood his words, and when he came to pay for the field, he weighed out the sum agreed upon between them in the best current coin. A deed, signed by four witnesses, was drawn up, and the field of Ephron, which was in Machpelah, the field, and the cave which was therein, were made sure unto Abraham and his descendants for all times.

The burial of Sarah then took place, amid great magnificence and the sympathy of all. Shem and his son Eber, Abimelech king of the Philistines, Aner, Eshcol, and Mamre, as well as all the great of the land, followed her bier. A seven days' mourning was kept for her, and all the inhabitants of the land came to condole with Abraham and Isaac.

When Abraham entered the cave to place the body of Sarah within, Adam and Eve refused to remain there, "because," they said, "as it is, we are ashamed in the presence of God on account of the sin we committed, and now we shall be even more ashamed on account of your good deeds." Abraham soothed Adam. He promised to pray to God for him, that the need for shame be removed from him. Adam resumed his place, and Abraham entombed Sarah, and at the same time he carried Eve, resisting, back to her place.

—Louis Ginzberg
Legends of the Jews I

✳✳

The Lord Shall Keep Thee from All Evil

The Lord shall keep thee from all evil;
  He shall keep thy soul.
The Lord shall guard thy going out and thy coming in
  from this time forth and forever.

—Psalm 121:7–8

✳✳

The Death of Jacob

After Jacob had blessed each of his sons separately, he addressed himself to all of them together, saying: "According to my power did I bless you, but in future days a prophet will arise, and this man Moses will bless you, too, and he will continue my blessings where I left off." He added, besides, that the blessing of each tribe should redound to the good of all the other tribes: the tribe of Judah should have a share in the fine wheat of the tribe of Benjamin, and Benjamin should enjoy the goodly barley of Judah. The tribes should be mutually helpful, one to another.

Moreover, he charged them not to be guilty of idolatry in any form or shape and not to let blasphemous speech pass their lips, and he taught them the order of transporting his bier, thus: "Joseph, being king, shall not help to bear it, nor shall Levi, who is destined to carry the Ark of the Shekinah. Judah, Issachar, and Zebulon shall grasp its front end, Reuben, Simon, and Gad its right side, Ephraim, Manasseh, and Benjamin the hindmost end, and Dan, Asher, and Naphtali its left side." And this was the order in which the tribes, bearing each its standard, were to march through the desert, the Shekinah dwelling in the midst of them.

Jacob then spake to Joseph, saying: "And thou, my son Joseph, forgive thy brethren for their trespass against thee, forsake them not, and grieve them not, for the Lord hath put them into thine hands, that thou shouldst protect them all thy days against the Egyptians."

Also he admonished his sons, saying that the Lord would be with them if they walked in His ways, and He would redeem them from the hands of the Egyptians. "I know," he continued, "great suffering will befall your sons and your grandsons in this land, but if you will obey God, and teach your sons to know Him, then He will send you a redeemer, who will bring you forth out of Egypt and lead you into the land of your fathers."

In resignation to the will of God, Jacob awaited his end, and death enveloped him gently. Not the Angel of Death ended his life, but the Shekinah took his soul with a kiss. Beside the three Patriarchs, Abraham, Isaac, and Jacob, only Moses, Aaron, and Miriam breathed their last in this manner, through the kiss of the Shekinah. And these six, together with Benjamin, are the only ones whose corpses are not exposed to the ravages of the worms, and they neither corrupt nor decay.

Thus Jacob departed this world, and entered the world to come, a foretaste of which he had enjoyed here below, like the other two Patriarchs, and none beside among men. In another respect their life in this world resembled their life in the world to come, the evil inclination had no power over them, either here or there, wherein David resembled them.

Joseph ordered his father's body to be placed upon a couch of ivory, covered with gold, studded with gems, and hung with drapery of byssus and purple. Fragrant wine was poured out at its side, and aromatic spices burnt next to it. Heroes of the house of Esau, princes of the family of Ishmael, and the lion Judah, the bravest of his sons, surrounded the sumptuous bier of Jacob. "Come," said Judah to his brethren, "let us plant a high cedar tree at the head of our father's grave, its top shall reach up to the skies, its branches shall shade all the inhabitants of the earth, and its roots shall grow down deep into the earth, unto the abyss. For from him are sprung twelve tribes, and from him will arise kings and rulers, chapters of priests prepared to perform the service of the sacrifices, and companies of Levites ready to sing psalms and play upon sweet instruments."

The sons of Jacob tore their garments and girded their loins with sackcloth, threw themselves upon the ground, and strewed earth upon their heads until the dust rose in a high cloud. And when Asenath, the wife of Joseph, heard the tidings of Jacob's death, she came, and with her came the women of Egypt, to weep and mourn over him. And the men of Egypt that had known Jacob repaired thither, and they mourned day after day, and also many journeyed down into Egypt from Canaan, to take part in the seventy days' mourning made for him.

The Egyptians spake to one another, saying, "Let us lament for the pious man Jacob, because the affliction of the famine was averted from our land on account of his merits," for instead of ravaging the land for forty-two years according to the decree of God, the famine had lasted but two years, and that was due to the virtues of Jacob.

Joseph ordered the physicians to embalm the corpse. This he should have refrained from doing, for it was displeasing to God, who spoke, saying: "Have I not the power to preserve the corpse of this pious man from corruption? Was it not I that spoke the reassuring words, Fear not the worm, O Jacob, thou dead Israel?" Joseph's punishment for this useless precaution was that he was the first of the sons of Jacob to suffer death. The Egyptians, on the other hand, who devoted forty days to embalming the corpse and preparing it for burial, were rewarded for the veneration they showed. Before He destroyed their city, God gave the Ninevites a forty days' respite on account of their king, who was the Pharaoh of Egypt. And for the three score and ten days of mourning that the heathen made for Jacob, they were recompensed at the time of Ahasuerus. During seventy days, from the thirteenth of Nisan, the date of Haman's edict ordering the extermination of the Jews, until the twenty-third of Siwan, when Mordecai recalled it, they were permitted to enjoy absolute power over the Jews.

When all preparations for the burial of Jacob had been completed, Joseph asked permission of Pharaoh to carry the body up into Canaan. But he did not himself go to put his petition before Pharaoh, for he could not well appear before the king in the garb of a mourner, nor was he willing to interrupt his lamentation over his father for even a brief space and stand before Pharaoh and prefer his petition. He requested the family of Pharaoh to intercede for him with the king for the additional reason that he was desirous of enlisting the favor of the king's relations, lest they advise Pharaoh not to fulfil his wish. He acted according to the maxim, "Seek to win over the accuser, that he cause thee no annoyance."

Joseph applied first to the queen's hairdresser, and she influenced the queen to favor him, and then the queen put in a good word for him with the king. At first Pharaoh refused the permission craved by Joseph, who, however, urged him to consider the solemn oath he had given his dying father, to bury him in Canaan. Pharaoh desired him to seek absolution from the oath. But Joseph rejoined, "Then will I apply also for absolution from the oath I gave thee," referring to an incident in his earlier history. The grandees of Egypt had advised Pharaoh against appointing Joseph as viceroy, and they did not recede from this counsel until Joseph, in his conversation with the Egyptian king, proved himself to be master of the seventy languages of the world, the necessary condition to be fulfilled before one could become ruler over Egypt. But the conversation proved something else, that Pharaoh himself was not entitled to Egyptian kingship, because he lacked knowledge of Hebrew. He feared, if the truth became known, Joseph would be raised to his own place, for he knew Hebrew besides all the other tongues. In his anxiety and distress, Pharaoh made Joseph swear an oath never to betray the king's ignorance of Hebrew. Now when Joseph threatened to have himself absolved from this oath as well as the one to his dying father, great terror overwhelmed him, and he speedily granted Joseph permission to go up to Canaan and bury his father there.

Moreover, Pharaoh issued a decree in all parts of the land menacing those with death who would not accompany Joseph and his brethren upon their journey to Canaan with their father's remains, and accordingly the procession that followed the bier of Jacob was made up of the princes and nobles of Egypt as well as the common people. The bier was borne by the sons of Jacob. In obedience to his wish not even their children were allowed to touch it. It was fashioned of pure gold, the border thereof inlaid with onyx stones and bdellium, and the cover was gold woven work joined to the bier with threads that were held together with hooks of onyx stones and bdellium. Joseph placed a large golden crown upon the head of his father, and a golden sceptre he put in his hand, arraying him like a living king.

The funeral cortege was arranged in this order: First came the valiant men of Pharaoh and the valiant men of Joseph, and then the rest of the inhabitants of Egypt. All were girt with swords and clothed in coats of mail, and the trappings of war were upon them. The weepers and mourners walked, crying and lamenting, at some distance from the bier, and the rest of the people went behind it, while Joseph and his household followed together after it, with bare feet and in tears, and Joseph's servants were close to him, each man with his accoutrements and weapons of war. Fifty of Jacob's servants preceded the bier, strewing myrrh upon the road in passing, and all manner of perfumes, so that the sons of Jacob trod upon the aromatic spices as they carried the body forward.

Thus the procession moved on until it reached Canaan. It halted at the threshing-floor of Atad, and there they lamented with a very great and sore lamentation. But the greatest honor conferred upon Jacob was the presence of the Shekinah, who accompanied the cortege.

The Canaanites had no intention at first to take part in the mourning made for Jacob, but when they saw the honors shown him, they joined the procession of the Egyptians, loosing the girdles of their garments as a sign of grief. Also the sons of Esau, Ishmael, and Keturah appeared, though their design in coming was to seize the opportunity and make war upon the sons of Jacob, but when they saw Joseph's crown suspended from the bier, the Edomite and Ishmaelite kings and princes followed his example, and attached theirs to it, too, and it was ornamented with thirty-six crowns.

Nevertheless the conflict was not averted; it broke out in the end between the sons of Jacob and Esau and his followers. When the former were about to lower the body of their father into the Cave of Machpelah, Esau attempted to prevent it, saying that Jacob had used his allotted portion of the tomb for Leah, and the only space left for a grave belonged to himself. For, continued Esau, "though I sold my birthright unto Jacob, I yet have a portion in the tomb as a son of Isaac." The sons of Jacob, however, were well aware of the fact that their father had acquired Esau's share in the Cave, and they even knew that a bill of sale existed, but Esau, assuming properly that the document was left behind in Egypt, denied that any such had ever been made out, and the sons of Jacob sent Naphtali, the fleet runner, back to Egypt to fetch the bill. Meantime, while this altercation was going on between Esau and the others, Hushim the son of Dan arose and inquired in astonishment why they did not proceed with the burial of Jacob, for he was deaf and had not understood the words that had passed between the disputants. When he heard what it was all about, and that the ceremonies were interrupted until Naphtali should return from Egypt with the bill of sale, he exclaimed, with indignation, "My grandfather shall lie here unburied until Naphtali comes back!" and he seized a club and dealt Esau a vigorous blow, so that he died, and his eyes fell out of their sockets and dropped upon Jacob's knees, and Jacob opened his own eyes and smiled. Esau being dead, his brother's burial could proceed without hindrance, and Joseph interred him in the Cave of Machpelah in accordance with his wish.

His other children had left all arrangements connected with the burial of their father's body to their brother Joseph, for they reflected that it was a greater honor for Jacob if a king concerned himself about his remains rather than simple private individuals.

The head of Esau, as he lay slain by the side of Jacob's grave, rolled down into the Cave, and fell into the lap of Isaac, who prayed to God to have mercy upon his son, but his supplications were in vain. God spoke, saying, "As I live, he shall not behold the majesty of the Lord."

—Louis Ginsberg
Legends of the Jews II

❋

A Good Man Leaveth an Inheritance

A good man leaveth an inheritance to his children's children.

—Proverbs 13:22

❋

Rav Sheshet and the Angel

Moed Katan 28a

"In the street like an animal?
You would take me here
among the shops and flies?
How dare you!"
Thus did Sheshet scream defiance
at Death.
"Come home with me!
Let me die in my bed
like a Mensch!"

Was it the cry, or
was it because no one
had said such things
to the Angel before?
Whichever it was,
Death followed Rav Sheshet
to his home
and waited for his family
to gather his last words.

Then,
and only then.
did he dare
to take his soul.

—Danny Siegel
Between Dust and Dance

✳

Blessed Is the Lord

Blessed is the Lord, God of Israel,
From eternity to eternity.
Amen and Amen.

—Psalm 41:14

✳

First You Mourn

Yahrzeit builds the fulfillment of the promise [to think of the deceased often] into the rhythm of their years.

—Carol P. Hausman in
Moment

✳

Consolation

It is a law of nature that however much one may grieve over the death of a dear one, at the end of a year consolation finds its way to the heart of the mourner.

—Louis Ginzberg
Legends of the Jews II

✳

Ten Hard Things

There are ten hard things in the world.

(Bava Batra 10a)

Mountains are hard,
but iron can level them.
Iron is hard,
but flames melt the metals
that make tunnels and mines.
And water, (such a simple thing,)
smothers fire that turns iron to liquid
and people to ash.
Yet water is lifted by cloudpuffs
that hold it well until it bursts with rain,
clouds which, as children,
we thought were soft as pillows
till we rode thunderstorms in planes,
whispering desperate snatches of the *Shema*.
And the *ruach*-wind blows clouds apart,
and wind-of-a-sort, our breath,
is held by our bodies in in-and-out rhythms
that keep us alive.
The body is, indeed, awesomely strong.
But fear breaks the body in flashes,
and wine—
even the cheapest homemade spirits—
dispels the greatest terrors.
Sleep, in turn, dissipates wine
that made us so brave,
and sleep, we know, is a hint of Death.

Death is beyond the Tenth Degree of mighty
and hard, in some other world.
and some say nothing is tougher,
more unbreaking than Death.

And yet,
another yet—
Solomon tells us

(he was wise,
so wise)
Tzedakah is stronger than Death
and the Angel holds no sway
where the heart is open.

—Danny Siegel
Between Dust and Dance

✳✳

The Righteous

The righteous even after their death are called alive.

—Talmud

✳✳

The Shortfalls of Knowledge

Derech Eretz Zuta 1

And suppose I learned
every single ancient Jewish tale
on Death.
Until I knew each eye, each smell,
every blade of the Angel.
And what if I found
a hundred scattered stories
in the more-than-Lifesized pages
of the Talmud
proving this rabbi's victory
and that potter's triumph
over the Killer.
Would this make the darkness
one candlelight brighter?
Would this, then, be a something
in the great endless nothing
waiting for me,
one scared Jew?

Not even the tricks and incantations
  of a Kabbalist
  can help.
Though I am pleased to note
  some few
  squeezed out some extra years,
  and nine, I read,
  entered Paradise alive.

—Danny Siegel
Nine Entered Paradise Alive

❃❃

To Hold with Open Arms

It is a sound convention which requires that a sermon begin with a
text—some verse from Scripture, or from Rabbinic literature, which
summarizes the theme. But it is well to understand that a text is, after
all, only the soul-experience of some man boiled down to the size of an
epigram. At some time in the past a prophet or a saint met God,
wrestled with good or evil, tasted of life and found it bitter or sweet,
contemplated death, and then distilled the adventure into a single line,
for those that would come after him. That is a text.

But it is not only the great, the saints, the prophets, and the heroes
who contemplate God, life, and death. We, too, the plainer folk of the
world, live, love, laugh, and suffer, and by no means always on the
surface. We, too, catch glimpses of eternity and the things that people
do. Not only of Moses, but of us, too, it may be said, as Lowell put it:

Daily with souls that cringe and plot
We Sinais climb and know it not.

There are texts in us, too, in our commonplace experiences, if only
we are wise enough to discern them.

One such experience, a *textual* experience, so to speak, fell to my lot
not so long ago. There was nothing dramatic about its setting nor
unusual in its circumstances. And yet to me it was a moment of
discovery, almost of revelation.

Let me recount it very briefly, as befits a text. After a long illness, I
was permitted for the first time to step out-of-doors. And as I crossed
the threshold sunlight greeted me. This is my experience—all there is to
it. And yet, so long as I live, I shall never forget that moment. It was

mid-January—a time of cold and storm up North, but in Texas, where I happened to be, a season much like our spring. The sky overhead was very blue, very clear, and very, very high. Not, I thought, the *shamayim* heaven, but *shemei shamayim*, a heaven of heavens. A faint wind blew from off the western plains, cool and yet somehow tinged with warmth—like a dry, chilled wine. And everywhere in the firmament above me, in the great vault between the earth and sky, on the pavements, the buildings—the golden glow of the sunlight. It touched me, too, with friendship, with warmth with blessing. And as I basked in its glory there ran through my mind those wonderful words of the prophet about the sun which someday shall rise with healing on its wings.

In that instant I looked about me to see whether anyone else showed on his face the joy, almost the beatitude, I felt. But no, there they walked—men and women and children, in the glory of the golden flood, and so far as I could detect, there was none to give it heed. And then I remembered how often I too, had been indifferent to sunlight, how often, preoccupied with petty and sometimes mean concerns, I had disregarded it. And I said to myself, How precious is the sunlight but alas, how careless of it are men. How precious—how careless. This has been a refrain sounding in me ever since.

It rang in my spirit when I entered my own home again after months of absence; when I heard from a nearby room the excited voices of my children at play; when I looked once more on the dear faces of some of my friends; when I was able for the first time to speak again from my pulpit in the name of our faith and tradition, to join in worship of the God who gives us so much of which we are so careless.

And a resolution crystallized within me. I said to myself that at the very first opportunity I would speak of this. I knew full well that it is a commonplace truth, that there is nothing clever about my private rediscovery of it, nothing ingenious about my way of putting it. But I was not interested in being original or clever or ingenious. I wanted only to remind my listeners, as I was reminded, to spend life wisely, not to squander it.

I wanted to say to the husbands and wives who love one another: "How precious is your lot in that it is one of love. Do not be, even for a moment, casual with your good fortune. Love one another while yet you may."

And to parents: "How precious is the gift of your children. Never, never be too busy for the wonder and miracle of them. They will be grown up soon enough and grown away, too."

We human beings, we frail reeds who are yet, as Pascal said, *thinking* reeds, *feeling* reeds, how precious are our endowments—minds to know, eyes to see, ears to listen, hearts to stir with pity, and to dream of justice and of a perfected world. How often are we indifferent to all these!

And we who are Jews and Americans, heirs of two great traditions, how fortunate our lot in both, and how blind we are to our double good fortune.

This is what struggled in me for utterance—as it struggled in Edna St. Vincent Millay when she cried out:

> O world I cannot hold thee close enough.

I want to urge myself and all others to hold the world tight—to embrace life with all our hearts and all our souls and all our might. For it is precious, ineffably precious, and we are careless, wantonly careless of it.

And yet, when I first resolved to express all this, I knew that it was only a half-truth.

Could I have retained the sunlight no matter how hard I tried? Could I have prevented the sun from setting? Could I have kept even my own eyes from becoming satiated and bored with the glory of the day? That moment had to slip away. And had I tried to hold on to it, what would I have achieved? It would have gone from me in any case. And I would have been left disconsolate, embittered, convinced that I had been cheated.

But it is not only the sunlight that must slip away—our youth goes also, our years, our children, our senses, our lives. This is the nature of things, an inevitability. And the sooner we make our peace with it the better. Did I urge myself a moment ago to hold on? I would have done better, it now begins to appear, to have preached the opposite doctrine of letting go of the doctrine of Socrates who called life a *peisithanatos*, a persuader of death, a teacher of the art of relinquishing. It was a doctrine of Goethe who said: *Entsagen sollst du, sollst entsagen*, Thou shalt renounce. And it was the doctrine of the ancient rabbis who despite their love of life said: He who would die, let him hold on to life.

It is a sound doctrine.

First, because, as we have just seen, it makes peace with inevitability. And the inevitable is something with which everyone should be at peace. Second, because nothing can be more grotesque and more undignified than a futile attempt to hold on.

Let us think of the men and women who cannot grow old gracefully because they cling too hard to a youth that is escaping them; of the parents who cannot let their children go free to live their own lives; of the people who in times of general calamity have only themselves in mind.

What is it that drives people to such unseemly conduct, to such flagrant selfishness, except the attitude which I have just commended—a vigorous holding on to life? Besides, are there not times when one ought to hold life cheap, as something to be lightly surrendered? In defense of one's country, for example, in the service of truth, justice, and mercy, in the advancement of mankind?

This, then, is the great truth of human existence. One must not hold life too precious. One must always be prepared to let it go.

And now we are indeed confused. First we learn that life is a privilege—cling to it! Then we are instructed: Thou shalt renounce!

A paradox, and a self-contradiction! But neither the paradox nor the contradiction are of my making. They are a law written into the scheme of things—that a man must hold his existence dear and cheap at the same time.

Is it not, then, an impossible assignment to which destiny has set us? It does not ask of us that we hold life dear at one moment, and cheap at the next, but that we do both simultaneously. Now I can grasp something in my fist or let my hand lie open. I can clasp it to my breast or hold it at arm's length. I can embrace it, enfolding it in my arms, or let my arms hang loose. But how can I be expected to do both at once?

To which the answer is: With your body, of course not. But with your spirit, why not?

Is one not forever doing paradoxical and mutually contradictory things in his soul?

One wears his mind out in study and yet has more mind with which to study. One gives away his heart in love and yet has more heart to give away. One perishes out of pity for a suffering world and is the stronger therefor.

So, too, it is possible at one and the same time to hold on to life and let it go, provided—well, let me put it this way:

We are involved in a tug-o-war: Here on the left is the necessity to renounce life and all it contains. Here on the right, the yearning to affirm it and its experiences. And between these two is a terrible tension, for they pull in opposite directions.

But suppose that here in the center I introduce a third force, one that lifts upward. My two irreconcilables now swing together, both pulling down against the new element. And the harder they pull, the closer together they come.

God is the third element, that new force that resolves the terrible contradiction, the intolerable tension of life.

And for this purpose it does not especially matter how we conceive God. I have been a great zealot for a mature idea of God. I have urged again and again that we think through our theology, not limping along on a child's notion of God as an old man in the sky. But for my immediate purpose, all of this is irrelevant. What is relevant is this: that so soon as a man believes in God, so soon indeed as he wills to believe in Him, the terrible strain is eased; nay, it disappears, and that for two reasons.

In the first place, because a new and higher purpose is introduced into life, the purpose of doing the will of God, to put it in Jewish terms, of performing the *mitzvot*. This now becomes the reason for our existence. We are soldiers whose commander has stationed us at a post. How we like our assignment whether we feel inclined to cling to it or to let it go, is an irrelevant issue. Our hands are too busy with our duties to be either embracing the world or pushing it away.

That is why it is written: "Make thy will conform to His then His will be thine, and all things will be as thou desirest."

But that, it might be urged, only evades the problem. By concentrating on duty we forget the conflicting drives within ourselves. The truth is, however, that, given God, the problem is solved not only by evasion but directly; that it is solved, curiously enough, by being made more intense. For, given God, everything becomes more precious, more to be loved and clung to, more embraceable; and yet at the same time easier to give up.

Given God, everything becomes more precious.

That sunshine in Dallas was not a chance effect, a lucky accident. It was an effect created by a great Artist, the master Painter of Eternity. And because it came from God's brush it is more valuable even than I had at first conceived.

And the laughter of children, precious in itself, becomes infinitely more precious because the joy of the cosmos is in it.

And the sweetness of our friends' faces is dearer because these are fragments of an infinite sweetness.

All of life is the more treasurable because a great and Holy Spirit is in it.

And yet, it is easier for me to let go.

For these things are not and never have been mine. They belong to the universe and the God who stands behind it. True, I have been privileged to enjoy them for an hour, but they were always a loan due to be recalled.

And I let go of them the more easily because I know that as parts of the divine economy they will not be lost. The sunset, the bird's song, the baby's smile, the thunder of music, the surge of great poetry, the dreams of the heart, and my own being, dear to me as every man's is to him, all these I can well trust to Him who made them. There is poignancy and regret about giving them up, but no anxiety. When they slip from my hands they will pass to hands better, stronger, and wiser than mine.

This then is the insight which came to me as I stood some months ago in a blaze of sunlight: Life is dear, let us then hold it tight while we yet may; but we must hold it loosely also!

And only with God can we ease the intolerable tension of our existence. For only when He is given, can we hold life at once infinitely precious and yet as a thing lightly to be surrendered. Only because of Him is it made possible for us to clasp the world, but with relaxed hands: to embrace it, but with open arms.

—Rabbi Milton Steinberg in
Jewish Reflections on Death

❋❋

My Father's Memorial Day

On my father's memorial day
I went out to see his mates—
All those buried with him in one row,
His life's graduation class.

I already remember most of their names,
Like a parent collecting his little son
From school, all of his friends.

My father still loves me, and I
Love him always, so I don't weep.
But in order to do justice to this place
I have lit a weeping in my eyes

With the help of a nearby grave—
A child's. "Our little Yossy, who was
Four when he died."

—Yehuda Amichai in
Amen

❈

Mothers

The measured flight of doves flying high
Is not so beautiful, neither is it
So near to the above, to heaven so nigh
As the look of mothers who lonely sit

And gaze through the window at night-black skies,
And hear wings hovering over the spot,
Recognise voices, one laughs and one cries,
And one is falling out of its cot.

And they wonder where their household has gone.
They look at the night and cannot realise
That they sit at the window all alone—
Their children laugh and weep in their eyes.

And they know good and just the Lord God is,
He is the ship on the clouds and the scent of the grass,
And those who came out of their wombs are his,
All, wherever they are, in His keeping He has.

Gardens of faith in their old hearts bloom,
That with their sons and daughters all goes right,
And their look as they sit alone in their room,
Is more beautiful than doves in flight.

—Israel Stern in
The Golden Peacock

❈

The Minyan Is a Community

My grandfather gave me a pair of *tefillin* when I became a *Bar Mitzvah*.
For three years I put them on six mornings a week at home, and I

davened. I participated in a minyan in the synagogue only on Sabbath and on festivals.

With each passing year I became more aware of two things about my daily davening: It took less and less time, and whatever good feelings I had had about it when I was thirteen were gone. So I put my *tefillin* away.

I took them out again only when our eldest son began to prepare for his Bar Mitzvah. I taught him how to put on *tefillin*, and I gave him my Bar Mitzvah set. I taught each son in turn, and each received a set of *tefillin*.

I attended a daily minyan when there was a death or when I was present in a synagogue at the right time, but not otherwise. I was content with the various services I conducted and attended.

For months now, I have been going to a traditional minyan most weekday mornings. My reason is the usual one: I'm saying Kaddish. But I do a lot more than say Kaddish during the forty to fifty minutes I spend in a small *bet hamidrash* each morning.

First, I have discovered a new and deeper dimension in the meaning of the word community. Our minyan is a community. There are twelve to twenty of us present on any given morning. Most of us put on *tefillin*. As I do so, I become aware only gradually of the other men, some already seated and quietly davening, others still standing as they competently put on their *tefillin* and say the requisite *berakhot*. I know most of the men by name now. But we do not speak beyond a nod and a good morning, and the presence of the other men is not a distraction to me.

At an unspoken point in time, one of the men goes to the *bima* and begins to chant the morning blessings. I have never quite figured out who decides who will lead the service. If a man has Yahrzeit, everyone seems to know it, and it is assumed he will lead the davening. Otherwise, without any conversation about it we take turns, all of us who wish to do so. Some mornings two men divide the service, but not always. On Monday and Thursday, on *Rosh Hodesh* and on festivals, if the cantor is present he reads from the Torah. If not, one or another of the men takes over. I am not sure how *aliyot* are apportioned to the required number of men when the cantor is not present. I have not kept a box score but I have the feeling that there is equity in the distribution of honors. I know there is no regard for bank account or status.

We are a quiet minyan. We are a competent minyan. No one has to announce pages. We sit, we stand, we turn pages, we sing parts of the service together, other parts we sing quietly, each to his own *nigun*. As we daven, we *shokel* each in his own pattern of body-swaying; some stand still. Our variety of Hebrew pronunciations goes from broad *Pailish* to clipped *Sefaradit* with stops along the way at every major Central and East European center of Jewish life. Rhythm is the hallmark of this communal coming-together—a rhythm of words, a rhythm of body movements, a rhythm of feeling. In some inexplicable way, individuals do their thing; yet the group feeling is intense.

Our minyan is not in a hurry. If I get caught up in a passage or a phrase or a word and I stop to think for half a minute, the minyan hasn't ripped off twenty pages during that time. We start on time, and we end within five minutes of forty minutes later—slow leader, fast leader, it makes little difference. Add five minutes for Torah reading. When we have to say Hallel and Musaf we start ten minutes earlier by prior agreement. No one should ever feel pressed for time.

So at our minyan there is no sense of being rushed. As a result, I have learned a lot about the meanings of many words, phrases, Psalms, passages in the Siddur. I am not alone in expanding my comprehension of the content of the service. From time to time, after services one of the men will comment on something which occurred to him for the first time as he was davening. We all listen whether or not we've known the "new" insight for years. Questions are asked. There are no *klotzkashes*; every question rates a respectful answer, or several answers.

We have a private caterer at our minyan. Charlie voluntarily sets out coffee and cake every morning. Sometimes there's a leftover, something from *Shabbat*, some special rolls someone has brought, a *mandelbrot* baked by someone else's wife. There's always a bottle of schnapps, too, but the "*lehayyim*-drinkers" are few at that time of morning. Mostly it's a cup of coffee, some *schmooz*, "have a good day," perhaps some coins into the *pushke* on the wall—and our minyan's members go out into the world to do its work.

In a normal weekday morning service, there are four opportunities to say the Kaddish. Not once have I felt casual about those moments—not within myself, and not in the feelings coming from the other men, both those saying Kaddish and those sitting and answering "Amen." We say the words quietly. I am completely absorbed in forcing once again to reality and acceptance the fact of my own loss. Yet I hear the other voices. I need to hear them. They support me. They add to my reality for standing and saying those words. I feel for my neighbors, too, and they feel for me. I know it deeply as I stand there.

Once in a while there is jarring note. A man wants to go faster than the rest of us. Without thinking, even without consciousness of what we are doing, the rest of us say the words a bit louder. Within a phrase or two the message has been received and we are in rhythm again, to the last amen.

Occasionally, before it is time to say Kaddish, or after the first Kaddish of the service, a scene may pop into my mind—my forefathers in Yavneh saying that Kaddish d'Rabbanan after a Sanhedrin debate about a matter of *halakhah* we now take for granted; the different accents of Jews in Yemen—or in Kai-Feng-fu—saying the same words; the anxiety in the voices of a minyan in the cellar of a Spanish home in the fourteenth century; my grandfather's minyan in Bialystock when he said Kaddish for his parents; the last minyan in Theresienstadt before we left it forever; the little *shtibl* in Jerusalem where I heard the most fervent Kaddish and said my amen with rare feeling. At those moments, like many Jews, I remember not only for myself and the bitter fact which brings me to the minyan each morning, but I remember for all Jews in all places at all times.

The last Kaddish is said, the *tefillin* and the *tallit* are removed. And in ways I cannot explain, as the effect of causes I do not comprehend, I am ready for my day. I am ready to do what I must do. I am ready to laugh and to enjoy and to fulfill. I am ready for the inevitable reminders of our son's life and death.

Could I be ready without the minyan? I do not know and I do not intend to try to find out. For I do know that those forty to forty-five minutes transform me each day I attend. They clear the way to a day of life.

—Rabbi Eugene J. Lipman in
Jewish Reflections on Death

✳✳

Kaddish for My Father

The Kaddish of the Prayer book is strange to me.
As strange as is God's Name.
So I say Kaddish for you with my poetry,
My heart filled with pain and shame.

I keep speaking to you without any words,
As though you were still here.
I adore your memory. You are to me
All that is good and fair.

My heart is entirely filled with you.
You are the pillar of fire on my road.
I have transplanted you into myself.
I stand where you stood.

> —Ezekiel Brownstone in
> *The Golden Peacock*

❊

Kaddish in Many Places

Thursday was a landmark date for me. It was the fifteenth day of
Shebat, an easy day to remember, for it was the new year of the trees.
Yesterday was the first day in eleven months that I was not required to
recite the Kaddish—to join the row of mourners in remembering their
sacred dead. Yesterday was the beginning of a new year in Israel and of
a new stage in my life. In Israel little saplings were planted on this day.
They will grow into beautiful trees, gracing the landscape of our Holy
Land. In my life many memories were planted during this year that has
now ended. Let me name some of them:

At times during this year I have said Kaddish in some most unusual
places. A few weeks ago, waiting for the plane to Israel in the El Al
terminal, I noticed a family in the corner of the waiting room who were
quite bereft, and whose garments had been torn with the traditional
keriah. I was asked, "Would you like to *daven* Minhah with us?" I
joined them in Minhah, and then, after the service, I asked discreetly
about the family. I learned that they were to fly on the same plane.
They were like the family of our ancestors, Jacob and Joseph, who
pleaded that they not be buried in Egypt, but that their remains be
brought back to the land of their birth. They were bringing back the
remains of a member of their family, born somewhere in Europe, but in
the spiritual sense, born in the land of Israel three thousand years ago.

On the plane, we had another minyan in the morning. The sun was
rising over the Mediterranean, or perhaps we were over the Italian
peninsula, and we read from a small Torah scroll that was going to be
presented by some congregation to Zahal, the Israeli defense forces. We
had no table, so the Torah was held up by two men. A Bar Mitzvah boy
read from the scroll, "*Bo el Pharaoh*"—"Go to Pharaoh and tell him to
let my people go." I was deeply touched by this. The Bar Mitzvah
boy's grandfather had been my teacher in high-school days and taught
me Talmud years ago. It was so symbolic. In the hold of the plane were

the remains of a Jew who had passed on, and above, in the passenger compartment, a vibrant dynamic minyan was reaffirming its continuity and its faith in God.

During the course of this last year I recited Kaddish many times in our own synagogue chapel. Day after day the minyan starts while it is still pitch-dark. It is an experience to come to this *bet hamidrash* and see how a handful of men make up this daily service and keep up the continuum of praise to God. The individual members of the minyan come and go but the minyan continues every single day of the year, every single year of the synagogue's life. It is touching to see how the members encourage each other, how their friendships develop, how concerned they become if one does not show up for a few days. They are truly a *havurah*, a fellowship, and they care for their *haverim*. In recent weeks, a fine woman has joined the minyan. She comes to pray for the well-being of her grown family and to recall the sacred memory of her mother. At first she seemed an outsider; now she is a part of the group.

During the course of the year I recited Kaddish at the *Kotel Maravi,* the Western Wall. There the tears of Israel have been shed since the destruction of the Temple. I felt privileged saying the ancient words there, and I felt that in a sense I was saying them there as my father's representative, since he never had the privilege of being there.

But there were jollier settings in which I said the Kaddish. There was the Hasidic *shtiblach* to which I had been introduced by my friend, Rabbi Abraham Karp. I had been to Meah Shearim many, many times, but I never knew that just a few yards away from the din of the Meah Shearim marketplace there was another din, not of peddlers and housewives debating the price of fish, but of men raising their voices in prayer. I had been to Jerusalem many times. I didn't know about this particular little set of miniature synagogues, these little spiritual diamonds in the rough. What a charming atmosphere pervades them. "Minhah, Minhah, Minhah," was the cry as I walked in, "we need a tenth man for the minyan." I needed them for my Kaddish, and they needed me for their minyan and so we felt connected, these Hasidim and I, even though we had never met before. The service was the service of the Sephardic ritual. I noticed that the prayer books that they used were very, very torn. My book dealer, Mr. Schreiber, was there, and so I said, "Perhaps you ought to get them some new prayer books. Order them for the synagogue, will you please, and inscribe my father's name." I had never been there before, and I do not know when or whether I will be back there again, but meantime something of me and something of my father's memory is there in those books.

Once a week, on Thursdays, the eve of the eve of the Sabbath, the little people of Jerusalem, the humble beggars, come in to that synagogue. With great dignity they receive their offerings. I noticed one beggar giving a bit of charity to another. This is the custom among these people—even the poorest of men has to help others.

One day, after leaving the "Minhah, Minhah, Minhah" setting, I saw people running. They were loading on lorries, small trucks. "Where are you going?" I asked.

"Why it's the *Yahrzeit* of the Or Hahayim," the answer came. The *Or Hahayim* is the famous mystical commentator on the Bible whose works are beloved and revered by both the *Ashkenazic* and *Sephardic* Jewish communities. (I once met a cab driver in Jerusalem who goes up to the grave of the *Or Hahayim* every morning at 4:00 A.M. to light an oil lamp at the grave of this great sage.) The old Yiddish expression has it that if the whole world runs you should run too, so I went to my Hertz car and followed them up to the Mount of Olives. There in one of the oldest burial grounds of Jewish history I came to the grave of the Or Hahayim, where I found the Jews of my little synagogue praying and reciting the words of the Psalms. In one corner there was a Minhah service. A little while later, as twilight came to Jerusalem, which is a glorious experience in itself, as the blue skies turned gradually to purple and finally to black, there was an Ashkenazic service. For the first time in my life I did not worship in an easterly direction, toward Jerusalem, but instead I prayed toward the west, for the Mount of Olives is east of the Temple site. There I could see the massive walls of Herodian stone that have stood as silent witnesses for thousands of years, testifying to the love of the Jewish people for the city of Jerusalem. I was praying for the first time in a westerly direction, for I was on the other side of the wall, but I could see the Jews at the wall in mind from where I stood, and in my mind I could join my prayers to theirs.

On the way home from Jerusalem last summer, I stopped off in London. One morning I went to a small synagogue near my hotel for services and for Kaddish. I noticed that the leader of the service prayed with the tallit draped over his head. The voice sounded vaguely familiar, but it was not until the service was over and he doffed his tallit and turned around that I realized who it was. It was the Chief Rabbi of England, in mourning for his mother, who was leading us that day in the Kaddish. But until the service was over and he turned around I did not know that. It could have been any ordinary Jew leading the prayers or mourning for his parent. The words were the same and the service was the same and the grief was the same no matter who happened to be leading the prayers.

Yes, there were many, many places and many occasions when I said Kaddish during these eleven months. Of all of them, however, this is the one that means the most to me. A week ago I visited the soldiers at *Hadassah* Hospital. Those who are still there are the ones who are most difficult to treat. They have been there since the Yom Kippur War, and as I went from bed to bed shaking hands and mumbling a few inadequate words of encouragement to them I felt so feeble, so helpless, so unable to say what I wanted to to them. Finally, after I had spent some time with them, I broke away from the group and went to the synagogue of the hospital to get some emotional relief. I went in there and sat down to look at the Chagall windows that are so lovely and to be by myself for a few minutes just to think. As I sat studying the windows, I noticed a *mohel*, a circumcisor, come in. I asked him, "When will the *Brith* be?" "In a little while," he replied. Then a modest Sephardic family and their guests came in. Soon they were joined by the proud father, who was one of the soldiers from the ward upstairs, still in his bandages and still in his cast. Then they brought the little child in, and the Brith began.

At the end of the service, they recited the Kaddish. I don't know for whom but I was delighted to join their quorum. As I did, I sensed the whole cycle of life revolving before me. I had said the Kaddish once on a plane carrying a man to his last resting place. Now I was saying it again as a new life entered the Covenant of Abraham. I was reciting Kaddish for my father, surrounded by the majestic beauty of the Chagall windows, but more than the creation by man was the creation of God. I was thinking of my father, who lay many thousands of miles away, but I was in the company of new kinsmen with whose path mine had now crossed. Somehow, I had the feeling that there is a wondrous continuity, a never-ending flow of life, to death and through death, and that therefore, despite all its aches and all its pains, there is great beauty and great meaning in our lives.

I have said Kaddish in many places and with many different people during these eleven months. The Kaddish has brought me into contact with many Jews, and with my father, and with myself. I think that he would be pleased.

—Rabbi Seymour J. Cohen in
Jewish Reflections on Death

✳✳

European Delicacy

Yitzchak took his tea
in Yohrtzeit glasses.
"It reminds me,"
he said,
placing a lump of sugar
between his teeth.

—Danny Siegel
Between Dust and Dance

✻✻

A Star Fell

A star fell and got lost
In the darkness.
It wasn't noticed. Many stars
Stayed shining up in space.

A tear dropped from my soul
For you, just now.
You won't see it. Many, many
Tears keep falling here below.

—Zalman Shneour
trans. A. C. Jacobs in
Anthology of Modern Hebrew Poetry

✻✻

III

YIZKOR: *PRAYER IN MEMORY FOR THE DEAD*

7

××

The Pain and Redemption of Remembrance

"Recalling the deceased during a synagogue service is not merely a convenient form of emotional release, but an act of solemn piety and an expression of profound respect. The *Yizkor* memorial service was instituted so that the Jew may pay homage to his forbears and recall the good life and traditional goals" (Rabbi Maurice Lamm, *The Jewish Way in Death and Mourning*).

Yizkor is for letting the music come back, softly and sweetly. Yizkor is to hush us and to heal us, because we are very tired under the burden which death has brought. Yizkor is to hush us with the quiet strength of prayer. Yizkor is to heal us with the wisdom that death gives urgency to life. Then sit quiet, without bitter tears, and let the silence flow in, bringing more love than grief, more gratitude than rebellion.

—Rabbi Jacob Philip Rudin
"Remembrance"
Religion and Bereavement

Yizkor, Rabbi Lamm informs, may be said for all Jewish dead: parents, grandparents, spouses, children, family, and friends.

The Memorial Service is primarily dedicated to those of our own family who have been called to life eternal; but it also recalls those countless Jews who were murderously cut down because they were Jews. Aspects of the Yizkor service can be traced to the days of the torturing martyrdom suffered by our forefathers in the time of the Crusades. In our own generation these memorial prayers have all too tragically become prayers through which anyone who bears the name Jew

249

can pour out his soul in lamentation for the millions of his fellow Jews who, after foulest torture, met their end in death chambers and organized massacre. Each of us standing in the synagogue can and should passionately exclaim: "In their memory I offer charity and would do good."

> —Rabbi David de Sola Pool
> *The Traditional Prayer Book*

Yizkor is a prayer service that for me as child was cloaked in mystery—a prayer my parents and grandparents offered on Yom Kippur, Day of Atonement; on *Shemini Atzeret-Simchat Torah;* on the last day of Passover; and on the second day of *Shavout*—a prayer they solemnly and tearfully chanted, a prayer I was not permitted to hear.

My sister and I were sent out of the synagogue moments before a *Yizkor* service, first by our grandparents and later our parents. When we were children, we were told to leave with words that frightened me with their urgency; later, when we were older, although not yet teenagers, we were dismissed with a loving glance and a firm touch on our shoulder. In time, we knew to leave without any sign from either our grandparents or our parents.

According to Rabbi Tzvi Rabinowicz, the object of having children whose parents are still alive leave the synagogue during *Yizkor* "may be either to leave the mourners undisturbed during this moving prayer, or to spare those who have not been bereaved any unnecessary grief" (*A Guide to Life*). In any case, Rabbi Lamm adds, "too often this results in an untidy and indecorous general exit that lowers the dignity of the service." For whatever reason my parents might have given, and they gave none (they were following the custom of their parents), my sister and I respected their wishes, and we quietly left the sanctuary during *Yizkor*. And never did I secretly turn to the pages in the prayer book for the memorial service.

There is wisdom to custom, I thought, and perhaps, too, as my father, I was governed by a notion of the ominous significance of knowing the *Yizkor* service before it was my time to know it. Today, my wife and I do not practice this custom. Our children, if they choose to do so, may remain with us when we chant *Kaddish* or the *Yizkor* prayers for the same reason I chose to stand with my wife when she chanted *Kaddish* for her father but before my father died, so she would not be alone with her sorrow. Dr. Mortimer Ostrow writes in *The Bond of Life*, "At a time when life seems so futile and fragile, the process of mourning and the rituals associated with it make us feel that we are not alone, but part of an enduring community." Rabbi Jules Harlow, editor of *The Bond of Life*, argues that "contrary to popular opinion, a person with a living parent may attend yizkor services."

Until my father died, then, I never knew the words of *Yizkor*, but I recognized the pain of memories it caused my parents, who were not immediately approachable when my sister and I rejoined them after the

Yizkor service. If my parents were so moved by the memories evoked by the *Yizkor* prayers, I, too, wanted to be a part of their experience; I wanted to know their memories without knowing their pain. But I could not.

Not being with my parents while they chanted the *Yizkor* prayers meant not being connected to a past of which I wanted so much to be a part, a past that included my father's and my mother's parents, my great-grandparents and my great-great-grandparents, and beyond them to the roots of my history and the roots of the Jewish people. *Yizkor* may have been a painful link but it was a necessary link. In remaining with us during our solem remembrances, our children become a real part of our familial and spiritual past in a way I could only imagine as child.

When it came my time to chant the *Yizkor* prayers for my father, I realized that without my father to chant the prayers for his parents, my prayers would have to serve them as well. And that is when I knew that a Jew prepares all his or her life to chant *Yizkor*, for without it—as without *Kaddish*—our ancestors, immediate and distant, would be spiritually and religiously lost to us. "We exist in memory as in time" (Wolpe).

In every person there is a private shrine of memory and love, and in that sanctuary our loved ones abide. We sense their presence, caress their spirits, and enfold them in our hearts. They talk to us; they tell tales. Thus the pain of separation is soothed by memory, the hurt sustained is healed by love; and we ourselves become purified and ennobled through our sorrow.

—Rabbi Jacob K. Shankman
"Remembrance"
Religion and Bereavement

Perhaps what I learned about *Yizkor* after my father's death that was most remarkable was that complementing the chanting of the prayer itself is the act of giving charity both on behalf of the living and in memory of the dead, the alms-giving an act of remembrance itself: the *Yizkor* service of recalling the dead is "based on the firm belief that the living, by acts of piety and goodness, can redeem the dead. The son can bring honor to the father. The 'merit of the children' can reflect the value of the parents. This merit is achieved, primarily, by living on a high ethical and moral plane, by being responsive to the demands of God and sensitive to the needs of fellowman. The formal expression of this merit is accomplished by prayer to God and by contributions to charity" (Lamm).

Tender memories fill our hearts as we think of whose words, actions, and personalities enriched our lives. This hour we pay humble tribute to thoughts that are ever with us, and to silent reflections that linger ever amidst the toil and turmoil of life. From the thought of them, let us receive that hallowed inspiration that will serve as a beacon as we proceed on our way in life.

—Rabbi David J. Seligson
"Remembrance"
Religion and Bereavement

Rabbi Rabinowicz explains that the *Yizkor* service was probably first introduced into the worship service during the Crusades:

The names of the martyrs who died for the "Sanctification of God's Name" were inscribed in special books known as Memorbuecher (Memorial Books) or Sefer Zikaron (Book of Remembrance), or Sefer Zikronot Neshamot (Memorial Book of the Souls) [*Jewish Encyclopedia*, vol. 8, p. 456]. One of the earliest of these books was begun at Nuremberg in 1296 and served as a model for other communities. The martyrs' names were read during the omer period, on the Sabbath before Pentecost, and on the Sabbath preceding the ninth of Av.

—Rabbi Tzvi Rabinowicz
A Guide to Life

Yizkor was included on Yom Kippur because

. . . when Jews seek redemption from their sins, they seek atonement as well for members of the family who have passed on. "Forgive Thy people, whom thou hast redeemed," says the Bible in Judges, chapter 21. Say the sages: "Forgive Thy people," which refers to the living; "Whom Thou hast redeemed," refers to the dead. The living can redeem the dead. Atonement must be sought for both. One scholar even suggests that the term Yom Ha'Kippurim, the technical name for the Day of Atonement, is written in the plural, ' 'atonements," because on that day the Jew must seek atonement for both those who are present and those who sleep in the dust.

—Rabbi Maurice Lamm
The Jewish Way in Death and Mourning

Later, the *Yizkor* service was added to the service on *Shemini Atzeret-Simchat Torah*, Passover, and *Shavuot*, when charity is given on behalf of the living and in memory of the dead (Rabinowicz). "It is a mitzvah to recite yizkor," writes Rabbi Maslin in *Gates of Prayer*, "and to devote a part of our festival prayers to the memories of the loved ones whose names we recall." On these three festivals, the reading of the law (Deuteronomy 14:22—16:17) includes the verse:

Three times a year—on the Feast of Unleavened Bread, on the Feast of Weeks, and on the Feast of Booths—all your males shall appear before the Lord your

God in the place that He will choose. They shall not appear before the Lord empty-handed, but each with his own gift, according to the blessing that the Lord your God has bestowed upon you.

—Deuteronomy 16:16–17

There are two distinct prayers that are traditionally referred to as hazkarat neshamot, recalling the dead. First is the malei rachamin, recited by the rabbi or cantor publicly at funeral and unveiling services, at holiday yizkor services, after the Torah readings on Monday and Thursday mornings, and on Saturday afternoons for yahrzeit. The second hazkarat neshamot prayer refers to the synagogue yizkor service. This is designed to be read by the individual congregant, silently on Yom Kippur and the three pilgrim festivals . . .

It is an ancient custom, on the four holidays when yizkor is recited, to kindle yahrzeit candles for the departed. It is best that the lights be flaming wicks, as the flame and candle symbolize the relation of the body and the soul.

—Rabbi Maurice Lamm
The Jewish Way in Death and Mourning

We attempt to help souls rise up after a death. To facilitate the ascent of the soul of a close relative, a neshamah, or soul light, is kindled on the anniversary (Yahrzeit) of the death, and also on the Day of Atonement, when even souls of the departed are judged anew and yizkor, the Prayer for Remembrance, is said. The Kaddish said during the period of mourning is a parallel means of evaluating the soul, through words rather than lights. The actual words are "raise up" and exalt God, but in doing so on behalf of the dead who can no longer speak for himself, the soul itself is raised. . . .

The "flame" of the Yahrzeit literally stands for the life and soul of the departed, and whole act of kindling is an image of the Soul ascending and returning to Her source.

—Freema Gottlieb
The Lamp of God

Rabbi Lamm reminds us:

Despite the common practice, yizkor should be recited beginning with the very first holiday after death. There is widespread belief that Yizkor may not be recited during the first year. This is an unfounded belief, which may well be discarded. Precisely because yizkor is a redemptive prayer for the dead is reason enough for it to be recited during the first year, when the soul is said to be judged. There is an no legitimate religious reason to delay it.

—Rabbi Maurice Lamm
The Jewish Way in Death and Mourning

And so *Yizkor* came for me on Yom Kippur 1989. In one hand I held our synagogue's *Book of Remembrance*, open to the page on which was written my father's name, and in my other hand, *Gates of Repentance: The New Union Prayerbook for the Days of Awe*, published by the Reform Movement's Central Conference of American Rabbis, open to the Memorial Service.

"Our days are like the grass," I read. "We shoot up like flowers that fade and die as the chill wind passes over them, yet Your love for those who revere You is everlasting. Lord, Your righteousness extends to all generations."

After the reading of Psalms 63, 90, and 121, there was time for silent meditation before the reading of Psalm 23. With Jo at my side and our children on both sides of us, I closed the prayer book and stared at my father's name in the *Book of Remembrance*. I think the only words my mind spoke were my father's names; "Milton Kay" was my first silent *Yizkor* meditation: "The Lord is my shepherd, I shall not want . . . May God remember the soul of my beloved father."

'He will swallow up death for ever. / And the Lord God will wipe away tears / From off all faces. . . " (Isaiah 25:8).

※

Readings

❋❋❋❋❋❋❋❋❋❋❋❋❋

Thou Shalt Be Missed

Thou shalt be missed because thy seat will be empty.

—1 Samuel 20:18

❋❋

A New Dress

Today for the first time
after seven long years
I put on
a new dress.

But it's too short for my grief,
too narrow for my sorrow,
and each white-glass button
like a tear
flows down the folds
heavy as a stone.

—Ruth Whitman in
An Anthology of Modern Yiddish Poetry

❋❋

I Am Sad, God

I am sad, God,
After the passing of years.
I encounter a day,
And I can find nothing
With which it pairs.

It is short,
Broken in two,
And it will not move towards the evening.
And there is no one here, no one who
Will watch over the rare minutes,

That they should not fly away like the wind.
A friend passes by.
Does he come? Does he come?
He does not come. He only passes by.
He is bewildered, and dumb.
I lift my arms, God, to you.
As I never lifted my arms before.
Your light dazzles my eyes.
I hear the rustle at my door.

I stand at the door, and I pray—
For what do I pray? For what do I need to pray?
I am ill of being a poet,
Free me from the Master of poets.

I am sad, God.
I say it, even if another poet
Said these words before.
The span of my tread shortens, more and more.

Therefore I would reach, before it is too late,
Your Holy Hill, your Holy Gate,
The place of all places, and there I will remain,
In the shelter of your wings.
Your shelter will shelter my unsheltered word.
And I will rest in the rest of your Mountain.

> —Halper Leivick in
> *The Golden Peacock*

Joseph

All this time in the desert Israel carried two shrines with them, the one the coffin containing the bones of the dead man Joseph, the other the Ark containing the covenant of the Living God. The wayfarers who saw the two receptacles wondered, and they would ask, "How doth the ark of the dead come next to the ark of the Ever-living?" The answer was. "The dead man enshrined in the one fulfilled the commandments enshrined in the other. In the latter it is written, I am the Lord thy God, and he said, Am I in the place of God? Here it is written, Thou shalt have no other gods before My face, and he said, I fear God. Here it is written, Thou shalt not take the name of the Lord thy God in vain, and therefore he did not swear by God, but said, By the life of Pharaoh. Here it is written, Remember the Sabbath day, and he said to the overseer of his palace on Friday, Slay and make ready, meaning for the Sabbath. Here it is written, Honor thy father and thy mother, and he said, when his father desired to send him to his brethren, Here am I, although he knew it was perilous for him to go. Here it is written, Thou shalt not kill, and he refrained from murdering Potiphar when Potiphar's wife urged him to do it. Here it is written. Thou shalt not commit adultery, and he scorned the adulterous proposals of Potiphar's wife. Here it is written, Thou shalt not steal, and he stole nothing from Pharaoh, but gathered up all the money and brought it unto Pharaoh's house. Here it is written, Thou shalt not bear false witness against thy neighbor, and he told his father nothing of what his brethren had done to him, though what he might have told was the truth. Here it is written, Thou shalt not covet, and he did not covet Potiphar's wife."

On their arrival in the Holy Land, the Israelites buried the bones of Joseph in Shechem, for God spake to the tribes, saying, "From Shechem did ye steal him, and unto Shechem shall ye return him."

God, who is so solicitous about the dead bodies of the pious, is even more solicitous about their souls, which stand before Him like angels, and do their service ministering unto Him.

—Louis Ginzberg
Legends of the Jews II

✳✳

A Tree Is Best Measured . . .

The closing chapter of Carl Sandburg's monumental work on Abraham Lincoln is entitled, "A tree is best measured when it is down." Here

Mr. Sandburg tells of the reaction in the United States and throughout the world to Mr. Lincoln's assassination. Not everyone spoke in the prophetic spirit of Edwin Stanton, who said, "Now he belongs to the ages." Some could not forget their harsh and cruel feelings toward the man who was swiftly destined to become America's greatest hero. But, for the most part, the reaction of the world was one of shock, horror, and uncontrollable grief.

"A tree is best measured when it is down" became a familiar proverb repeated in sermons, eulogies and editorials throughout the land. People no longer thought of Lincoln's unpolished manner, his political attitudes, his simple, undenominational faith, and his behavior in the conduct of the war. While he had held his high position in life, they saw his human failings; but now, as he lay before them in death, they saw his great human virtues. They were beginning to see the complete man.

This is what we all do when a beloved one is taken from us; we see and understand him only when, like the tree, he is down. The faults we found difficult to live with, the failings we learned to overlook, the shortcomings which were part of his character, are forgotten; we see and we remember only the good. Let us thank God that He made us so, for had He not, memory might be unbearable. "De mortuis nil nisi bonum," said Plutarch, and we say it too: "concerning the dead, nothing but good."

Our religion enjoins us to remember our departed loved ones, to think of them in life's sacred moments, as they were when they were engaged in prayer, celebrating joy, or in time of trouble. Long after all else is forgotten by the indifferent and neglectful Jew, two words of our religious vocabulary remain vivid: Kaddish and Yizkor. But there are too many for whom this aspect constitutes the whole of Judaism. Though they deny themselves the joys and serenity and wisdom that they might draw from our ancient faith, they yet find much to cling to in its consolations.

As we read the simple but moving memorial service which has been designed for the most sacred hour of our holiest day, our departed will spring before our mind's eye for a little while and we shall see the qualities for which we have come to idealize them: the mother's sacrificial love; the father's protective strength; the sister's or brother's sweet companionship; the consecrated love of the husband or wife; the child's unspoiled devotion; the friend's constancy. We see only the full measure of the good as we see a tree when it is down; what the mind's eye sees, the heart will enshrine.

How wonderful memory is: it preserves in glowing colors the

recollections we cherish; it obscures those experiences we would rather forget, and by its magic, it preserves our loved one as wholly good and altogether perfect.

Memory is a good thing. But there are none so tragic as those who wear the mantle of grief as if it were a coat of mail of which they cannot divest themselves, a coat of mail which is imprisoning from within and impenetrable from without. There are none so sad as the widowed, the orphaned, and the bereft to whom the urgencies of life and the passage of time can bring no consolation. It is not easy to measure the grief of another or to know how much a heart is broken. None of us is a stranger to sorrow, and we all know that there is no simple rule by which we can determine and weigh the amount of grief another should feel; yet, there are some for whom grief and tragedy become the all-absorbing concerns of life. Indeed, for such people, the sense of loss is so profound that even the image of their loved one is often obliterated because of preoccupation with the sorrow they bear in their hearts.

The inevitable effect of such preoccupation with sorrow is a withdrawal from life itself. Such people soon come to believe that no one can understand their heartache, and it is then but a short step to the conviction that theirs is a special kind of desolation. In extreme cases, their withdrawal from life is complete. They no longer want to be with the friends of a lifetime. The interests that absorbed them in a happier day begin to pall, their pursuits no longer have meaning, and they become like lost souls lurking in the shadows. This is tragic. Too often there is a deeper error that grows in the minds of those whose suffering is so profound: they think it is pious to suffer, that God ordains such self-rejection and self-hurt. But it is not so. God does not want to break our hearts—he gives us memory to make them whole again.

Psychologists tell us that much of our grief is bound up with feelings of guilt because we did not give more of ourselves to our loved ones during their lifetime. We feel guilty because there was unfinished business between us; because we did not deliver all the tokens of love that were due them; because we were more concerned with providing security for our loved ones than with giving ourselves to one another; because we were in search of a place among our friends and too little concerned with our place in the hearts of our loved ones. Our endless reasons for feeling guilty can be real enough, but very often they are meaningless.

The great truth which we must learn not only with our minds but with our hearts is that God intended life to go on; that our being here, even if bereft of our loved ones, has purpose and is part of a Divine plan.

Though we cannot comprehend its vastness, we can fulfill the tasks to which God assigns us.

Since nature abhors a vacuum, we must also learn that life is not fully realized as long as the places our loved ones occupied are left vacant. The good they did, the kindness they showed, the charities they sustained, the values they supported, we, the living, must now carry on. Beyond this life we sense that there exists an immortality of the soul; we shall have to wait our time to learn what lies beyond. But there is an immortality we do know—that is, the living memorial of good deeds by which we perpetuate the lives of those who inspire them in us. There is no better way to lighten the heart's burden of grief, or to keep the memory of our loved ones always fresh.

On this day, when we give thought to our departed, and whenever we contemplate the mystery and wonder of life, let us be thankful that when God gave us a fragment of His omniscience, He withheld for Himself the secret of life and death. For had He shared it with us, it would be too much for us to bear. It is far easier for us to live with this mystery than to attempt to penetrate it. Let us thank God for memory, for memory makes it possible for us to lick the sweet spoon of life again and again. More than in any other living experience, in a time of death we must depend on faith and trust. In unison with the poet whose song of praise we sing to the glory of God in the Adon Olam, we must say, "Into thy hand I commend my spirit, both when I sleep and when I wake, and with my spirit my body too; God is with me; I shall not fear."

—Rabbi Nathan A. Perilman in
Religion and Bereavement

✳✳

My Father

I have changed into my father's clothes,
Grown like him beard and earlocks.
I am now an old Jew.

I have gone into my room,
And by the light of a candle
Sit studying Mishna.

Before dawn I go to the Beth Medrash,

To say Psalms for my pious father,
As he said Psalms for his pious father.

The Jews in my father's Synagogue
Call me to the Reading of the Law,
As is right for an old Jew.

When the winter nights
Get into my old bones,
I sit with them by the stove,
Speaking words of Torah.

I sit waiting for letters from my children.
And each Friday, before the Sabbath begins,
I write letters to each of them.

I have changed into my father's clothes,
Grown like him beard and earlocks.
I am now an old Jew.

—Ezekiel Brownstone in
The Golden Peacock

꘎꘎

Preludes to Kaddish

To My Father

You gathered incredible strength
in order to die
to seem calm and fully conscious
without complaint, without trembling
without a cry
so that I would not be afraid

Your wary hand
slowly grew cold in mine
and guided me carefully
beyond into the house of death
so I might come to know it

Thus in the past you used to take my hand
and guide me through the world
and show me life
so I would not fear

I will follow after you
confident as a child
toward the silent country
where you went first
so I would not feel a stranger there

And I will not be afraid.

                              —Blaga Dmitrova in
                                Kol Haneshamah

                    ❈❈

The Death of My Father

The anniversary of the death of a certain Shlomo ben Nissel falls on the
eighteenth day of the month of Shebat. He was my father, the day is
tomorrow; and this year, as every year since the event, I do not know
how to link myself to it.

Yet, in the Shulhan Aruk, the great book of precepts by Rabbi Joseph
Karo, the astonishing visionary-lawmaker of the sixteenth century,
precise, rigorous rules on the subject do exist. I could and should simply
conform to them. Obey tradition. Follow in the footsteps. Do what
everyone does on such a day: Go to the synagogue three times, officiate
at the service, study a chapter of Mishnah, say the orphan's Kaddish,
and in the presence of the living community of Israel, proclaim the
holiness of God as well as his greatness. For his ways are tortuous but
just, his grace heavy to bear but indispensable, here on earth and
beyond, today and forever. May his will be done. Amen.

This is undoubtedly what I would do had my father died of old age,
of sickness, or even of despair. But such is not the case. His death did
not even belong to him. I do not know to what cause to attribute it, in
what book to inscribe it. No link between it and the life he had led. His
death, lost among all the rest, had nothing to do with the person he had
been. It could just as easily have brushed him in passing and spared him.
It took him inadvertently, absentmindedly. By mistake. Without
knowing that it was he; he was robbed of his death.

Stretched out on a plank of wood amid a multitude of blood-covered
corpses, fear frozen in his eyes, a mask of suffering on the bearded,
stricken mask that was his face, my father gave back his soul at
Buchenwald. A soul useless in that place and one he seemed to want to
give back. But he gave it up, not to the God of his fathers, but rather

to the impostor, cruel and insatiable, to the enemy God. They had killed his God, they had exchanged him for another. How, then, could I enter the sanctuary of the synagogue tomorrow and lose myself in the sacred repetition of the ritual without lying to myself, without lying to him? How could I act or think like everyone else, pretend that the death of my father holds a meaning calling for grief or indignation?

Perhaps, after all, I should go to the synagogue to praise the God of dead children, if only to provoke him by my own submission.

Tomorrow is the anniversary of the death of my father, and I am seeking a new law that prescribes for me what vows to make and no longer to make, what words to say and no longer to say.

In truth, I would know what to do had my father, while alive, been deeply pious, possessed by fervor or anguish of a religious nature. I then would say: It is my duty to commemorate this date according to Jewish law and custom, for such was his wish.

But though he observed tradition, my father was in no way fanatic. On the contrary, he preached an open spirit toward the world. He was a man of his time. He refused to sacrifice the present to an unforeseeable future, whatever it might be. He enjoyed simple everyday pleasures and did not consider his body an enemy. He rarely came home in the evening without bringing us special fruits and candies. Curious and tolerant, he frequented Hasidic circles because he admired their songs and stories, but refused to cloister his mind, as they did, within any given system.

My mother seemed more devout than he. It was she who brought me to heder to make me a good Jew, loving only the wisdom and truth to be drawn from the Torah. And it was she who sent me as often as possible to the Rebbe of Wizsnitz to ask his blessing or simply to expose me to his radiance.

My father's ambition was to make a man of me rather than a saint. "Your duty is to fight solitude, not to cultivate or glorify it," he used to tell me. And he would add: "God, perhaps, has need of saints; as for men, they can do without them."

He could be found more often in government offices than in the synagogue—and, sometimes, in periods of danger, even more often than at home. Every misfortune that befell our community involved him directly. There was always an impoverished, sick man who had to be sent in an emergency to a clinic in Kolozsvar or Budapest; an unfortunate shopkeeper who had to be bailed out of prison; a desperate refugee who had to be saved. Many survivors of the Polish ghettos owed their lives to him. Furnished with money and forged papers, thanks to him and his friends, they were able to flee the country for Rumania and from there to the United States or Palestine. His activities cost him three months in a Hungarian prison cell. Once released, he did not utter a word of the tortures he had undergone. On the very day of his release, he took up where he had left off.

My mother taught me love of God. As for my father, he scarcely spoke to me about the laws governing the relations between man and his creator. In our conversations, the Kaddish was never mentioned. Not even in camp. Especially not in camp.

So I do not know what he would have hoped to see me do tomorrow, the anniversary of his death. If only, in his lifetime, he had been a man intoxicated with eternity and redemption.

But that is not the problem. Even if Shlomo ben Nissel had been a faithful servant of the fierce God of Abraham, a just man, of demanding and immaculate soul, immune against weakness and doubt, even then I would not know how to interpret his death.

For I am ignorant of the essentials: what he felt, what he believed, in that final moment of his hopeless struggle, when his very being was already fading, already withdrawing toward that place where the dead are no longer tormented, where they are permitted at last to rest in peace, or in nothingness—what difference does it make?

His face swollen, frightful, bloodless, he agonized in silence. His cracked lips moved imperceptibly. I caught the sounds, but not the words of his incoherent memory. No doubt, he was carrying out his duty as father by transmitting his last wishes to me, perhaps he was also entrusting me with his final views on history, knowledge, the world's misery, his life, mine. I shall never know. I shall never know if he had the name of the Eternal on his lips to praise him—in spite of everything—or, on the contrary, because of everything, to free himself from him.

Through puffy, half-closed eyelids, he looked at me, and at times, I thought, with pity. He was leaving and it pained him to leave me behind, alone, helpless, in a world he had hoped would be different for me, for himself, for all men like him and me.

At other times, my memory rejects this image and goes its own way. I think I recognize the shadow of a smile on his lips: the restrained joy of a father who is leaving with the hope that his son, at least, will remain alive one more minute, one more day, one more week, that perhaps his son will see the liberating angel, the messenger of peace. The certitude of a father that his son will survive him.

In reality, however, I do not hesitate to believe that the truth could be entirely different. In dying, my father looked at me, and in his eyes where night was gathering, there was nothing but animal terror, the demented terror of one who, because he wished to understand too much, no longer understands anything. His gaze fixed on me, empty of meaning. I do not even know if he saw me, if it was me he saw. Perhaps he mistook me for someone else, perhaps even for the exterminating angel. I know nothing about it because it is impossible to grasp what the eyes of the dying see or do not see, to interpret the death rattle of their last breath.

I know only that that day the orphan I became did not respect tradition: I did not say Kaddish. First, because no one there would have heard and responded "Amen." Also because I did not yet know that beautiful and solemn prayer. And because I felt empty, barren: a useless object, a thing without imagination. Besides, there was nothing more to say, nothing more to hope for. To say Kaddish in that stifling barracks, in the very heart of the kingdom of death, would have been the worst of blasphemies. And I lacked even the strength to blaspheme.

Will I find the strength tomorrow? Whatever the answer, it will be wrong, at best incomplete. Nothing to do with the death of my father.

The impact of the Holocaust on believers as well as unbelievers, on Jews as well as Christians, has not yet been evaluated. Not deeply, not enough. That is no surprise. Those who lived through it, lack objectivity: They will always take the side of man confronted with the Absolute. As for the scholars and philosophers of every genre who have had the opportunity to observe the tragedy, they will—if they are capable of sincerity and humility—withdraw without daring to enter into the heart of the matter; and if they are not, well, who cares about their grandiloquent conclusions? Auschwitz, by definition, is beyond their vocabulary.

The survivors, more realistic if not more honest, are aware of the fact that God's presence at Treblinka or Maidanek—or, for that matter, his absence—poses a problem which will remain forever insoluble.

I once knew a deeply religious man who, on the Day of Atonement, in despair, took heaven to task, crying out like a wounded beast, "What do you want from me, God? What have I done to you? I want to serve you and crown you ruler of the universe, but you prevent me. I want to sing of your mercy, and you ridicule me. I want to place my faith in you, dedicate my thought to you, and you do not let me. Why? Why?"

I also knew a freethinker who, one evening, after a selection, suddenly began to pray, sobbing like a whipped child. He beat his breast, became a martyr. He had need of support, and even more, of certitude: If he suffered, it was because he had sinned; if he endured torment, it was because he had deserved it.

Loss of faith for some equaled discovery of God for others. Both answered to the same need to take a stand, the same impulse to rebel. In both cases, it was an accusation. Perhaps someday someone will explain how, on the level of man, Auschwitz was possible; but on the level of God, it will forever remain the most disturbing of mysteries.

Many years have passed since I saw my father die. I have grown up, and the candles I light several times a year in memory of departed members of my family have become more and more numerous. I should have acquired the habit, but I cannot. And each time the eighteenth day of the month of Shebat approaches, I am overcome by desolation and futility: I still do not know how to commemorate the death of my father, Shlomo ben Nissel, a death which took him as if by mistake.

Yes, a voice tells me that in reality it should suffice, as in previous years, to follow the trodden path: to study a chapter of Mishnah and to say Kaddish once again, that beautiful and moving prayer dedicated to the departed, yet in which death itself figures not at all. Why not yield? It would be in keeping with the custom of countless generations of sages and orphans. By studying the sacred texts, we offer the dead continuity if not peace. It was thus that my father commemorated the death of his father.

But that would be easy. The Holocaust defies reference analogy. Between the death of my father and that of his, no comparison is possible. It would be inadequate, indeed unjust, to imitate my father. I should have to invent other prayers, other acts. And I am afraid of not being capable or worthy.

All things considered, I think that tomorrow I shall go to the synagogue after all. I will light the candles, I will say Kaddish, and it will be for me a further proof of my impotence.

—Elie Wiesel in
Jewish Reflections on Death

✳✳

Meditations on Visits to the Cemetery

"Though I walk through the valley of the shadow of death, I fear no evil, for Thou art with me, Thy rod and Thy staff they sustain me."

Deep within our being hast Thou planted the longing for Thee, the desire to draw nigh unto Thee. Amidst all the vicissitudes of life we may find Thee; for Thou art nigh unto those who call on Thee in truth.

The whole world is Thy temple, and everywhere we see the wonders and signs of Thine all-sustaining Providence. But here in this gathering place of those who pass through the vale of death, consecrated by the tears of dear ones they left behind, I feel more vividly than in any other spot how near Thou art to the humble and contrite heart. In this restful habitation of the dead, a peace, as if descending from another world, enfolds the soul and lifts it to the contemplation of Thy mercy and Thy grace. The unrest of the world is far away and shut out; the voice of passion and conflict is hushed. The more distinctly do we hear and heed the inner voice, which reminds us that we are only pilgrims and sojourners here and that this earth is only the forecourt of Eternity. O that this faith may ever sustain us in our trials, make us humble and grateful in prosperity, confident and hopeful in adversity. May it teach us to employ our experiences to purify our souls, to strengthen all that is good within us and keep us from all that is evil, so that, when our time comes, we may be gathered in peace to our own resting places. Amen.

—Rabbi Israel Goldstein
Mourners' Devotions

❈❈

Meditations and Prayers at the Grave

At the Grave of a Father

Peace be to thy spirit, dear father! Well do I know, that safely thou dwellest under the shadow of God. And yet, to think that thou no more art with me on earth, grieves the heart and saddens the thought. Thou hast so lovingly cared for me, Thou hast so long supported me, hast watched over me, and, from the first, awakened my mind and tried to improve my capacities.

I have come to the place where the earthly part of thee has been laid to rest, and at thy grave I pray unto Him, who has revealed Himself to us as a Father, that He grant me the strength and the will to emulate the good example set by thee, that I may practice the good thou hast taught me, and lead a pure and virtuous life, so that, when my time shall come to enter eternity, I may be worthy to be called thy child. The glory of God be upon thee, and His peace surround thee. Amen.

At the Grave of a Mother

Almighty Father! The thought of my dear mother, whom Thou hast called to her everlasting home, brings to my mind the many blessings which Thou didst vouchsafe to me through her; for through her didst Thou bless me with Thy choicest bounties, the sweet joys of home. From her lips was I first taught of Thine unseen presence, while her life, by her affection and self-denial, made me feel Thine own love, O God.

May I ever cherish the memory of her loving care among the dearest and the holiest treasures of my life. By her sweet example she strove to lead me in Thy ways.

O help me to honor her precepts still, though her lips are closed forever. May her grave be like a sanctuary, to draw me nearer to Thee. May it teach me the urgency of duty to the living, especially to those on whom I am dependent, and who are dependent on me.

May her love and faithfulness that guarded and guided my childhood, be forever written upon the tablet of my heart and set up as a memorial before my eyes, that I may ever find grace and favor in the eyes of God and of man.

—Rabbi Israel Goldstein
Mourners' Devotions

✳

God, You Are My God

A psalm of David, when he was in the Wilderness of Judah.

> God, You are my God;
>   I search for You,
>   my soul thirsts for You,
>   my body yearns for You,
>   as a parched and thirsty land that has no water.
> I shall behold You in the sanctuary,
>   and see Your might and glory,
> Truly Your faithfulness is better than life;
>   my lips declare Your praise.
> I bless You all my life;
>   I lift up my hands, invoking Your name.

I am sated as with a rich feast,
   I sing praises with joyful lips
   when I call You to mind upon my bed,
   when I think of You in the watches of the night;
   for You are my help,
   and in the shadow of Your wings
   I shout for joy.
My soul is attached to You;
   Your right hand supports me.

May those who seek to destroy my life
   enter the depths of the earth.
May they be gutted by the sword;
   may they be prey to jackals.
But the king shall rejoice in God;
   all who swear by Him shall exult,
   when the mouth of liars is stopped.

—Psalm 63

✴

O Lord, You Have Been Our Refuge in Every Generation

A prayer of Moses, the man of God.

O Lord, You have been our refuge in every generation.
Before the mountains came into being,
   before You brought forth the earth and the world,
   from eternity to eternity You are God.

You return man to dust,
   You decreed, "Return you mortals!"
For in Your sight a thousand years
   are like yesterday that has past,
   like a watch of the night.
You engulf men in sleep;
   at daybreak they are like grass that renews itself;
   at daybreak it flourishes anew;
   by dusk it withers and dries up.
So we are consumed by Your anger,
   terror-struck by Your fury.
You have set our iniquities before You,
   our hidden sins in the light of Your face.

All our days pass away in Your wrath;
  we spend our years like a sigh.
The span of our life is seventy years.
  or, given the strength, eighty years;
  but the best of them are trouble and sorrow.
They pass by speedily, and we are in darkness.
Who can know Your furious anger?
Your wrath matches the fear of You.
Teach us to count our days rightly,
  that we may obtain a wise heart.

Turn, O Lord!
How long?
Show mercy to Your servants.
Satisfy us at daybreak with Your steadfast love
  that we may sing for joy all our days.
Give us joy for as long as You have afflicted us,
  for the years we have suffered misfortune.
Let Your deeds be seen by Your servants,
  Your glory by their children.
May the favor of the Lord, our God, be upon us;
  let the work of our hands prosper,
  O prosper the work of our hands!

—Psalm 90

❈❈

I Turn My Eyes to the Mountains

A song for ascents.

I turn my eyes to the mountains;
  from where will my help come?
My help comes from the Lord,
  maker of heaven and earth.
He will not let your foot give way;
  your guardian will not slumber.
See, the guardian of Israel
  neither slumbers nor sleeps!
The Lord is your guardian,
  the Lord is your protection
  at your right hand.

By day the sun will not strike you,
    nor the moon by night.
The Lord will guard you from all harm;
    He will guard your life.
The Lord will guard your going and coming
    now and forever.

                                   —Psalm 121

✴

Protect Me, O God, for I Seek Refuge in You

Protect me, O God, for I seek refuge in You.
I say to the Lord,
    "You are my Lord, my benefactor;
    there is none above You."
As to the holy and mighty ones that are in the land,
    my whole desire concerning them is that
    those who espouse another [god]
    may have many sorrows!
I will have no part of their bloody libations;
    their names will not pass my lips.
The Lord is my allotted share and portion;
    You control my fate.
Delightful country has fallen to my lot;
    lovely indeed is my estate.
I bless the Lord who has guided me;
    my conscience admonishes me at night.
I am ever mindful of the Lord's presence;
    He is at my right hand; I shall never be shaken.
So my heart rejoices,
    my whole being exults,
    and my body rests secure.
For You will not abandon me to Sheol,
    or let Your faithful one see the Pit.
You will teach me the path of life.
In Your presence is perfect joy;
    delights are ever in Your right hand.

                                   —Psalm 16

✴

The Lord Is My Shepherd

The Lord is my shepherd; I shall not want.
He maketh me to lie down in green pastures;
    He leadeth me beside the still waters;
    He restoreth my soul;
    He guideth me in straight paths for His name's sake.
Yea, though I walk through the valley of the shadow of death,
    I will fear no evil,
    For Thou art with me
    Thy rod and Thy staff, they comfort me.
Thou preparest a table before me in the presence of mine enemies;
    Thou hast anointed my head with oil; my cup runneth over.
Surely goodness and mercy shall follow me all the days of my life,
    And I shall dwell in the house of the Lord forever.

—Psalm 23

❊❊

Yizkor

יִזְכּוֹר אֱלֹהִים נִשְׁמוֹת יַקִּירַי ＿＿＿＿ שֶׁהָלְכוּ
לְעוֹלָמָם. אָנָּא תִּהְיֶינָה נַפְשׁוֹתֵיהֶם צְרוּרוֹת בִּצְרוֹר הַחַיִּים
וּתְהִי מְנוּחָתָם כָּבוֹד. שֹׂבַע שְׂמָחוֹת אֶת־פָּנֶיךָ,
נְעִימוֹת בִּימִינְךָ נֶצַח. אָמֵן.

May God remember for ever my dear ones . . . who have gone to their eternal rest. May they be at one with the One who is life eternal. May the beauty of their lives shine for evermore, and may my life always bring honor to their memory.

יִזְכּוֹר אֱלֹהִים נִשְׁמוֹת כָּל־אַחֵינוּ בְּנֵי יִשְׂרָאֵל שֶׁמָּסְרוּ
אֶת־נַפְשׁוֹתֵיהֶם עַל קִדּוּשׁ הַשֵּׁם. אָנָּא תִּהְיֶינָה
נַפְשׁוֹתֵיהֶם צְרוּרוֹת בִּצְרוֹר הַחַיִּים וּתְהִי מְנוּחָתָם
כָּבוֹד. שֹׂבַע שְׂמָחוֹת אֶת־פָּנֶיךָ, נְעִימוֹת בִּימִינְךָ נֶצַח.
אָמֵן.

May God remember for ever our brothers and sisters of the House of Israel who gave their lives for the Sanctification of the Divine Name. May they be at one with the One who is life eternal. May the beauty of their lives shine for evermore, and may my life always bring honor to their memory.

אֵל מָלֵא רַחֲמִים, שׁוֹכֵן בַּמְּרוֹמִים, הַמְצֵא מְנוּחָה
נְכוֹנָה תַּחַת כַּנְפֵי הַשְּׁכִינָה עִם קְדוֹשִׁים וּטְהוֹרִים
כְּזֹהַר הָרָקִיעַ מַזְהִירִים לְנִשְׁמוֹת יַקִּירֵינוּ שֶׁהָלְכוּ
לְעוֹלָמָם. בַּעַל הָרַחֲמִים יַסְתִּירֵם בְּסֵתֶר כְּנָפָיו
לְעוֹלָמִים, וְיִצְרוֹר בִּצְרוֹר הַחַיִּים אֶת־נִשְׁמָתָם. יְיָ
הוּא נַחֲלָתָם. וְיָנוּחוּ בְּשָׁלוֹם עַל מִשְׁכָּבָם, וְנֹאמַר:
אָמֵן.

O God full of compassion, Eternal Spirit of the universe, grant perfect
rest under the wings of Your Presence to our loved ones who have
entered eternity. Master of Mercy, let them find refuge for ever in the
shadow of Your wings, and let their souls be bound up in the bond of
eternal life. The Eternal God is their inheritance. May they rest in peace,
and let us say: Amen.

※※

O Lord, My God

O Lord, my God,	אֵלִי, אֵלִי,
	Ei·li, Ei·li,
I pray that these things never end:	שֶׁלֹּא יִגָּמֵר לְעוֹלָם
	she·lo yi·ga·meir le·ol·am
The sand and the sea,	הַחוֹל וְהַיָּם,
	ha·chol ve·ha·yam,
The rush of the waters,	רִשְׁרוּשׁ שֶׁל הַמַּיִם,
	rish·rush shel ha·ma·yim,
The crash of the heavens,	בְּרַק הַשָּׁמַיִם,
	be·rak ha·sha·ma·yim,
The prayer of the heart.	תְּפִלַּת הָאָדָם.
	te·fi·lat ha·a·dam.
The sand and the sea,	הַחוֹל וְהַיָּם,
	ha·chol ve·ha·yam,
The rush of the waters,	רִשְׁרוּשׁ שֶׁל הַמַּיִם,
	rish·rush shel ha·ma·yim,
The crash of the heavens,	בְּרַק הַשָּׁמַיִם,
	be·rak ha·sha·ma·yim,
The prayer of the heart.	תְּפִלַּת הָאָדָם.
	te·fi·lat ha·a·dam.

※※

IV

PASSAGES:
GOING AND COMING

8

When Death Comes There Are Many Ways to Heal

I began this book with a section called "Passages: Coming and Going," telling of my father Milton's death at 73 following a four-month illness with lymphoma, and sharing the aftereffects of his death on my life and on those whose lives were tied to his, aftereffects which, like his life itself, have left lasting imprints: I cannot ever think of my father's living without also thinking of my father's dying; I cannot ever think of my father's life without also thinking of my father's death.

> Spending time with someone who is loved and dying is a reminder that nothing can be made to stay. For it is not only the person who will be gone. However tightly we hold his or her hand, however deeply we breathe of his or her presence and essence, memories gently fade, presence ebbs away in the course of time. Even knowing this, we cannot impress others deeply enough on ourselves to make them stay as they are in life. Human memory is too fragile a vessel to carry the vitality of a person. The immmediacy of presence is as nothing else. Next to being, memory is a delicate thread, hazily seen, indifferently spun, slack and worn.
>
> I remember someone I loved. The first meaning of that sentence is that the loved one is gone.
>
> —Rabbi David J. Wolpe
> *The Healer of Shattered Hearts*

> Time does not make my sadness any less,
> Time does not make my memory any less painful,
> Time does not change

277

and Time will not change
what I have lost
and what I will always love.

There is no time,
There is only grief and mourning
for what happened once
and will last forever.

—Seymour Freedman
"Time Does Not Make My Sadness Any Less"
Mourning for My Father

As I wrote the first chapter of this book, it was midsummer and I heard the sounds of cicadas outside my open window. As I write this final chapter, it is late spring and I hear not the sounds of cicadas (they have not yet begun their treetop buzzings); rather, I hear the shouts and laughter of children at play and the songs of birds, together creating a chorus of rejoicing: living is a wonder to be cherished! "Hallelujah," writes the psalmist. "It is good to chant hymns to our God; it is pleasant to sing glorious praise" (Psalm 147:1).

I have lived more than one life cycle since my father's death; I have lived more than one cycle of the seasons, the passages of coming and going and coming, from summer to fall to winter to spring to summer; I have lived the passages from *Shavuot* to Rosh Hashanah and Yom Kippur to Sukkot to Hanukkah to Purim to *Shavuot*; I have lived the passages of birth and death, the death of an 80-year-old man in his sleep after a long illness and of a boy not yet 20 in a sudden and violent automobile accident and of a young woman in her forties struck abruptly by a failed heart as she crossed a city street. And I have lived through them all without my father, and though my heart aches for the losses that my family and friends have suffered during the years following my father's death, it cannot ache more than it does for my own loss.

My heart aches that I have laughed without my father's smile to share my joy; that I have shed tears without my father's words to dry them. But to think only of what I have lost is to be unjust to all I still have: my wife and children, my mother and sister, my relatives and friends, the songs of children and birds, my work and my prayers, and the memories of my father's life.

While I cannot ever think of my father's life without also thinking of my father's death, I cannot ever think of my father's death without also thinking of my father's life. Coming and going and coming: the cycle of the seasons, of the festivals, of birth and death and birth. "The Lord rebuilds Jerusalem," the psalmist writes; "He gathers in the exiles of Israel. /He heals their broken hearts, /and binds up their wounds" (Psalm 147:2-3).

Time will not make me love you less,
but will I pray diminish the pain,
so that I can remember you,

and all the time of our life together,
not simply with sadness,
but with a sense of blessedness and gratitude.
No one in the world ever had
a father,
difficult in greatness, interesting in complexity,
as you, Dad.
I thank G-d for having given me you as a father,
I thank G-d, I thank you Dad,
I will love you always.

> —Seymour Freedman
> "Time Will Not Make Me Love You Less"
> *Mourning for My Father*

My father's heart ached when he, too, laughed and cried without his father to share his joy and his sorrow. His father's heart ached when he laughed and cried without his father to share his joy and sorrow. And his father's father's heart ached. "What is occurring occurred long since, /And what is to occur occurred long since" (Eccesiastes 3:15). Human beings will die and human beings will mourn.

And the Lord God said, "Now that the man has become like one of us, knowing good and bad, what if he should stretch out his hand and take also from the tree of life and eat, and live forever!" So the Lord God banished him from the garden of Eden, to till the soil from which he was taken. He drove the man out, and stationed east of the garden of Eden the cherubim and the fiery ever-turning sword, to guard the way to the tree of life.

> —Genesis 3:22–24

"He reckoned the number of the stars; /to each He gave its name," the psalmist continues. "Great is our Lord and full of power; /His wisdom is beyond reckoning" (Psalm 147:4–5). God did not promise humankind eternal life on earth. God did promise humankind eternal God: "The Lord shall reign forever, /your God, O Zion, for all generations. /Hallelujah" (Psalm 146:10).

"A work that describes the rites and customs of mourning," counsels Rabbi Tzvi Rabinowicz, "would be incomplete without some mention of the Jewish approach to the hereafter. At the same time, it should be pointed out that Judaism does not encourage too much probing into this subject" (*A Guide to Life*). Creation remains a mystery. Death is part of that creation.

O Lord, You have examined me and know me.
When I sit down or stand up You know it;
You discern my thoughts from afar.

You observe my walking and reclining,
  and are familiar with all my ways.
There is not a word on my tongue
  but that You, O Lord, know it well.
You hedge me before and behind;
  You lay Your hand upon me.
It is beyond my knowledge;
  it is a mystery; I cannot fathom it.

—Psalm 139:1–6

The nature of this book would seem to preclude anything more than a mention of the Jewish approach to the hereafter. After all, I knew my father—and God (and still do know God) —in the finite world and not in any infinite world. A belief in the world to come, or a belief in resurrection, may bring added solace to me as a mourner, but it is only part of the foundation of my belief in God, not the foundation itself. An examination of the Jewish approach to the hereafter is for a different book, although included in the readings following this chapter are provided some individual Jewish perspectives on the hereafter.

"If the searcher chooses to remain with eternity, the searcher looses [sic] eternity! If the searcher chooses this finite world, the searcher is rewarded with eternity! This is expressed in a slightly different way by the saying that the pious are not in paradise, paradise is in the pious" (Rabbi Lawrence Kushner, *The River of Light*). To illustrate his perspective, Rabbi Kushner refers his readers to Rabbi Heschel.

A story is told about a rabbi who once entered heaven in his dream. He was permitted to approach the temple in Paradise where the great sages of the Talmud, the Tannaim, were spending their eternal lives. He saw that they were just sitting around tables studying the Talmud. The disappointed rabbi wondered, "Is this all there is to Paradise?" But suddenly he heard a voice: "You are mistaken. The Tannaim are not in Paradise. Paradise is in the Tannaim."

—Rabbi Abraham Joshua Heschel
The Sabbath

My finite world is the world of my wife and children, my mother and my sister, my relatives and friends, my here and now. My finite world is to be lived now, for in my living now do I give honor to the life God gave to my father and to the life my father lived. I am part of his legacy as he was part of his father's.

As reference to the Jewish approach to the hereafter is appropriate for a book on the rituals and customs of mourning, so, too, is reference to ethical wills. The first widely read collection of ethical wills was the two-volume *Hebrew Ethical Wills*, by Israel Abrahams, published in 1926. In 1983, *Ethical*

Wills: A Modern Jewish Treasury was published, edited by Jack Riemer and Nathaniel Stampfer. A revised edition of this book, edited by Rabbi Riemer and Dr. Stampfer, was published in 1991 as *So That Your Values Live On— Ethical Wills And How To Prepare Them*. Recently, in 1990, Jason Aronson published *This I Believe: Documents of American Jewish Life,* written and edited by Jacob Rader Marcus. The first ethical wills in our tradition are those by Jacob and Moses.

And Jacob called his sons and said, "Come together that I may tell you what is to befall you in days to come.

Assemble and hearken, O sons of Jacob;
Hearken to Israel your father:

Reuben, you are my first-born,
My might and first fruit of my vigor,
Exceeding in rank
And exceeding in honor.
Unstable as water, you shall excel no longer;
For when you mounted your father's bed,
You brought disgrace—my couch he mounted!

Simeon and Levi are a pair;
Their weapons are tools of lawlessness.
Let not my person be included in their council,
Let not my being be counted in their assembly.
For when angry they slay men,
And when pleased they maim oxen.
Cursed be their anger so fierce,
And their wrath so relentless.
I will divide them in Jacob,
Scatter them in Israel.

You, O Judah, your brothers shall praise;
Your hand shall be on the nape of your foes;
Your father's sons shall bow low to you.
Judah is a lion's whelp;
On prey, my son, have you grown.
He crouches, lies down like a lion,
Like the king of beasts—who dare rouse him?
The scepter shall not depart from Judah,
Nor the ruler's staff from between his feet;
So that tribute shall come to him
And the homage of people be his.

He tethers his ass to a vine,
His ass's foal to a choice vine;
He washes his garment in wine,
His robe in blood of grapes.
His eyes are darker than wine;
His teeth are whiter than milk.

Zebulun shall dwell by the seashore;
He shall be a haven for ships,
And his flank shall rest on Sidon.

Issachar is a strong-boned ass,
Crouching among the sheepfolds.
When he saw how good was security,
And how pleasant was the country,
He bent his shoulder to the burden,
And became a toiling serf.

Dan shall govern his people,
As one of the tribes of Israel.
Dan shall be a serpent by the road,
A viper by the path,
That bites the horse's heels
So that his rider is thrown backward.

I wait for Your deliverance, O LORD!

Gad shall be raided by raiders,
But he shall raid at their heels.

Asher's bread shall be rich,
And he shall yield royal dainties.

Naphtali is a hind let loose,
Which yields lovely fawns.
Joseph is a wild ass,
A wild ass by a spring
—Wild colts on a hillside.

Archers bitterly assailed him;
They shot at him and harried him.
Yet his bow stayed taut,
And his arms were made firm
By the hands of the Mighty One of Jacob—
There, the Shepherd, the Rock of Israel—
The God of your father who helps you,
And Shaddai who blesses you
With blessings of heaven above,
Blessings of the deep that couches below,
Blessings of the breast and womb.
The blessings of your father
Surpass the blessings of my ancestors,
To the utmost bounds of the eternal hills.
May they rest on the head of Joseph,
On the brow of the elect of his brothers.

Benjamin is a ravenous wolf;
In the morning he consumes the foe,
And in the evening he divides the spoil."

All these were the tribes of Israel, twelve in number, and this is what their father said to them as he bade them farewell, addressing to each a parting word appropriate to him.

Then he instructed them, saying to them, "I am about to be gathered to my kin. Bury me with my fathers in the cave which is in the field of Ephron the Hittite, the cave which is in the field of Machpelah, facing Mamre, in the land of Canaan, the field that Abraham bought from Ephron the Hittite for a burial site—there Abraham and his wife Sarah were buried; there Isaac and his wife Rebekah were buried; and there I buried Leah—the field and the cave in it, bought from the Hittites." When Jacob finished his instructions to his sons, he drew his feet into the bed and, breathing his last, he was gathered to his people.

—Genesis 49

This is the blessing with which Moses, the man of God, bade the Israelites farewell before he died. He said:

> The Lord came from Sinai;
> He shone upon them from Seir;
> He appeared from Mount Paran,
> And approached from Ribeboth-kodesh,
> Lightning flashing at them from His right.

> Lover, indeed, of the people,
> Their hallowed are all in Your hand.
> They followed in Your steps,
> Accepting Your pronouncements,
> When Moses charged us with the Teaching
> As the heritage of the congregation of Jacob.
> Then He became King in Jeshurun,
> When the heads of the people assembled,
> The tribes of Israel together.

> May Reuben live and not die,
> Though few be his numbers.

And this he said of Judah:
> Hear, O Lord the voice of Judah
> And restore him to his people.
> Though his own hands strive for him,
> Help him against his foes.

And of Levi he said:
> Let Your Thummim and Urim
> Be with Your faithful one,
> Whom You tested at Massah,
> Challenged at the waters of Meribah;
> Who said of his father and mother,

"I consider them not."
His brothers he disregarded,
Ignored his own children.
Your precepts alone they observed,
And kept Your covenant.
They shall teach Your norms to Jacob
And Your instructions to Israel.
They shall offer You incense to savor
And whole-offerings on Your altar.
Bless, O Lord, his substance,
And favor his undertakings.
Smite the loins of his foes;
Let his enemies rise no more.

Of Benjamin he said:
Beloved of the Lord,
He rests securely beside Him;
Ever does He protect him,
As he rests between His shoulders.

And of Joseph he said:
Blessed of the Lord be his land
With the bounty of dew from heaven,
And of the deep that couches below;
With the bounteous yield of the sun,
And the bounteous crop of the moons;
With the best from the ancient mountains,
And the bounty of hills immemorial;
With the bounty of earth and its fullness,
And the favor of the Presence in the Bush.
May these rest on the head of Joseph,
On the crown of the elect of his brothers.
Like a firstling bull in his majesty,
He has horns like the horns of the wild-ox;
With them he gores the peoples,
The ends of the earth one and all.
These are the myriads of Ephraim,
Those are the thousands of Manasseh.

And of Zebulun he said:
Rejoice, O Zebulun, on your journeys,
And Issachar, in your tents.
They invite their kin to the mountain,
Where they offer sacrifices of success.
For they draw from the riches of the sea
And the hidden hoards of the sand.

And of Gad he said:
  Blessed be He who enlarges Gad!
  Poised is he like a lion
  To tear off arm and scalp.
  He chose for himself the best,
  For there is the portion of the revered chieftain,
  Where the heads of the people come.
  He executed the Lord's judgments
  And His decisions for Israel.

And of Dan he said:
  Dan is a lion's whelp
  That leaps forth from Bashan.

And of Naphtali he said:
  O Naphtali, sated with favor
  And full of the Lord's blessing,
  Take possession on the west and south.

And of Asher he said:
  Most blessed of sons be Asher;
  May he be the favorite of his brothers,
  May he dip his foot in oil.
  May your doorbolts be iron and copper,
  And your security last all your days.
  O Jeshurun, there is none like God,
  Riding through the heavens to help you,
  Through the skies in His majesty.
  The ancient God is a refuge,
  A support are the arms everlasting.
  He drove out the enemy before you
  By His command: Destroy!
  Thus Israel dwells in safety,
  Untroubled is Jacob's abode,
  In a land of grain and wine,
  Under heavens dripping dew.
  O happy Israel! Who is like you,
  A people delivered by the Lord,
  Your protecting Shield, your Sword triumphant!
  Your enemies shall come cringing before you,
  And you shall tread on their backs.

Moses went up from the steppes of Moab to Mount Nebo, to the summit of
Pisgah, opposite Jericho, and the Lord showed him the whole land: Gilead as
far as Dan; all Naphtali; the land of Ephraim and Manasseh; the whole land of
Judah as far as the Western Sea; the Negeb; and the Plain—the valley of Jericho,

the city of palm trees—as far as Zoar. And the Lord said to him, "This is the land of which I swore to Abraham, Isaac, and Jacob, 'I will give it to your offspring.' I have let you see it with your own eyes, but you shall not cross there."

So Moses the servant of the Lord died there, in the land of Moab, at the command of the Lord.

—Deuteronomy 33—34:5

My father did not write an ethical will and I would not presume to suggest what he might have written had he done so. But in the many *b'nai mitzvah* cards and graduation autograph books he inscribed, and in the letters my father so frequently wrote to his children and grandchildren, he taught us that love is unconditional; society must be just and merciful; the tension of success is in the struggle between personal satisfaction and material gain and can be eased but not eliminated; Judaism has roots and wings and we are more Jewishly alive when we live by both.

Perhaps in some measure, this book, dedicated to my father's memory, acknowledges my ethical inheritance.

"The route of grief appears to be one of tangled and complex pathways, with trails looping back and forth," writes Herman Feifel. I have come to the end of one pathway now on my journey to understand, accept, and live with the loss of my father. And as I take the hand of my wife to start on another pathway, I only ask that God and the strength of my own body and soul continue to guide me on my way.

It is hard to sing of oneness when our world is not complete, when those who once brought wholeness to our life have gone, and naught but memory can fill the emptiness their passing leaves behind.

But memory can tell us only what we were, in company with those we loved; it cannot help us find what each of us, alone, must now become. Yet no one is really alone; those who live no more, echo still within our thoughts and words, and what they did is part of what we have become.

We do best homage to our dead when we live our lives most fully, even in the shadow of our loss. For each of our lives is worth the life of the whole world; in each one is the breath of the Ultimate One. In affirming the One, we affirm the worth of each one whose life, now ended, brought us closer to the Source of Life, in whose unity no one is alone and every life finds purpose.

—*Gates of Prayer*

I do not know
if it is consolation to you now,
But you did not live your life
for nothing.
You made something of it.

You left behind a family who loves you,
the children and grandchildren,
and their love for you
which will go on and on,
until we ourselves
are too, if worthy,
granted our own consolation.

—Seymour Freedman
"I Do Not Know"
Mourning for My Father

And may God bless you.

※※

Readings

※※※※※※※※※※※※※※※

The General Mourning for Aaron

When Israel beheld the funeral rites prepared in honor of Aaron by God and by the angels, they also prepared a funeral ceremony of thirty days in which all the people, men and women, adults and children, took part. This universal mourning had its foundation not only in Israel's emulation of the Divine mourning and of the ceremonies arranged by Moses and Eleazar, or in their wish to show their reverence for the deceased high priest, but first and foremost in the truth that the people deeply loved Aaron and deeply felt his death. They mourned for him even more than they did later for Moses; for the latter only a part of the people shed tears, but for Aaron, everyone. Moses, as a judge, was obliged to mete out justice to the guilty, so that he had enemies among the people, men who could not forget that he had pronounced them guilty in court. Moses, furthermore, was sometimes severe with Israel when he held up to them their sins, but never Aaron. The latter "loved peace and pursued peace, loved men and brought them near to the Torah." In his humility, he did not consider his dignity hurt by offering greetings first to even the lowliest, yes, he did not even fail in offering his greeting when he was certain that the man before him was wicked or godless. The lament of the angels for Aaron as one "who did turn many away from iniquity" was therefore well justified. This kindliness of his led many a sinner to reform, who at the moment when he was about to commit a sin thought to himself: "How shall I be able to lift up my eyes to Aaron's face? I, to whom Aaron was so kind, blush to do evil." Aaron recognized his especial task as that of the peace-maker. If he discovered that two men had fallen out, he hastened first to the one, then to the other, saying to each: "My son, dost thou not know what he is doing with whom thou hast quarreled? He beats at his heart, rends his garments in grief, and says, 'Woe is me! How can I ever again lift up my eyes and look upon my companion against whom I have acted so?'" Aaron would then speak to each separately until both the former enemies would mutually forgive each other, and as soon as they were again face to face salute each other as friends. If Aaron heard that husband and wife lived in discord, he would hasten to the husband, saying: "I come to thee because I hear that thou and thy wife live in discord, wherefore thou must divorce her. Keep in mind, however, that if thou shouldst in place of thy present wife marry another, it is very questionable if thy second wife will be as good as this one: for at your first quarrel she will throw up to thee that thou art a quarrelsome man, as was shown by thy divorce from thy first wife." Many thousands of unions were saved from impending rupture by the efforts and urgings of Aaron, and the sons born to the couples brought together anew usually received Aaron's name, owing, as they did, their existence to his intercession. Not less than eighty thousand youths bearing his name took part in the mourning for Aaron.

When Moses beheld the deep-felt sorrow of the heavenly beings and of men for Aaron, he burst into passionate weeping, and said: "Woe is me, that am now left all alone! When Miriam died, none came to show her the last marks of honor, and only I, Aaron, and his sons stood about her bier, wept for her, mourned her, and buried her. At Aaron's death, I and his sons were present at his bier to show him the last marks of honor. But alas! How shall I fare? Who will be present at my death? I have neither father nor mother, neither brother nor sister,—who then will weep for me?" God, however, said to him: "Be not afraid, Moses, I myself shall bury thee amid great splendor, and just as the cave in which Aaron lies has vanished, that none may know the spot where Aaron is buried, so too shall no mortal know thy burial place. As the Angel of Death had no power over Aaron, who died 'by the kiss,' so shall the Angel of Death have no power over thee, and thou shalt die 'by the kiss.'" Moses grew calm at these words, that he had his place among the blessed pious. Blessed are they, for not only does God in person gather them to Him, but as soon as they are dead, the angels go joyously to meet them and with beaming faces go to greet them, saying, "Enter into peace."

—Louis Ginzberg
Legends of the Jews III

✻✻✻

Samael's Vain Search

Samael, the Angel of Death, had not heard that God had taken Moses' soul from his body and received it under the Throne of Glory. Believing that Moses was still among the living, he betook himself to Moses' house in order to seize his soul, for he feared to return before God without having executed His command to take Moses' soul. He did not, however, find Moses in his accustomed place, so he hastened into the land of Israel, thinking, "Long did Moses pray to be permitted to enter this land, and perhaps he is there." He said to the land of Israel, "Is Moses perchance with thee?" But the land replied, "Nay, he is not found in the land of the living."

Samael then thought: "I know that God once said to Moses, 'Lift up thy rod and divide the sea,' so perhaps he is by the sea." He hastened to the sea and said, "Is Moses here?" The sea replied: "He is not here, and I have not seen him since the day when he clove me into twelve parts, and with the twelve tribes passed through me."

Samael then betook himself to Gehenna asking, "Hast thou seen Moses, the son of Amram?" Gehenna replied, "With mine ears have I heard his cry, but I have not seen him."

He betook himself to Sheol, Abaddon, and Tit-ha-Yawen, to whom he said, "Have ye seen the son of Amram?" They replied: "Through Pharaoh, king of Egypt, have we heard his call, but we have not seen him."

He betook himself to the Abyss and asked. "Hast thou seen the son of Amram?" The answer arose, "I have not seen him, but heard indeed his call."

He asked Korah's sons, that dwell within the Abyss, "Have ye seen the son of Amram?" They replied, "We have not seen him since the day upon which at Moses' bidding the earth opened its mouth and swallowed us."

He betook himself to the clouds of glory and asked, "Is Moses perchance with you?" They answered, "He is hid from the eyes of all living."

He went to the heavens and asked, "Have ye seen the son of Amram?" The answer was, "We have not seen him since at God's command he mounted to us to receive the Torah."

He hastened to Paradise, but when the angels that guard its gates beheld Samael, they drove him away and said, "Wicked one! Wicked one! 'This is the gate of the Lord; the righteous shall enter into it.'" Samael thereupon flew over the gates of Paradise at a height of four thousand parasangs, descended into Paradise and asked Paradise, "Hast thou perchance seen Moses?" Paradise answered, "Since in Gabriel's company he visited me to look upon the reward of the pious, I have not seen him."

He went to the tree of life, but even at the distance of three hundred parasangs, it cried out to him: "Approach me not." He therefore asked from afar, "Hast thou seen the son of Amram?" The tree replied, "Since the day on which he came to me to cut him a staff, I have not seen him."

He betook himself to the tree of the knowledge of good and evil, and said, "Hast thou seen the son of Amram?" The tree replied, "Since the day on which he came to me to get a writing reed, wherewith to write the Torah, I have not seen him."

He betook himself to the mountains with his query. These replied, "Since he hewed the two tables out of us, we have not seen him."

He went to the deserts and asked, "Have ye seen the son of Amram?" These replied, "Since he has ceased to lead Israel to pasture upon us, we have not seen him."

He betook himself to mount Sinai, for he thought God had formerly commanded Moses to ascend it, and that he might now be there. He asked Sinai, "Hast thou seen the son of Amram?" Sinai said, "Since the day on which out of God's right hand he received the Torah upon me, I have not seen him."

He betook himself to the birds and said, "Have ye seen Moses?" They replied, "Since the day whereon he separated the birds into clean and unclean we have not seen him."

He went to the quadrupeds and asked: "Have ye seen Moses?" They answered: "Since the day on which he determined which beasts might be eaten, and which might not, we have not seen him." The answer of the birds and beasts referred to the day on which God assembled all the species of animals, led them before Moses, and instructed him which of these were clean and which were not, which might, and which might not be eaten.

Samael then betook himself to the "Court of the Dead," where the angel Dumah guards the souls of the deceased, and asked this angel, "Hast thou seen the son of Amram?" He replied: "I heard the words of lamentation for him in heaven, but I have not seen him."

He betook himself to the angels and asked, "Have ye seen the son of Amram?" These made the same reply as Dumah, and advised him to go to the mortals, who might possibly give him information concerning Moses' whereabouts.

He betook himself to the mortals and asked, "Where is Moses?" These replied: "Our teacher Moses is not like human beings. He is the peer of the angels of ministry, for he ascended into heaven and dwelt in heaven like the angels, 'he hath gathered the wind in his fists' like an angel, and God took his soul to Himself in the place of His sanctity.

—Louis Ginzberg
Legends of the Jews III

✳✳

Outrage and Faith

The afterlife is not simply a psychological crutch with which we appease ourselves. Nor is it a theological stick with which we threaten those who perpetuate evil. It is, rather, God's commitment to us, part of His responsibility as our Creator. By endowing us with souls, with aspirations, and with the potential for perfection—characteristics that have no limit—He has indicated that He intended us to be infinite, to exist beyond our physical lives. For me that belief is as fundamental as the belief in God. You cannot have one without the other.

But I cannot prove these matters of faith in any of the conventional ways we recognize as proof. People can rarely prove the beliefs they cherish. How do you prove that all people are created equal? That slavery is immoral? That feeding the hungry is a virtuous act? To me these truths are self-evident, as clear as though they'd been proven by scientific experiment or logical argument. So it is with religious belief.

In this way, outrage and faith coexist in delicate balance—the one forcing us out of complacency into lives of value; the other leading us forward, like the Israelites' pillar of fire, stretching us beyond ourselves and promising to reward our journey.

Outrage preserves our dignity, the dignity of the mortal whose nature inclines to rebel against finitude and despair. Faith represents the divine spark in all humans that burns upward toward its source and helps us to strain toward perfection. Together outrage and faith impel us to strive to the limits of our given abilities and leave the rest to God.

Trusting in God in this way frees us to concentrate on the immediate duties of the here and now. Just as we live in the tension between outrage and faith, so we live in the tension between present and future, this world and the world to come. And though we are destined for eternal life, Judaism cautions us not to dwell upon it, not to muse excessively on the imponderable issues it raises, but instead to give pride of place to the present and to make of our earthly behavior proud reflections of our Maker.

—Arlene Agus in
What Happens After I Die?

✳✳

Is There Life After Death?

Last year a dear friend died very suddenly. I felt a massive grief at his loss not only because I loved the man but also because of his death at this particular time of his life. Simmy, age seventy-four, had recovered from a nasty bout of shingles two years earlier. After years of urging by his wife, Anne, he finally agreed to semiretirement from his busy law practice in Boston, which meant he now worked only twelve hours a day. They had recently purchased an apartment in Jerusalem, directly across the street from their younger son, daughter-in-law, and four young grandchildren. The latter were very close to him and, like their father, called him "Dad." Simmy and Anne planned to spend several months a year in their Jerusalem apartment.

Simmy was a true *tzadik*, albeit in bon vivant's clothing. Courtly and polished, he could also be opinionated and contentious. Beneath that colorful exterior, beneath even an occasional goddam and what in hell, lay the gentlest, tenderest of souls. He did more acts of *chesed*, more favors for people, than anyone I've ever met. Any of his acquaintances who ever encountered an underdog would instinctively advise, "Go ask Simmy G. for help." And somehow he always managed to find a way to avoid even the merest thanks. He could have called in one-tenth of his personal IOUs—which he never had anyone sign—and lived out his years, unto one hundred and twenty, in luxury and dignity. Yet just as he was poised at a moment when he could finally enjoy a most happy time of life, it was snuffed out. He should have had another fifteen years, ten at least. I wept for a solid week after his funeral. I grieved for his wife, for his children and grandchildren, as did the many hundreds of people who attended his funeral and walked in his cortege, the great and famous rabbis who eulogized him, the bank clerk who burst into tears a week later upon learning of his death. For weeks and then months I grieved at the premature end of his life and could find no consolation anywhere inside of me.

More than any saint I've ever read or heard of, Simmy deserved a place in *olam haba*; by dint of a single act of *chesed*, the scales of the heavenly court would have been tipped, and he would have been sent express to the world of the righteous. Yet in the weeks and months immediately following his death, this did not once occur to me. He was dead, very dead. If he was not here, he was nowhere. It was totally unfair, unjust.

But my system simply could not handle that. It rebelled against so blatant a violation of fairness. In recent weeks, as the pain has become a bit less raw, as time has given a small measure of respite, I find myself occasionally thinking that Simmy is probably arguing and cajoling his way through heaven, helping a few helpless saints. And I've heard his extremely bright and sophisticated twelve-year-old grandson Noah say, "I talked to Dad . . ." All of this doesn't take away the sadness that he's not here, but somehow it makes it more manageable. Otherwise we might just throw up our hands in total bewilderment. . . .

—Blu Greenberg in
What Happens After I Die?

⁂

Ani Maamin
אני מאמין

ma·a·min be·e·mu·na she·lei·ma	אֲנִי מַאֲמִין בֶּאֱמוּנָה שְׁלֵמָה
be·vl·at ha·ma·shl·ach.	בְּבִיאַת הַמָּשִׁיחַ.
Ve·af al pl she·ylt·ma·he·mei·a,	וְאַף עַל פִּי שֶׁיִּתְמַהְמֵהַּ,
im kol zeh a·nl ma·a·min,	עִם כָּל זֶה אֲנִי מַאֲמִין,
im kol zch a·cha·kch lo	עִם כָּל זֶה אֲחַכֶּה לּוֹ
be·chol yom she·ya·vo.	בְּכָל יוֹם שֶׁיָּבוֹא.

I believe with perfect faith in the Messiah's coming. And even if he be delayed, I will await him.

—*Gates of Prayer*

⁂

Yigdal
יִגְדַּל

Yig·dal E·lo·him chai ve·yish·ta·bach,	יִגְדַּל אֱלֹהִים חַי וְיִשְׁתַּבַּח,
nim·tsa ve·ein elt el me·tsi·u·to.	נִמְצָא וְאֵין עֵת אֶל־מְצִיאוּתוֹ.
E·chad ve·ein ya·chid ke·yi·chu·do,	אֶחָד וְאֵין יָחִיד כְּיִחוּדוֹ,
ne·lam ve·gam ein sof le·ach·du·to.	נֶעְלָם וְגַם אֵין סוֹף לְאַחְדּוּתוֹ.
Ein lo de·mut ha·guf ve·ei·no guf,	אֵין לוֹ דְמוּת הַגּוּף וְאֵינוֹ גוּף,
lo na·a·roch el·lav ke·du·sha·to.	לֹא נַעֲרוֹךְ אֵלָיו קְדֻשָּׁתוֹ.
Kad·mon le·chol da·var a·sher niv·ra,	קַדְמוֹן לְכָל־דָּבָר אֲשֶׁר נִבְרָא,
ri·shon ve·ein rei·shit le·rei·shi·to.	רִאשׁוֹן וְאֵין רֵאשִׁית לְרֵאשִׁיתוֹ.
Hi·no a·don o·lam, le·chol no·tsar	הִנּוֹ אֲדוֹן עוֹלָם, לְכָל־נוֹצָר
yo·reh ge·du·la·to u·mal·chu·to.	יוֹרֶה גְדֻלָּתוֹ וּמַלְכוּתוֹ.
She·fa ne·vu·a·to ne·ta·no,	שֶׁפַע נְבוּאָתוֹ נְתָנוֹ,
el a·ne·shei se·gu·la·to ve·tif·ar·to.	אֶל־אַנְשֵׁי סְגֻלָּתוֹ וְתִפְאַרְתּוֹ.
Lo kam be·yis·ra·eil ke·mo·sheh od	לֹא קָם בְּיִשְׂרָאֵל כְּמֹשֶׁה עוֹד
na·vi u·ma·bit et te·mu·na·to,	נָבִיא וּמַבִּיט אֶת־תְּמוּנָתוֹ,
To·rat e·met na·tan le·a·mo Eil,	תּוֹרַת אֱמֶת נָתַן לְעַמּוֹ אֵל,
al yad ne·vi·o ne·e·man bei·to.	עַל יַד נְבִיאוֹ נֶאֱמַן בֵּיתוֹ.
Lo ya·cha·lif ha·eil,ve·lo ya·mir	לֹא יַחֲלִיף הָאֵל, וְלֹא יָמִיר
da·to, le·o·la·mim le·zu·la·to.	דָּתוֹ, לְעוֹלָמִים לְזוּלָתוֹ.
Tso·feh ve·yo·del·a se·ta·rei·nu,	צוֹפֶה וְיוֹדֵעַ סְתָרֵינוּ,
ma·bit le·sof da·var be·kad·ma·to.	מַבִּיט לְסוֹף דָּבָר בְּקַדְמָתוֹ.
Go·mell le·ish che·sed ke·mif·a·lo,	גּוֹמֵל לְאִישׁ חֶסֶד כְּמִפְעָלוֹ,
no·tein le·ra·sha ra ke·rish·a·to.	נוֹתֵן לְרָשָׁע רַע כְּרִשְׁעָתוֹ.
Yish·lach le·keits ya·min pe·dut o·lam,	יִשְׁלַח לְקֵץ יָמִין פְּדוּת עוֹלָם,
Kol chai ve·yeish ya·kir ye·shu·a·to.	כָּל־חַי וְיֵשׁ יַכִּיר יְשׁוּעָתוֹ.
Cha·yel o·lam na·ta be·to·chei·nu,	חַיֵּי עוֹלָם נָטַע בְּתוֹכֵנוּ,
ba·ruch a·dei ad sheim te·hi·la·to.	בָּרוּךְ עֲדֵי עַד שֵׁם תְּהִלָּתוֹ.

Magnified and praised be the living God; His existence is eternal. He is One and unique in His unity; He is unfathomable, and His Oneness is unending. He has no bodily form, He is incorporeal; His holiness is beyond compare. He preceded all creation; He is the First, and He Himself has no beginning.

Behold the eternal Lord, who reveals His greatness and sovereignty to every creature. He inspired with the gift of prophecy those whom He chose to make known His glory.

Never has there been a prophet like Moses, whose closeness to God is unmatched. A Torah of truth did God give to His people, through His prophet, His faithful servant.

God does not change; His teaching will not be supplanted; He will always be the same. He watches us and knows our secret thoughts; He perceives the end of every matter before it begins.

He deals kindly with those who merit kindness, and brings upon the wicked the evil consequences of their deeds. At the end of days He will send an everlasting redemption; all that lives and breathes shall witness His deliverance.

He has implanted eternal life within us. Blessed is His glorious name to all eternity.

—Gates of Prayer

❊❊❊

Yigdal (A Metrical Version)

We praise the living God,
For ever praise His name,
Who was and is and is to be
For e'er the same;
The One eternal God
Before our world appears,
And there can be no end of time
Beyond His years.
Without a form is He,
Nor can we comprehend
The measure of His love for us—
Without an end.
For He is Lord of all,
Creation speaks His praise.
The human race and all that grows
His will obeys.
He knows our every thought,

Our birth and death ordains;
He understands our fervent dreams,
Our hopes and our pains.
Eternal life has He
Implanted in our soul.
We dedicate our life to Him—
His way, our goal!

—*Gates of Prayer*

❈

Adon Olam
אדון עולם

A·don o·lam, a·sher ma·lach	אֲדוֹן עוֹלָם, אֲשֶׁר מָלַךְ
be·te·rem kol ye·tsir niv·ra,	בְּטֶרֶם כָּל־יְצִיר נִבְרָא,
le·eit na·a·sa ve·chef·tso kol,	לְעֵת נַעֲשָׂה בְחֶפְצוֹ כֹּל,
a·zai me·lech she·mo nik·ra.	אֲזַי מֶלֶךְ שְׁמוֹ נִקְרָא.
Ve·a·cha·rei ki·che·lot ha·kol,	וְאַחֲרֵי כִּכְלוֹת הַכֹּל,
le·va·do yim·loch no·ra,	לְבַדּוֹ יִמְלוֹךְ נוֹרָא,
ve·hu ha·ya, ve·hu ho·veh,	וְהוּא הָיָה, וְהוּא הֹוֶה,
ve·hu yi·he·yeh be·tif·a·ra.	וְהוּא יִהְיֶה בְּתִפְאָרָה.
Ve·hu e·chad, ve·ein shei·ni	וְהוּא אֶחָד, וְאֵין שֵׁנִי
le·ham·shil lo, le·hach·bi·ra,	לְהַמְשִׁיל לוֹ, לְהַחְבִּירָה,
be·li rei·shit, be·ll tach·lit,	בְּלִי רֵאשִׁית, בְּלִי תַכְלִית,
ve·lo ha·oz ve·ha·mis·ra.	וְלוֹ הָעֹז וְהַמִּשְׂרָה.
Ve·hu Ei·li, ve·chai go·a·li,	וְהוּא אֵלִי, וְחַי גּוֹאֲלִי,
ve·tsur chev·li be·eit tsa·ra,	וְצוּר חֶבְלִי בְּעֵת צָרָה,
ve·hu ni·si u·ma·nos li,	וְהוּא נִסִּי וּמָנוֹס לִי,
me·nat ko·si be·yom ek·ra.	מְנָת כּוֹסִי בְּיוֹם אֶקְרָא.
Be·ya·do af·kid ru·chi	בְּיָדוֹ אַפְקִיד רוּחִי
be·eit i·shan ve·a·i·ra,	בְּעֵת אִישַׁן וְאָעִירָה,
ve·im ru·chi ge·vi·ya·tl:	וְעִם־רוּחִי גְּוִיָּתִי:
A·do·nai ll, ve·lo i·ra.	יְיָ לִי, וְלֹא אִירָא.

He is the eternal Lord, who reigned before any being had yet been created; when all was done according to His will, already then His name was King.

And after all has ceased to be, still will He reign in solitary majesty; He was, He is, and He shall be in glory.

And He is One; none other can compare to Him, or consort with Him; He is without beginning, without end; to Him belong power and dominion.

And He is *my* God, my living Redeemer, my Rock in time of trouble and distress; He is my banner and my refuge, my benefactor when I call on Him.

Into His hands I entrust my spirit, when I sleep and when I wake; and with my spirit, my body also: the Lord is with me, I will not fear.

—Gates of Prayer

❋❋

The Lord of All

The Lord of all, who reigned supreme,
Ere first creation's form was framed;
When all was finished by His will,
His name Almighty was proclaimed.
When this, our world, shall be no more,
In majesty He still shall reign,
Who was, who is, who will remain,
His endless glory we proclaim.
Alone is He, beyond compare,
Without division or ally,
Without initial date or end,
Omnipotent He rules on high.
He is my God, my Savior He,
To whom I turn in sorrow's hour—
My banner proud, my refuge sure,
Who hears and answers with His pow'r.
Then in His hand myself I lay,
And trusting sleep, and wake with cheer;
My soul and body are His care;
The Lord does guard, I have no fear.

—Gates of Prayer

❋❋

Be Honest & Upright to Your Self & Fellow Man
A Jewish New Year Letter to a Son

September 5, 1918

My Dear Boy Armand:

This morning I wrote you a short letter, because I had no time to write a long one, but now while I have lots of important work yet to do, & that is paying bills, yet I feel it is just as important to write you, for the fact that New Year is fast approaching & also that you are now practically starting out in life, to become a factor not only for your self but also for others.

To the New Year I wish you such wich only a good parent can wish a son who so far has held the utermost confidence of his parent. While you have had & possibly still have some minor faults wich are only due to your young years, but as a total your parents feel that they have an ideal son & our heart & everything els is with you constandly, & may the Almighty keep you & watch over you for us.

Now my dear boy, I recall the first letter I have received from my dear father, *Selig* [of blessed memory], in wich he asked me not to forget the teachings of my parents & in this he said above all be honest & upright to you self & fellow man. This very advise I can [not] impress to strongly open you, for the temptations at times are great & trying, & it takes a strong character to allways withsdand it but those that withsdans it will have great satisfaction throut theire lifes.

Be kind to your fellow man & allways before acting aske your self how would I like this? By asking your self this question & with honesty of purpose you will always then treat your fellowman as he should be treated.

As to your education, I have spoken to your personally, never the less I shall put a few words in writing by saying that you know my pocket book is open for you to get all such education that you need & ought to have. I am ready to go to the full length but I will aske [you] to beware of temptations that might be put before you at times wich would mean neglect of your education. Remember you can not know too much & lost time can not be made up. In writing you all this I do not want you to misconstru the meaning of my advise for, as stated in the beginning of my letter, your parent have the utmost confidence in you. But no one knows better than I what temptations you likely have to content with. In advising you as I do I feel that it might take deep root in your heart & mind, so that no mather what comes before you that you allways have my advise in mind. That we miss you greatly goes without saying & when I notice your dear mother when she gets your letters how she tries to supress her feelings then I realize the more the sacrifice we are making for your future, but all is done willingly & with an abundance of love that you can only repay by doing the right thing at the right time, wich I am sure you will. In conclusion I will say do not be unmindful of your body & soul for only by doing this, you can acoplish the other duties as outlined above.

We received your letter & sorry that you have such a hart bed but no doubt by the time you get trough a days exersise you can sleep on wood. I am going to take this letter home to mother & will send it to morrow as mother wishes to write, so will close again sending my best wishes for the New Year and, for all time, a parent's love.

God bless you is the wish to your ever loving Dad,

Herman

—Herman Hecht in
This I Believe

✳✺✳

Life Has Been Inexpressibly Sweet to Me

Whensoever death shall come, it will find me unafraid. I pray that it may find me ready. I have ever tried so to live that I might be prepared to meet my God. I love life and the exquisite gifts of work, of play, of joy, . . . of light, of laughter, and most of all, of love that it has brought me. I am, and have always been, deeply grateful for the abundance of life with which I have been blessed. Life has been inexpressibly sweet to me. Yet, come death when it may, I yield up life as gladly, as gratefully, as I have accepted its gift for the while. . . . it would be selfish to ask for more. All my life long I have been blessed with the gifts of love, far, far beyond my deserving, I have tried, haltingly, inadequately but sincerely. . . . to repay through service some of the debt I owe to life for its profuse bounty towards me. I gave three years (the happiest of my life because the richest in service) to the Holy Land. I have tried at all times, and for all who called upon me, rich as well as poor, gentile as well as Jew, to give service through such poor gifts, as my physical strength, my mental power and my spiritual resources enabled me to offer. I have tried so to do. More than that I cannot say, for I know that often, pitifully often, I have failed through weakness and inadequacy—physical, mental, and spiritual. Yet the stimulus and the joy of trying have been mine.

From anyone towards whom I have failed in human kindness I ask forgiveness. I do not feel, and I never have felt, any unkindness or malice in my heart towards anyone. Where I have failed, it has been through my insufficiency, never through ill will.

But I would not leave with you who care to hear, and even perchance to cherish, a message from me, any emphasis on failure. Though in tangible achievement I have not done what perhaps I dreamed of doing and what the world may rightly have expected me to achieve; the very living of my life has been supremely successful. There has been no day in which my heart has not leaped with gratitude to God for the joy of life and its fulfillment in the perfect love that has been given to me both as a child and in every moment of my sacred married life. There has yet never dawned the day when I have not been able to give thanks unto God for His goodness, and the day of death shall be but one more such day.

Therefore I would not have my death darken the life of anyone. Life to me has always been joy with humor and laughter and happiness. I would have it so, and I have tried to make it so for all others with whom my lot has been cast. I have tried to comfort others in their sorrow and to show them the sunshine of life's path. So if any would remember me, let my name be mentioned with a smile, with brightness, with humor, with happy memory, with wholesome gladness. Paint not my memory with tears or regrets, but let my spirit live among you after death as it has on earth, with joyousness. I would have the children of the religious school of my congregation gladdened on the Sunday nearest its anniversary or, should that be in the summer, then I would have some other children's lives made sweeter on that day, and at all times I would have my wife and children and those who have been the sweetest blessings in my life recall me with a smile as they think how much of heartwarming love they gave to me.

I can never even begin to express my thanks to all whose goodness, whose forbearance and whose friendships have made my life so wondrous an adventure. May God bless you all for the blessings you have given to me. I have had all and more than man could dare ask for—a life that has known no want, a life of wide and varied interests, with music, travel, humor, work, opportunities of spiritual service. But most of all I have had friendship and kindness from everyone, and a perfect, exquisite love from my life's partner.

Many waters cannot quench love
Rivers cannot drown it. . . . [Song of Songs 8:7]

To all I would sum up what I have tried to be in the deep wisdom of
the ancient words: "The end of it, when all has been heard, is to revere
God and keep His commandments, for this is the whole of man"
[Ecclesiastes 12:13].
So,

I rest my spirit in His hand,
Asleep, awake by Him I'm stayed.
God with me still, in life, in death,
I face my future unafraid.

—Rabbi David de Sola Pool in
This I Believe

※※

I Know I Cannot Impose My Values and Judgments on You

It was a custom in ancient times for the father to leave an ethical will
together with the legal testament. I hesitate to follow in this fine
tradition for fear of imposing my will on yours. The state of the world
which I leave you hardly testifies to the wisdom of my generation, or
those immediately before. I would be remiss, however, if I did not warn
your generation that, in your anger and frustration, you fail to
distinguish between the conventions that enshrine the past because it is
the past and the traditions which have in them the seed of a more
meaningful future. There is no single, simple, or automatic way in
which one can learn the art of this discretion—but I sincerely believe
that the history and teachings of Judaism contain implicit and explicit
guidelines for achieving a viable synthesis between the tried values of the
past and the liberating needs of the present and the future. This belief
and the understandable, though inarticulate, loyalty to the choices of a
lifetime compel me to urge you to consider well the rock whence you
were digged.

[Because of] the attrition of the tradition in my lifetime . . . there is
a real danger that it will disappear in your children's lives. I would
consider this an affront to principle of continuity and a loss of a fine
family resource. I know I cannot impose my values and judgments on

you, but I can and do request that you not let this heritage go by default—but that you study it, participate in it, and make your decision on the basis of knowledge as well as sentiment. You will find that it may be a very real help in holding you together as a family. One of the most painful experiences I have had as a rabbi has been to witness the weakening of family ties—brothers and sisters who come together at funerals and weddings as strangers asking querulously of each other: "Why have we not heard from you? Why do we have to wait for a funeral to bring us together?" As love becomes more ambient, less focused, more dependent on necessity and convenience, it will need the more elemental instinctive support of family affection, of common womb genesis. So hold fast to the family affection you have so far maintained and try to pass it on to your children.

—Jacob J. Weinstein in
This I Believe

Afterword

I wrote in my first chapter about the importance of ritual in my life and that "I was conscious of learning as I observed and participated in the rituals associated with dying, death, burial and *shivah*." And I was comforted.

I also wrote about the meaning of God in my life, as "a real presence that is embodied in a grandmother's fingers and in all the actions of the people who conceived me, gave birth to me, and who raised me and nurtured my mind and heart, my body and soul. God is not outside my human existence, God is within, because God is a part of every human existence and waits only to be discovered by each individual."

Although God did not inspire me to write this book, I believe my friend Arthur Kurzweil was guided by divine influence to request that I consider it.

> All my thoughts of Death beforehand,
> all my understanding,
> did not teach me,
> what Death is.
>
> Only through your death,
> have I come to know Death,
> and in truth,
> I have learned, now,
> all I ever want
> to know,
> though not, I fear
> all I will come to know.
>
> —Seymour Freedman
> "All My Thoughts of Death Beforehand"
> *Mourning for My Father*

I believe Arthur knew even during his *shivah* visit to my home, although he said nothing about it then, that through my father's death, I would come to know not what death is (only my father knows death) but first what losing is and later what loss is, and that through my writing and scholarship, I could find in my own words and in the words of others the insights into bereavement that would bring comfort not only to me but also to others. Therefore my manuscript is titled *A Jewish Book of Comfort*. It is not, however, a textbook in the manner that a student uses a textbook as a standard work for a particular branch of study. Rather, *A Jewish Book of Comfort* is intended as a companion to the bereaved and to those who seek to console the bereaved.

Whether Arthur's faith in me is justified can be known only by the readers of *A Jewish Book of Comfort*. But my faith in Arthur's vision is justified by my having written it.

I also wrote in the first chapter about the importance of family and friends in my life and that in moments of deep despair, "we could each call upon each other's strength." I am grateful for my mother Rose's strength and wisdom and love; for my sister Barbara's companionship and love, and for my children Cory, Lisa, and Adina's compassion and love. As an adult, the love my wife, Jo, had for me and for my father enabled me to be the son I wanted to be for my dad. The love she has today for me and my mother enables me to be the son I want to be for my mom. I am indebted to Jo for her friendship and love and patient and inspired reading of my manuscript from first page of yellow pad paper to galley page. Finally, I am grateful for the professional skills of the staff at Jason Aronson: Muriel Jorgensen, Director of Editorial Production; Janet Warner, Production Editor; Diane Berman, Editorial Assistant; Gail Katz, Editorial Assistant; and Pamela Roth, Managing Editor, the Jewish Book Club.

Rabbi Nahman of Bratslav reminds us, "The entire world is a very narrow bridge. The main thing is to have no fear at all."

May we all go from strength to strength. Amen.

Glossary

Adar Twelfth month of the Hebrew calendar (approximately February–March).

Adon Olam "Eternal Lord." A traditional prayer book hymn attributed to various medieval poets, particularly Solomon Ibn Gabriol.

Aggadah, Aggadot Part of the Talmud that complements the legal parts (*halachah*), stressing its ethical and inspirational meanings. Includes picturesque similes, epigrams, metaphor, wordplay, and dramatic colloquy.

Alav ha-Shalom "May he rest in peace."

Aleinu "It is our duty." A prayer read at the end of services.

Aliyah, Aliyot "Going up." A term used when one is called up to the Torah.

Amidah Name by which the Prayer of the Eighteen Blessings (*Shemonah Esray*) is known. The term *Amidah* (prayer said standing) is also known as *Tefillah*.

Amora, Amoraim Speaker or interpreter. The name given to the scholars responsible for the *Gemara*.

Ani Maamin "I believe." A song of faith sung by Holocaust victims on their way to their deaths.

Aninut Interval between death and burial.

Annos Sephardic term for anniversary of a death.

Arafel Darkness.

Ashkenazic Jew of Germany or elsewhere in Eastern Europe.

Avel, Avelim Mourner.

Avelut Mourning; the periods of formal mourning.

307

Bar Mitzvah, *Bat Mitzvah* (*B'nei Mitzvah*) Son or daughter of the Commandment.

Bechi In a euology, the expression of grief and sense of loss experienced by the mourners and the entire Jewish community.

Ben-oni "Son of my suffering," from which is derived *onen*: mourner during the time between death and burial.

Berakhot Blessings.

Bet Ha-Midrash House of study.

Bet Olam Eternal house (cemetery).

Bimah Platform in a synagogue on which the Torah is read and from which the reader leads the congregation in prayer.

Bo el Pharaoh "Go to Pharaoh."

Bom From the Shema: "*V'dibarta bom*: . . . and thou shalt talk of them. . . ."

Brit Convenant.

Chasidic, *Chasidim* (Hasidic, *Hasidim*) Traditional religious movement devoted to strict observance of Jewish ritual and tradition, founded by the Baal Shem Tov (Master of the Good Name) in the eighteenth century.

Chaver, *Chaverim* (*Haver*, *haverim*) Friend. Literally, "an associate."

Chavurah (*Havurah*) Study and worship group founded as an alternative to established synagogues.

Cheder (*Heder*) (Yiddish) Hebrew school.

Chesed (*Hesed*) Kindness, love, goodness, benevolence.

Chevrah Kadisha (*Hevrah Kadisha*) Holy Brotherhood. Title applied to charitable society now generally limited to associations for burial of the dead.

Chol Ha-Moed (*Hol Ha-Moed*) The half festive days or the secular days of Passover and Sukkot.

Cohain (*Kohain*) Priest; a descendant of Aaron.

Daven (Yiddish) Pray.

"Dayenu" "It would have been enough for us." A song sung at the Passover *seder*.

Edah Community; group.

Edelkeit (Yiddish) Gentility.

Eilu Megalchin Chapter in Jeremiah dealing with laws of mourning and excommunication.

El Malay Rachamim "O God, full of compassion." A memorial prayer.

Ephah Biblical measure, as in a measure of barley.

Gaon, *Geonim* Leading academician in Babylonia.

Gemara Commentary on the Mishnah by a group of scholars known as the *Amoraim*.

Goy, *Goyim* Non-Jew; literally, and in the plural, nations, peoples, Gentiles.

Hadassah   Women's Zionist Organization of America, founded in 1912 by Henrietta Szold; another name for Esther, heroine of the story of Esther.

Hagiographa   "Holy writings." Greek word used to designate the third division of the Hebrew Bible, called *Ketuvim* in Hebrew.

Halachah, Halachot   Guidance. Jewish law or legal literature.

Hallel   Hymns of praise consisting of six psalms and recited on certain festive days.

Hanukkah   (Chanukah) Festival of Lights, which begins on the twenty-fifth day of Kislev and lasts eight days. It commemorates the victory of the Maccabees over the Assyrian-Greek army in 164 B.C.E and the rededication of the Temple.

Hazkarah   A memorial.

Hazkarat neshamot   Memorial services.

Hesped   Euology.

Hevel   Vanity.

Iyar   Second month of the Hebrew calendar (approximately April–May).

Kaddish   Holy or sacred. The mourner's prayer recited during the period of mourning and on the anniversary of a death.

Karavi   In a eulogy, balance and appropriateness: a eulogy may not grossly exaggerate, or invent, qualities that the deceased did not in fact possess.

Kavorah   Burial.

Kedushah   Sanctification in the liturgy: "Holy, Holy, Holy is the Lord of Hosts, the whole earth is full of God's glory."

Keriah   Rending. The custom of rending or tearing the garment worn by relatives before burial as a sign of deep grief.

Kesitah   A biblical unit of unknown value.

Kefi'at Ha-mitah   Ancient custom during *shivah* of overturning the bed or couch; a means of discouraging marital relations.

Kiddush Hashem   "Sanctification of God's name." Martyrdom.

Klal Yisrael   People (community) of Israel.

Klotzkashes   (Yiddish) Foolish questions.

Kotel Maaravi   Western Wall in Jerusalem.

Le-chayyim   To life.

Maariv   Evening service.

Maftir   Concluding. The last portion of the *Sidrah*.

Maggid   Wandering preacher or storyteller found among the early chasidic communities in eighteenth-century Poland.

Mamzer   Hebrew for "bastard." Any child of a forbidden relationship.

Mandelbrot   (Yiddish) Almond cookie.

Matzevah   Monument, tombstone.

Mavet   Death.

Mazel Tov   Good luck.

Memorbuecher   (Yiddish) Memorial book.

Menorah   Seven-branched candelabrum used in the ancient Tabernacle and Temple.

Menorat Ha-Maor   *Candelabrum of Light*, written by Rabbi Isaac Aboab the Elder, a religioethical writer of the fourteenth century.

Mensch   (Yiddish) Good person.

Mezuzah   Parchment on which portions of the Torah are written and the case in which it is placed, set on doorposts.

Midrash, *Midrashim*   Nonlegal sections of the Talmud and the rabbinic books containing biblical interpretations in the spirit of the *Aggadah* (legend).

Midrash Mishle   Midrash on the Book of Proverbs.

Mikveh   Ritual bath.

Minchah   Afternoon service.

Minyan   Ten adults above the age of 13 (men only in traditional Judaism) required for the recitation of prayers.

Mishnah   Repetition. The collection of the statements of the *Taanaim* (teachers) expounding on the bible and constituting the core of Oral Law. The Mishnah together with the *Gemara* comprise the Talmud.

Mitzvah, *Mitzvot*   One of the 613 commandments of God. Refers also to "good deed."

Moed Katan   Minor festival. The name of a book of the Talmud that records the laws of mourning.

Mohel   One who performs the ritual of *brit milah*, the covenant of circumcision.

Musaf   Additional prayers on the Sabbath, holidays, and *Rosh Chodesh* (new moon).

Nachalah meldado   *Yahrzeit* as called by the Sephardim. (See *Annos*.)

Ner daluk   Kindled light.

Ner Tamid   Eternal light in the synagogue in front of the *Aron Kodesh* (Holy Ark).

Neshamah   Soul.

Netaneh Tokef (*Unetaneh Tokef*)   "Let us recount the power." Rosh Hashanah prayer.

Nigun   Melody.

Nisan   First month of the Hebrew calendar (approximately April–May).

Olam Ha-Ba   "The world to come."

Olam Ke-minhago noheg   "Nature pursues its own course."

Omer   Sheaf. The seven weeks counted between Pesach (Passover) and Shavuot.

Onen   Mourner during the time between death and burial.

Or Ha-Chayyim   Famous mystical commentator on the Bible.

Pailish   (Yiddish) Ashkenazic style of pronunciation.

Pentateuch   Five Books of Moses. The Torah.

Perenes   (Yiddish) Thick old feather blankets.

Pesach   (Passover) The 8-day festival commemorating the liberation of the
Jews from Egyptian bondage.

Prozdor   Anteroom, a room that leads to a larger room.

Purim   Lots. Festival celebrated on the fourteenth of *Adar* in commemoration of the deliverance of the Jews in Persia from the hands of Haman.

Pushke   (Yiddish) *Tzedakah* (charity) box.

Rebbe   A leading rabbi among the *hasidim*.

Refuat ha-guf   Healing of the body.

Refuat ha-nefesh   Healing of the spirit.

Rosh Chodesh (Rosh Hodesh)   New moon.

Ruach   Soul, spirit.

Schmooz   (Yiddish) Chat.

Seder   Order. The order of the home service on Pesach (Passover).

Sefer Zikaron   Book of Remembrance.

Semachot   Talmudic tractate known by this name and by the name *Evel
Rabbati* (Hebrew for "great mourning"), dealing with death and mourning
customs.

Sephardic (*Sefaradit*, Hebrew)   Pertaining to the *Sephardim*, descendants of
the Jews of Spain expelled from Spain in the fifteenth century. (Also, as an
adjective, Sephardic Jews.)

Seudah (Seudat) havraah   Meal provided for mourners by neighbors upon
return from funeral.

Shabbat   Sabbath.

Shacharit   Morning service.

Shalom   Hello, good-bye, peace.

Shames, Shammos (Yiddish); *Shammash* (Hebrew)   Sexton or usher in a
synagogue and the helper candle used to light the Hanukkah *menorah*
(*hanukkiyah*).

Shavuot   Pentecost or Festival of Weeks celebrated 50 days after Passover
as a festival of nature, of offering the first fruits of the harvest.

Shechinah   Divine Presence.

Shema   Hear, listen. The *Shema* prayer proclaims the unity of one God.

Shemei shamayim   Heaven of heavens.

Shemini Atzeret-Simchat Torah   Shemini Atzeret is the last day of
Sukkot. Simchat Torah, rejoicing the law, is the festival immediately
following Shemini Atzeret.

Sheol   Afterlife, netherworld.

Shevat   Eleventh month of the Hebrew calendar (approximately January–
February).

Shivah   Seven. The seven days of mourning.

Shloshim   Thirty. The thirty days of full mourning.

Shokel (Shukel) (Yiddish)   Swaying to and fro during prayer.

Shomer   Watcher. One who keeps guard over the body until burial.

Shtetl (Yiddish)   Small community in Eastern Europe.

Shtibl, *Shtiblach* (Yiddish)   Small synagogue.

Shulchan Aruch   Table prepared. *The Code of Jewish Law* by Rabbi Joseph Caro, first published in the sixteenth century.

Siddur   Prayer book.

Sitra achra   The other side, the demon world.

Sukkah   Booth or hut. The temporary structure built for the celebration of Sukkot in recognition of the temporary dwellings built by the Israelites as they journeyed from Egypt to Canaan.

Tachrichim   Shrouds worn by the dead.

Taharah   Ritual of cleansing a corpse.

Tallit   Prayer shawl.

Talmud   Comprised of Mishnah and *Gemara*, commentary on the Pentateuch.

Tefillah, *Tefillot* Prayers.

Tefillin   Phylacteries. Small boxes containing passages from the Scriptures and affixed to the forehead and arm during recital of the morning prayers.

Tefillat shov   Prayers that seek to reverse the laws of nature.

Tetzaveh   *Sidra Tetzaveh*, Torah portion. Exodus 27:20–30:10: "You shall further instruct the Israelites. . . ."

Tisha B'Av   Fast of the ninth of *Av* that commemorates the destruction of both the First and the Second Temples (586 B.C.E. and 70 C.E.).

Teshuvah   Repentance.

Tsimmis (Yiddish)   A carrot and prune stew. Lit., all mixed up.

Tzadik   Righteous man.

Tzedakah   Righteousness, charity.

Tzidduk Ha-Din   Acknowledgment of divine judgment. Part of burial service.

Yahrzeit (*Yahrtzeit*) (Yiddish)   Anniversary of a death.

Yah-veh   God.

Yarmulke (Yiddish), (*Kippah*, Hebrew)   Head covering or skullcap.

Yavneh   City south of Jaffa where Rabbi Yochanan Ben Zakkai opened an academy and established the Sanhedrin, which functioned until the Bar Kokhba revolt.

Yerushah   Inheritance.

Yigdal   Hymn. "*Yigdal Elohim chai* . . ." magnified and praised be the living God.

Yitgadal ve-yitkadash shmei rabba   "Let the glory of God be extolled." The first phrase in the Mourner's *Kaddish*.

Yizkor   Memorial service.

Yom Ha-Kippurim   Technical name for Yom Kippur, Day of Atonement.

Yom Ha-Shoah   Holocaust Memorial Day.

Yom Kippur   Day of Atonement.

Zahal   Israel Defense Forces.

Zichronah Livrachah   May her memory be a blessing.

Zichrono Livrachah   May his memory be a blessing.

Zocheir Kol Ha-Nishkachot   God remembers all the forgotten.

Zohar   Title of the mystical work introduced into Spain by Moses de Leon at the end of the thirteenth century and attributed to Rabbi Simeon bar Yochai of the second century.

References

Abrahams, Israel. *Hebrew Ethical Wills*. 2 vols. Philadelphia: The Jewish Publication Society, 1926.

Adler, Morris. "We Do Not Stand Alone." In *Jewish Reflections on Death*, ed. Jack Riemer. New York: Schocken Books, 1976, pp. 164–165.

_____ . "Sorrow Can Enlarge the Domain of Our Life." In *Light from Jewish Lamps: A Modern Treasury of Jewish Thoughts*, ed. Rabbi Sidney Greenberg. Northvale, NJ: Jason Aronson Inc., 1986, pp. 312–313.

Agus, Arlene. "Outrage and Faith." In *What Happens After I Die? Jewish Views of Life After Death*, ed. Rifat Sonsino and Daniel B. Syme. New York: UAHC Press, 1990, pp. 116–125.

Amichai, Yehuda. "My Father's Memorial Day." In *Amen*. New York: Harper & Row, 1977, p. 57.

Angel, Rabbi Marc. *The Orphaned Adult: Confronting the Death of a Parent*. New York: Human Sciences Press, 1977.

Ausubel, Nathan, ed. *A Treasury of Jewish Folklore: Stories, Traditions, Legends, Humor, Wisdom and Folk Songs of the Jewish People*. New York: Crown Publishers, 1975, pp. 111–112.

Bialik, Hayyim Nahman. "After My Death." In *Anthology of Modern Hebrew Poetry*, vol. 1, ed. S. Y. Penueli and A. Ukhmani. Jerusalem: Institute for the Translation of Hebrew Literature and Israel Universities Press, 1966, pp. 33–34.

_____ . "You're Leaving Me." In *Selected Poems of Hayyim Nahman Bialik*, ed. Israel Efros. New York: Bloch Publishing Company, 1965, pp. 200–201.

Blaustein, Reba. "Loss." In *A Singing in My Soul: A Pocket Full of Poems*. San Francisco, 1983, p. 1.

Bokser, Ben Zion. *The Gift of Life: A Treasury of Inspirations*. London: Abelard-Schuman, 1958, pp. 15–16, 67–68.

Brenner, Anne. "Surviving the Loss of a Spouse." *Journal of Jewish Communal Service*, Summer 1989, pp. 298–304.

Browne, Lewis, ed. *The Wisdom of the Jewish People*. Northvale, NJ: Jason Aronson Inc., 1987, pp. 291–292.

Brownstone, Ezekiel. "Kaddish for my Father"; "My Father." In *The Golden Peacock: A*

Worldwide Treasury of Yiddish Poetry, ed. Joseph Leftwich. New York: Thomas Yoseloff, 1961, pp. 402–403.

Cohen, Hershel, and Victor M. Solomon. *Nahalat Shafra: A Book of Eulogettes*. Hoboken, NJ: Ktav Publishing House, 1990.

Cohen, Seymour J. "Kaddish in Many Places." In *Jewish Reflections on Death*, ed. Jack Riemer. New York: Schocken Books, 1976, pp. 173–177.

de Sola Pool, David. "Life Has Been Inexpressibly Sweet to Me: The Spiritual Testament of Rabbi David de Sola Pool." In *This I Believe: Documents of American Jewish Life*, ed. Jacob Rader Marcus. Northvale, NJ: Jason Aronson Inc., 1990, pp. 239–241.

———. *The Traditional Prayer Book*. New York: Behrman House, 1960, p. 474.

Deutsch, Babette. "Maariv." In *The Menorah Journal*, April 1922, pp. 79–80.

Dmitrova, Blaga. "To My Father." In *Kol Haneshamah; Shabbat Eve*. Wyncote, PA: The Reconstructionist Press, 1989, p. 206.

Elkins, Joshua Charles. "An Exploration of Alternatives for Educating Jewish Adolescents to Dying, Death, and Bereavement: A Pre-Deliberation Research Project." Ph.D. diss. Columbia University Teachers College, 1979.

Epstein, Helen. "A Death in the Family 1989." *New York*, November 27, 1989, pp. 34–43.

Feifel, Herman, Ph.D. "Grief and Bereavement: Overview and Perspective." *Bereavement Care for All Who Help the Bereaved*, Spring 1988, pp. 2–4.

———. *Meanings of Death*. New York: McGraw-Hill, 1959.

———. *New Meanings of Death*. New York: McGraw-Hill, 1977.

Feldman, Emanuel. "Death as Estrangement: The Halakhah of Mourning." In *Jewish Reflections on Death*, ed. Jack Riemer. New York: Schocken Books, 1976, pp. 84–94.

Freedman, Seymour. "After the Most Painful Grief"; "All My Thoughts of Death Beforehand"; "I Dare Not Go Deep in Memory"; "I Do Not Know"; "It Is a Dream"; "Time Does Not Make My Sadness Any Less"; "Time Will Not Make Me Love You Less"; "Why Does the Human Being." In *Mourning for My Father*. Jerusalem: Field Publishing House Ltd., 1989, pp. 1, 41, 12, 57, 15, 122, 128, 9.

Gates of Prayer: The New Union Prayerbook; Afternoon and Evening Services and Prayers for the House of Mourning. New York: CCAR, 1978, p. 8.

Gates of the House: The New Union Prayerbook: Prayers and Readings for Home and Synagogue. New York: CCAR, 1977, pp. 130, 217.

Gates of Prayer: The New Union Prayerbook; Weekdays, Sabbaths, and Festival Services and Prayers for Synagogue and Home. New York: CCAR, 1975, pp. 166, 267, 625, 731–733, 753.

Gates of Repentance: The New Union Prayerbook for the Days of Awe. New York: CCAR, 1978, pp. 491–492.

Gelb, Alan. "Finally Answering the Call." *New York Times Magazine*, January 7, 1990, pp. 18, 20.

Gilboa, Amir. "I Know I Won't Come This Way Again." In *The Light of Lost Suns: Selected Poems of Amir Gilboa*, trans. Shirley Kaufman. New York: Persea Books, 1979, p. 51.

Ginzberg, Louis. *Legends of the Jews*. Vol. I, pp. 99–102, 286–290, 299–306; vol. II, pp. 29, 148–154, 183–184; vol. III, pp. 471–479. Philadelphia: The Jewish Publication Society, 1954.

Goldberg, Rabbi Chaim Binyamin. *Mourning in Halachah: The Laws and Customs of the Year of Mourning*. New York: Mesorah Publications, Ltd., 1991.

Goldstein, Israel. "Evening Service"; "Meditations on Visits to the Cemetery"; "Meditations and Prayers at the Grave"; "The Uses of Adversity." In *Mourners' Devotions*. New York: Bloch Publishing Company, 1941, pp. 7, 73, 76–77, 69–70.

Gottlieb, Freema. *The Lamp of God: A Jewish Book of Light*. Northvale, NJ: Jason Aronson Inc., 1989, pp.10, 262, 337.

Greenberg, Blu. "Is There Life After Death?" In *What Happens After I Die? Jewish Views of Life*

After Death, ed. Rifat Sonsino and Daniel B. Syme. New York: UAHC Press, 1990, pp. 79–95.

Greenberg, Rabbi Sidney, ed. *A Treasury of Comfort*. North Hollywood, CA: Wilshire Book Company, 1954.

_____ . *Light from Jewish Lamps: A Modern Treasury of Jewish Thoughts*. Northvale, NJ: Jason Aronson Inc., 1986, pp. 236, 307.

_____ . *Words to Live By: Selected Writings of Rabbi Sidney Greenberg*, ed. Arthur Kurzweil. Northvale, NJ: Jason Aronson Inc., 1990, pp. 130, 139, 154, 161, 162.

Greenberg, Uri Zvi. "Man in Time." In *Anthology of Modern Hebrew Poetry*, vol. 2, ed. S. Y. Penueli and A. Ukhmani. Jerusalem: Institute for the Translation of Hebrew Literature and Israel Universities Press, 1966, pp. 252–253.

Grollman, Rabbi Earl A. "Bereavement and Faith: Passover—A Season of Triumph, But Tears." *Bereavement: A Magazine of Hope and Healing*, March/April 1989, pp. 19, 43.

_____ . *Explaining Death to Children*. Boston: Beacon Press, 1967, pp. 224–225.

Hall, Trish. "Solace after Bereavement: Counseling Services Grow." *New York Times*, May 20, 1990, pp. A1, A32.

Hausman, Carol P. "First You Mourn." *Moment*, September 27, 1987, pp. 43–45.

Hecht, Herman. "Be Honest & Upright to Your Self & Fellow Man; A Jewish New Year Letter to a Son." In *This I Believe: Documents of American Jewish Life*, ed. Jacob Rader Marcus. Northvale, NJ: Jason Aronson Inc., 1990, pp. 163–164.

Heschel, Abraham Joshua. *The Earth Is the Lord's and the Sabbath*. New York: Harper & Row, 1966.

_____ . *God in Search of Man: A Philosophy of Judaism*. Northvale, NJ: Jason Aronson Inc., 1987, pp. 103, 265, 367.

Hoffman, Edward. *The Way of Splendor: Jewish Mysticism and Modern Psychology*. Northvale, NJ: Jason Aronson Inc., 1989.

Hubscher, Rabbi Jacob. *The Kaddish Prayer: Its Meaning, Significance and Tendency*. Berlin: M. Jacobowitz, 1929, pp. 12, 29.

Jung, Leo. "The Meaning of the Kaddish." In *Jewish Reflections on Death*. New York: Schocken Books, 1976, pp. 160–163.

Klagsbrun, Francine. *Voices of Wisdom: Jewish Ideals and Ethics for Everyday Living*. Philadelphia: The Jewish Publication Society, 1980, pp. 499, 510–511.

Kompert, L. "The Kaddish." In *Mourners' Devotions*. New York: Bloch Publishing Company, 1941, pp. 62–63.

Kulback, Moshe. "Grandfather Dies"; "My Grandmother." In *The Golden Peacock: A Worldwide Treasury of Yiddish Poetry*, ed. Joseph Leftwich. New York: Thomas Yoseloff, 1961, pp. 155, 154.

Kushner, Harold. *When Bad Things Happen to Good People*. New York: Schocken Books, 1981, pp. 139–140.

_____ . *Who Needs God*. New York: Summit Books, 1989, pp. 105, 136.

Kushner, Lawrence. *The River of Light: Spirituality, Judaism, and the Evolution of Consciousness*. Woodstock, VT: Jewish Lights Publishing, 1990, pp. 46–47, 54–55, 112, 124–125, 128, 130, 139, 142.

_____ . *GOD was in this PLACE & I, i did not know: Finding SELF, SPIRITUALITY and ULTIMATE MEANING*. Woodstock, VT: Jewish Lights Publishing, 1991.

Lamm, Maurice. *The Jewish Way in Death and Mourning*. New York: Jonathan David Publishers, 1969.

_____ . "A Parable." In *Understanding Bereavement and Grief*, ed. Norman Linzer. New York: Ktav and Yeshiva University Press, 1977, pp. 88–89.

Leivick, Halper. "I Am Sad, God." In *The Golden Peacock: A Worldwide Treasury of Yiddish Poetry*, ed. Joseph Leftwich. New York: Thomas Yoseloff, 1961, pp. 125–126.

Liebman, Rabbi Joshua Loth. *Peace of Mind*. New York: Simon & Schuster, 1946.

Linzer, Norman, ed. *Understanding Bereavement and Grief*. New York: Ktav and Yeshiva University Press and Jewish Funeral Directors of America, Inc., 1977, pp. 88–89, 90–94.

Lipman, Eugene J. "The Minyan Is a Community." In *Jewish Reflections on Death*, ed. Jack Riemer. New York: Schocken Books, 1976, pp. 169–172.

Lipsett, Beatrice. "Refuge." In *The Journal Project: Pages from the Lives of Old People*, ed. Marc Kaminsky. New York: Teachers & Writers Collaborative Publications, 1980, p. 55.

Lowenthal, Marvin, trans. *The Memoirs of Glückel of Hameln*. New York: Schocken Books, 1977, p. 150.

Marcus, Jacob Rader. *This I Believe: Documents of American Jewish Life*. Northvale, NJ: Jason Aronson Inc., 1990, pp. 163–164, 251–252.

Maslin, Simeon J., ed. *Gates of Mitzvah: A Guide to the Jewish Life Cycle*. New York: CCAR, 1979, pp. 53, 54, 57, 61, 63, 64, 96, 103.

Moses, Isaac, ed. "The Rose Is Queen." In *The Sabbath-School Hymnal: A Collection of Songs, Services and Responsive Readings for the School, Synagogue and Home*. New York: Bloch Publishing Company, 1911, p. 348.

Nadich, Judah. *Jewish Legends of the Second Commonwealth*. Philadelphia: The Jewish Publication Society, 1983, pp. 267–268.

Ostrow, Dr. Mortimer. "Grief and Mourning." In *The Bond of Life: A Book for Mourners*, ed. Rabbi Jules Harlow. New York: The Rabbinical Assembly, 1983, pp. 22–34.

Perilman, Rabbi Nathan A. "A Tree Is Best Measured . . ." In *Religion and Bereavement: Counsel for the Physician, Advice for the Bereaved, Thoughts for the Clergyman*, Austin H. Kutscher and Lillian G. Kutscher. New York: Health Sciences Corporation, 1972, pp. 33–36.

Polsky, Howard W., and Yaella Wozner. *Everyday Miracles: The Healing Wisdom of Hasidic Stories*. Northvale, NJ: Jason Aronson Inc., 1989, p. 382.

Potok, Chaim. *The Gift of Asher Lev*. New York: Alfred A. Knopf, 1990, pp. 67–70, 122–124, 249, 326.

Prophets, The. A New Translation of "The Holy Scriptures" According to the Masoretic Text, second section. Philadelphia: The Jewish Publication Society, 1978.

Rabinowicz, Rabbi Tzvi. *A Guide to Life: Jewish Laws and Customs of Mourning*. Northvale, NJ: Jason Aronson Inc., 1989.

Rawitch, Melech. "Kaddish." In *A Treasury of Yiddish Poetry*, ed. Irving Howe and Eliezer Greenberg. New York: Holt, Rinehart & Winston, 1969, p. 204.

Riemer, Jack, ed. *Jewish Reflections on Death*. New York: Schocken Books, 1976, pp. 34–39, 138–140, 160–163, 164–165, 166–168, 169–172, 173–177, 239–241.

————. *Understanding Bereavement and Grief*, ed. Norman Linzer, Ph.D. New York: Ktav Publishing House, Inc., Yeshiva University Press, and Jewish Funeral Directors of America, Inc., 1977, pp. 90–94.

Riemer, Jack, and Nathaniel Stampfer, eds. *Ethical Wills: A Modern Jewish Treasury*. New York: Schocken Books, 1983.

————. *So That Your Values Live On—Ethical Wills and How To Prepare Them*. Woodstock, VT: Jewish Lights Publishing, 1991.

Rosenblatt, Roger. "The Face of God." *Life*, December 1990, pp. 47–78.

Roth, Philip. *Patrimony: A True Story*. New York: Simon & Schuster, 1991, pp. 233–234.

Rudin, Rabbi Jacob Philip. "Remembrance." In *Religion and Bereavement: Counsel for the Physician, Advice for the Bereaved, Thoughts for the Clergyman*, Austin H. Kutscher and Lillian G. Kutscher. New York: Health Sciences Publishing Corporation, 1972, pp. 36–38.

Sachs, Nelly. "How Long Have We Forgotten How to Listen." *Shirim: A Jewish Poetry Journal*, 1990, p. 12.

Sacks, Rabbi Dr. Jonathan. "Practical Implications of Infinity." In *To Touch the Divine: A Jewish Mysticism Primer*. Brooklyn, NY: Merkos L'inyonei Chinuch, Inc., 1989, pp. 59–90.

Schaalman, Herman E. "The Divine Authority of the Mitzvah." In *Gates of Mitzvah: A Guide to the Jewish Life Cycle*, ed. Simeon J. Maslin. New York: CCAR, 1979, pp. 100–103.

Scholem, Gershon G., ed. *Zohar, the Book of Splendor: Basic Readings from the Kabbalah*. New York: Schocken Books, 1949, pp. 72–73.

Schulweis, Rabbi Harold M. "Conversation with the Angel of Death" (sermon); "Between"; "Beyond Judgment"; "It Is Never Too Late"; "Personal Credo"; "Strange Envy" (poems).

_____. "Hold On and Let Go." In "Immortality Through Goodness and Activism." *What Happens After I Die? Jewish Views of Life After Death*, ed. Rifat Sonsino and Daniel B. Syme. New York: UAHC Press, 1990, pp. 96–106.

Seligson, Rabbi David J. "Remembrance." In *Religion and Bereavement: Counsel for the Physician, Advice for the Bereaved, Thoughts for the Clergyman*, ed. Austin H. Kutscher and Lillian G. Kutscher. New York: Health Sciences Publishing Corporation, 1972, pp. 43–44.

Shankman, Rabbi Jacob K. "Remembrance." In *Religion and Bereavement: Counsel for the Physician, Advice for the Bereaved, Thoughts for the Clergyman*, Austin H. Kutscher and Lillian G. Kutscher. New York: Health Sciences Publishing Corporation, 1972, pp. 38–41.

Shneour, Zalman. "A Star Fell." In *Anthology of Modern Hebrew Poetry*, vol. 2, ed. S. Y. Penueli and A. Ukhmani. Jerusalem: Institute for the Translation of Hebrew Literature and Israel Universities Press, 1966, p. 182.

Siegel, Dr. Bernie S. *Love, Medicine & Miracles: Lessons Learned about Self-Healing from a Surgeon's Experience with Exceptional Patients*. New York. Harper & Row, 1986.

_____. *Peace, Love & Healing: Bodymind Communication and the Path to Self-Healing: An Exploration*. New York: Harper & Row, 1989.

Siegel, Danny. "Ben"; "Death and Fear of Death"; "European Delicacy"; "Losses"; "Rav Sheshet and the Angel"; "Ten Hard Things"; "The Passing of Tzirel Dvorah Siegel." In *Between Dust and Dance*. New York: United Synagogue of America, 1978, pp. 51–52, 67, 77, 57, 66, 68, 54–55.

_____. "A Day with My Mother and Aunt Phyllis, Her Sister." In *Angels*. Spring Valley, NY: The Town House Press, 1980, pp. 129–131.

_____. "The Shortfalls of Knowledge." In *Nine Entered Paradise Alive*. Spring Valley, NY: The Town House Press, 1980, p. 66.

Silver, Abba Hillel. *Where Judaism Differed*. Northvale, NJ: Jason Aronson Inc., 1987, p. 276.

Silverman, Rabbi William B., and Dr. Kenneth M. Cinnamon. *When Mourning Comes: A Book of Comfort for the Grieving*. Northvale, NJ: Jason Aronson Inc., 1990, pp. 14–15, 69.

Sonsino, Rifat, and Daniel B. Syme, eds. *What Happens After I Die? Jewish Views of Life After Death*. New York: UAHC Press, 1990, pp. 79–95, 103–104, 116–125.

Steinberg, Milton. "To Hold With Open Arms." In *Jewish Reflections on Death*, ed. Jack Riemer. New York: Schocken Books, 1976, pp. 138–140.

Steinsaltz, Adin. *The Strife of the Spirit*. Northvale, NJ: Jason Aronson Inc., 1988, pp. 193, 151, 154.

Stern, Israel. "Mothers." In *The Golden Peacock: A Worldwide Treasury of Yiddish Poetry*, ed. Joseph Leftwich. New York: Thomas Yoseloff, 1961, p. 437.

Szold, Henrietta. "Letter to Haym Peretz." In Marvin Lowenthal, *Henrietta Szold: Life and Letters*. New York: The Viking Press, 1942, pp. 92–93.

Tanakh: The Holy Scriptures. Philadelphia: The Jewish Publication Society, 1988.

Toback, Phyllis. "Kaddish." In *Invisible Thread: A Portrait of Jewish American Women, Interviews by Diana Bletter*. Philadelphia: The Jewish Publication Society, 1989, pp. 190–192.

Torah, The. The Five Books of Moses; A New Translation of "The Holy Scriptures" According to the Masoretic Text. First section. Philadelphia: The Jewish Publication Society of America, 1962.

Trepp, Rabbi Leo. *The Complete Book of Jewish Observance: A Practical Manual for the Modern Jew*. New York: Behrman House, Inc./Summit Books, 1980, p. 342.

Tussman, Malka Heifetz. "I Know Not Your Ways," trans. Marcia Falk. In *Shirim: A Jewish Poetry Journal*, 1990, p. 11.

Weinstein, Jacob J. "I Know I Cannot Impose My Values and Judgments on You: Rabbi Weinstein Offers Advice in Troubled Times." In *This I Believe: Documents of American Jewish Life*, ed. Jacob Rader Marcus. Northvale, NJ: Jason Aronson Inc., 1990, pp. 251–252.

Whitman, Ruth. "A New Dress." In *An Anthology of Modern Yiddish Poetry*. New York: October House Inc., 1966, p. 47.

Wiesel, Elie. "The Death of My Father." In *Jewish Reflections on Death*, ed. Jack Riemer. New York: Schocken Books, 1976, pp. 34–39.

Wolpe, David J. *The Healer of Shattered Hearts: A Jewish View of God*. New York: Henry Holt and Company, 1990, pp. 8, 24–26, 30–31, 37–43, 45, 58, 93, 107, 109.

Writings, The. A New Translation of "The Holy Scriptures" According to the Masoretic Text, third section. Philadelphia: The Jewish Publication Society, 1982.

Zashin, Joseph. "The Fraternity of Mourners." In *Jewish Reflections on Death*, ed. Jack Riemer. New York: Schocken Books, 1976, pp. 166–168.

Zelda. "Light a Candle," trans. Marcia Falk. In *Shirim: A Jewish Poetry Journal*, 1990, p. 13.

Acknowledgments

Every effort has been made to ascertain the owner of copyrights for the selections used in this volume and to obtain permission to reprint copyrighted passages. For the use of the passages indicated, the author expresses his gratitude to those whose names appear below. The author will be pleased, in subsequent editions, to correct any inadvertent error or omission that may be pointed out.

"About Men; Finally Answering the Call" by Alan Gelb, January 7, 1990, the *New York Times Magazine*. Copyright © 1990 by the New York Times Company. Reprinted by permission.

"A Day with My Mother and Aunt Phyllis, Her Sister" by Danny Siegel, from *Angels*, published by the Town House Press. Copyright © 1980 by Danny Siegel. Reprinted by permission of the author.

"After the Most Painful Grief"; "All My Thoughts of Death Beforehand"; "I Dare Not Go Deep in Memory"; "I Do Not Know"; "It Is a Dream"; "Time Will Not Make Me Love You Less"; "Why Does the Human Being" by Seymour Freedman, from *Mourning for My Father*, published by Gefen Publishing House. Copyright © 1989. Reprinted by permission of the publisher.

"After My Death" by Hayyim Nahman Bialik, from *Anthology of Modern Hebrew Poetry*, vol. 1, edited by S. Y. Penueli and A. Ukhmani. © 1966 by Dvir Publ., Israel. Used by permission of ACUM Ltd. and the Institute for the Translation of Hebrew Literature.

"A New Dress" by Ruth Whitman, from *An Anthology of Modern Yiddish Poetry*, edited by Ruth Whitman. Copyright © 1966. Reprinted by permission of Ruth Whitman.

"A Parable" by Rabbi Maurice Lamm, from *Understanding Bereavement and Grief*, edited by Norman Linzer, published by Ktav Publishing House, Inc., Yeshiva University Press, and Jewish Funeral Directors of America, Inc. Copyright © 1977. Reprinted by permission of Ktav Publishing House, Inc.

"A Star Fell" by Zalman Shneour, from *Anthology of Modern Hebrew Poetry*, vol. 2, edited by S. Y. Penueli and A. Ukhmani. © 1966 by Zalman Shneour, ACUM, Israel. Used by permission of ACUM Ltd. and the Institute for the Translation of Hebrew Literature.

"A Tree Is Best Measured" by Nathan A. Perilman, from *Religion and Bereavement; Counsel for the*

321

Greenberg. Copyright © 1986 by Jason Aronson Inc. Reprinted by permission of the publisher.

From *Patrimony: A True Story*. Copyright © 1990 by Philip Roth. Reprinted by permission of Simon & Schuster.

From *Peace of Mind*. Copyright 1946 by Joshua Loth Liebman. Renewed © 1973 by Fan Liebman. Reprinted by permission of Simon & Schuster.

From *River of Light: Spirituality, Judaism, and the Evolution of Consciousness* by Lawrence Kushner, published by Jewish Lights Publishing, P. O. Box 237, Woodstock, VT 05091. $17.95 inc. s/h.

From "Solace After Bereavement: Counseling Services Grow," by Trish Hall, the *New York Times*, May 20, 1990. Copyright © 1990 by the New York Times Company. Reprinted by permission.

From *The Gift of Asher Lev* by Chaim Potok. Copyright © 1990 by Chaim Potok. Reprinted by permission of Alfred A. Knopf, Inc., and William Heinemann Ltd.

From *The Healer of Shattered Hearts* by David J. Wolpe. Copyright © 1990 by David J. Wolpe. Reprinted by permission of Henry Holt and Company, Inc., and reprinted with the permission of the Author, c/o The Mitnick Agency, 91 Henry Street, San Francisco, CA 94114.

From *The Jewish Way in Death and Mourning* by Maurice Lamm. Copyright © 1969. Reprinted by permission of the author and Jonathan David Publishers, Middle Village, New York.

From *The Lamp of God: A Jewish Book of Light* by Freema Gottlieb. Copyright © 1989 by Freema Gottlieb. Reprinted by permission of Jason Aronson Inc.

From *The Prophets: A New Translation of "The Holy Scriptures" According to the Masoretic Text*. Second Edition. Copyright © 1978 by The Jewish Publication Society of America. Reprinted by permission of the publisher.

From *The Strife of the Spirit* by Rabbi Adin Steinsaltz. Copyright © 1988 by Adin Steinsaltz. Reprinted by permission of Jason Aronson Inc.

From *The Torah: The Five Books of Moses; A New Translation of "The Holy Scriptures" According to the Masoretic Text*. First Edition. Copyright © 1962 by The Jewish Publication Society of America. Reprinted by permission of the publisher.

From *The Way of Splendor: Jewish Mysticism and Modern Psychology* by Edward Hoffman. Copyright © 1989 by Edward Hoffman. Reprinted by permission of Jason Aronson Inc.

From *The Wisdom of the Jewish People*, edited by Lewis Browne. Copyright © 1987 by Jason Aronson Inc. Reprinted by permission of the publisher.

From *The Writings: A New Translation of "The Holy Scriptures" According to the Masoretic Text*. Third Edition. Copyright © 1982 by The Jewish Publication Society of America. Reprinted by permission of the publisher.

From *When Bad Things Happen to Good People* by Harold S. Kushner. Copyright © 1981 by Harold S. Kushner. Reprinted by permission of Pantheon Books, a division of Random House, Inc., and Pan Books Ltd., London.

From *Where Judaism Differed* by Abba Hillel Silver. Copyright © 1987 by Jason Aronson Inc. Reprinted by permission of the publisher.

From *When Mourning Comes: A Book of Comfort for the Grieving* by Rabbi William B. Silverman and Dr. Kenneth M. Cinnamon. Copyright © 1990 by William B. Silverman. Reprinted by permission of Jason Aronson Inc.

From *Words to Live By: Selected Writings of Rabbi Sidney Greenberg*, edited by Arthur Kurzweil. Copyright © 1990 by Sidney Greenberg. Reprinted by permission of Jason Aronson Inc.

"Grief and Bereavement: Overview and Perspective" by Dr. Herman Feifel from *Bereavement Care* Spring 1988. The journal is available from Cruse-Bereavement Care, 126 Sheen Road, Richmond, Surrey TW12 1UR, England. Reprinted by permission of the publisher.

"Hold On and Let Go" by Rabbi Harold M. Schulweis from *What Happens After I Die? Jewish*

Views of Life After Death, edited by Rifat Sonsino and Daniel B. Syme. Copyright © 1990 by UAHC (Union of American Hebrew Congregations) Press. Reprinted by permission of the publisher.

"I Am Sad, God" by Halper Leivick; "My Grandmother"; and "Grandfather Dies" by Moshe Kulback; "Kaddish for My Father" and "My Father" by Ezekiel Brownstone; "Mother" by Israel Stern, from *The Golden Peacock; A Worldwide Treasury of Yiddish Poetry*, compiled, translated, edited by Joseph Leftwich. Copyright © 1961. Reprinted by permission of Thomas Yoseloff and Associated University Presses.

"I Know I Cannot Impose My Values and Judgments on You: Rabbi Weinstein Offers Advice in Troubled Times" by Jacob Weinstein, from *This I Believe: Documents of American Jewish Life*, edited by Jacob Rader Marcus. Copyright © 1990 by Jacob Rader Marcus. Reprinted by permission of Jason Aronson Inc.

"I Know I Won't Come This Way Again" by Amir Gilboa, translated by Shirley Kaufman, from *The Light of Lost Suns; Selected Poems of Amir Gilboa*, published by Persea Books. Copyright © 1979. Reprinted by permission of Shirley Kaufman.

"I Know Not Your Ways" by Malka Heifetz Tussman from *Teeth in the Earth: Selected Poems of Malka Heifetz Tussman*, translated, edited, and introduced by Marcia Falk (Wayne State University Press, 1992). Copyright © 1992 by Marica Lee Falk. Used by permission of the translator.

"Light a Candle" by Zelda, translated by Marcia Falk. Copyright © 1978 by Marcia Lee Falk. Used by permission of the translator.

"Is There Life After Death?" by Blu Greenberg, from *What Happens After I Die? Jewish Views of Life After Death*, edited by Rifat Sonsino and Daniel B. Syme. Copyright © 1990 by UAHC (Union of American Hebrew Congregations) Press. Reprinted by permission of the publisher.

Julie Hilton Danan for permission to quote from her eulogy for her grandmother, Fanny Hilton.

"Kaddish" by Melech Ravitch, translated by Nathan Halper, from *A Treasury of Yiddish Poetry* by Irving Howe and Eliezer Greenberg. Reprinted by permission of Henry Holt and Company, Inc.

"Kaddish" by Phyllis Toback, from *Invisible Thread: A Portrait of Jewish American Women, Interviews by Diana Bletter*. Copyright © 1989. Reprinted by permission of The Jewish Publication Society of American.

"Kaddish in Many Places" by Seymour J. Cohen, from *Jewish Reflections On Death*, edited by Jack Riemer. Copyright © 1976. Reprinted by permission of Seymour J. Cohen.

"Life Has Been Inexpressibly Sweet to Me: The Spiritual Testament of Rabbi David de Sola Pool" by David de Sola Pool, from *This I Believe: Documents of American Jewish Life*, edited by Jacob Rader Marcus. Copyright © 1990 by Jacob Rader Marcus. Reprinted by permission of Jason Aronson Inc.

"Loss" by Reba Blaustein, from *A Singing in My Soul*, published by the author. Copyright © 1983. Reprinted by permission of Donna Mumford.

"Man in Time" by Uri Zvi Greenberg, from *Anthology of Modern Hebrew Poetry*, vol. 2, edited by S. Y. Penueli and A. Ukhmani. © 1966 by Uri Zvi Greenberg, ACUM, Israel. Used by permission of ACUM Ltd. and the Institute for the Translation of Hebrew Literature.

Michelle Schlein for permission to quote from her personal letter to the author.

"My Father's Memorial Day," from *Amen* by Yehuda Amichai. Copyright © 1977. Reprinted by permission of Harper Collins Publishers and by permission of Oxford University Press.

"On Death and Dying" by Rabbi Jack Riemer, from *Understanding Bereavement and Grief*, edited by Norman Linzer, published by Ktav Publishing House, Inc., Yeshiva University Press, and Jewish Funeral Directors of America, Inc. Copyright © 1977. Reprinted by permission of Ktav Publishing House, Inc.

"Outrage and Faith" by Arlene Agus, from *What Happens After I Die? Jewish Views of Life After*

Death, edited by Rifat Sonsino and Daniel B. Syme. Copyright © 1990 by UAHC (Union of American Hebrew Congregations) Press. Reprinted by permission of the publisher.

Permission is granted by the family of the late Rabbi Leo Jung to reprint "The Meaning of the Kaddish."

Rabbi Harold M. Schulweis for permission to include his unpublished sermon and poems.

"Refuge" by Beatrice Lipsett. Reprinted from *The Journal Project: Pages from the Lives of Old People*, edited by Marc Kaminsky, by permission of Teachers & Writers Collaborative, 5 Union Square West, New York, NY 10003. Copyright © 1980 Teachers & Writers Collaborative, Inc.

"Remembrance" by David J. Seligson, from *Religion and Bereavement; Counsel for the Physician—Advice for the Bereaved, Thoughts for the Clergyman*. Copyright © 1972. Reprinted by permission of Foundation of Thanatology.

"Remembrance" by Jacob Rudin, from *Religion and Bereavement; Counsel for the Physician—Advice for the Bereaved, Thoughts for the Clergyman*. Copyright © 1972. Reprinted by permission of Foundation of Thanatology.

"Remembrance" by Jacob K. Shankman, from *Religion and Bereavement; Counsel for the Physician—Advice for the Bereaved, Thoughts for the Clergyman*. Copyright © 1972. Reprinted by permission of Foundation of Thanatology.

Roger Rosenblatt, *Life* magazine, Copyright © 1990 Time Warner Inc.

The essay "The Death of My Father" is included in *Legends From Our Time* by Elie Wiesel. Copyright © 1968 by Elie Wiesel. Reprinted by permission of Georges Borchardt, Inc., for the author.

"The Kaddish" by L. Kompert, from *Mourners' Devotions* by Israel Goldstein. Copyright © 1941. Reprinted by permission of Bloch Publishing Company.

"The Minyan Is a Community" by Eugene J. Lipman, from *Jewish Reflections On Death*, edited by Jack Riemer. Copyright © 1976. Reprinted by permission of Eugene J. Lipman and B'nai B'rith National Jewish Monthly.

"The Rose Is Queen" from *The Sabbath—School Hymnal; A Collection of Songs and Responsive Readings for the School, Synagogue and Home*, edited by Isaac Moses. Copyright © 1911. Reprinted by permission of Bloch Publishing Company.

"The Shortfalls of Knowledge" by Danny Siegel, from *Nine Entered Paradise Alive*, published by The Town House Press. Copyright © 1980 by Danny Siegel. Reprinted by permission of the author.

"To Hold with Open Arms," from *A Believing Jew* by Milton Steinberg, copyright © 1951 by Edith Steinberg and renewed 1979 by Jonathan Steinberg and David Joel Steinberg. Reprinted by permission of Harcourt Brace Jovanovich, Inc. Reprinted by permission of Russell & Volkening as agents for the author. Copyright © 1951 by Edith Steinberg, © copyright renewed 1979 by Edith Steinberg.

"We Do Not Stand Alone" by Morris Adler, from *Jewish Reflections On Death*, edited by Jack Riemer. Copyright © 1976. Reprinted by permission of Shulamith Adler Benstein.

"Where Does It End?" and "The Existence of God" by Ben Zion Bokser, from *The Gift Of Life; A Treasury of Inspirations* by Ben Zion Bokser. Copyright © 1958 by Abelard-Schuman. Reprinted by permission of Kallia H. Bokser.

"You're Leaving Me" by Hayyim Nahman Bialik, from *Selected Poems of Hayyim Nahman Bialik*, edited by Israel Efros. Copyright © 1965. Reprinted by permission of Bloch Publishing Company.

Index

About the Author

Alan A. Kay is a professor of English and coordinator of weekly peace seminars at New York City Technical College, The City University of New York, Brooklyn, New York, as well as a religious school teacher of eleventh- and twelfth-grade students at Merrick Community Hebrew High School, Merrick, Long Island. Professor Kay earned his doctorate in English Education from New York University. He is the author of *A Teacher's Guide to My Generations: A Course in Jewish Family History* and the founding editor of *Shofar*—a magazine for Jewish children—and several publications, including *Perspectives*, the faculty journal; *Brooklyn Bridge to the World*, the student literary magazine; and *Journeys to a New World*, collections of student family histories, all at New York Technical College. Professor Kay lives on Long Island with his wife, Jo, and their three children, Corinne, Lisa, and Adina.